Acupuncture Points Are Holes:
A Case Study in Social Entrepreneurship

Lisa Rohleder

POCA *

PEOPLE'S ORGANIZATION of
COMMUNITY ACUPUNCTURE

Cover art by James Shelton and Kate Kampmann.
Somnambulistic Mystic Productions

Thank you, St. Jude.

Author's Note

This is a work of creative nonfiction. Its subject is myself as a social entrepreneur. Its purpose is to help teach certain practices of social entrepreneurship within the POCA Cooperative by means of using me as a case study. Most community acupuncturists are either entrepreneurs themselves, or they work for entrepreneurs, so they need a grasp of the subject. Also, if you're a community acupuncturist or a social entrepreneur, your primary resource is yourself: your focus, your passion, your willingness to take risks and build relationships. The purpose of this book is to give a detailed example of what that might look like.

In order to streamline the narrative as a teaching tool, I took all kinds of liberties: I changed some names and abbreviated others; I compressed certain timelines and edited out people, things, and events; I inserted poems and blog posts; I made up composite stories and portrayed everything I remembered only from my own point of view. Also, a Greek chorus of impatient capitalists showed up every so often to interject their (fictional) perspective into the narrative. I don't know where they came from; I tried to send them back but they wouldn't go.

I hope nobody approaches this book as a linear and factual account, because it isn't intended to be one.

Entrepreneurship of any kind is notoriously difficult to teach. Its expression varies from person to person and a great deal of it happens inside the head and heart. The goal of this book is to provide a window into the inside stuff, and so I prioritized that over a precise and objective presentation. I hope the results are instructive, or at least entertaining.

Introduction

This isn't a success story. It's more of a love story. It might be a cautionary tale.

The idea of social entrepreneurship is very broad: the use of entrepreneurial techniques and principles applied to solve social problems. This encompasses non-profits borrowing techniques from for-profits, for-profits borrowing principles from non-profits, for-profits owned by non-profits and vice versa – the list of variations goes on. In theory, social entrepreneurship can operate in an organization of any size.

I used to carry around a copy of Muhammad Yunus' *Banker to the Poor*,[1] even after I'd read it three times, just to keep me company. It was 2004 and I'd just learned the term *social entrepreneurship*. I needed to remind myself there were words for what I was trying to do. Words helped, when what I wanted to do felt so big and so urgent and so uncontainable I thought I couldn't stand it.

The problem, though, was that Dr. Yunus' work was so exalted compared to mine – he started out by loaning $27 to a group of village artisans and ended up with a billion-dollar bank – that it wasn't relatable.

In *How to Change the World: Social Entrepreneurs and the Power of New Ideas*, David Bornstein writes, "social entrepreneurship, like business entrepreneurship, has many levels to it".[2] It seems, though, that most of the visible examples in the US involve large international companies, leaders in micro finance, successful investors – in short, people who obviously have it together. Unlike me.

I'd be happy if this book contributed in any way to lowering perceived barriers to social entrepreneurship. Who's qualified to help build a better world? I hope the answer includes low class people, children of immigrants, and survivors of abuse, and I hope it's clear those people can practice social entrepreneurship on their own terms. If nobody's said that yet, well, here you go.

Alongside *Banker to the Poor*, what I would have liked to read when I was starting out was a confession of an intimate, messy, evolving relationship with capitalism, from someone who started their own business not because they wanted to but because they had to. Someone who wasn't an economist or a banker, someone unqualified to be an entrepreneur by anything but desperation. I would've liked to read something ragged and personal by somebody who had no idea what they were doing, but was driven to do it anyway.

So that's this book.

The Chorus: Cut to the Chase, Please

So what happened exactly?

I became an acupuncturist, and then discovered that the economic and clinical model for providing acupuncture in the US didn't allow me to treat anybody like my own family (working class people, lower middle class people, people with limited disposable income). I started my own business only because there were no jobs and nobody to hire me; at the time, I was alienated from my chosen field, intimidated by money and by business, and broke. I made a lot of mistakes.

And then I fell down the rabbit hole of social entrepreneurship.

Out of necessity I overhauled the economic and clinical model for providing acupuncture and then persuaded lots of other people to use the model that worked for people like me. I made a lot more mistakes – more interesting ones, at a bigger scale. I co-founded a group of clinics that provides 50,000 low-cost treatments a year, then I co-founded an international cooperative that provides somewhere around a million low-cost treatments a year, then I talked the cooperative into creating its own acupuncture school to promote the model, and now I'm the director of the school.

What's the big picture?

Acupuncture can be uniquely useful to American society and its health problems. The dominant model for providing acupuncture involves doling it out in tiny, expensive increments to a limited number of privileged individuals. Acupuncture works better when you deliver it by means of clinics that function less like boutiques, or even hospitals, and more like public libraries or public utilities: high volume, a diverse group of users, community-supported. Instead of trying to sell acupuncture in limited quantities like fancy bottled water, try pouring it out through a big pipe, and let people take as much as they need.

That's the vision of the community acupuncture movement. This book is about building the pipe.

Well, did you succeed?

I'm not sure what "success" even means when you're trying to solve a big social problem involving unequal access to healthcare – is success/failure even a useful binary? We built the pipe, but we need to keep building it.

Because on a certain level we're never going to succeed, right? Inequality will always be with us. But at this point in my trajectory, lots of people perceive me and my organizations as successful. It's all relative, I guess; we're certainly very busy, and we grow every year, and we haven't gone out of business yet. As Rebecca Solnit says about activism: *It's always too soon to go home.*[3]

What turned out to be your biggest problem?

Capitalism in healthcare is heartbreaking; there's no nifty fix. When people hear social entrepreneurship, they often think, do good and make lots of money. But if you make lots of money by delivering healthcare, you're profiting off of people's pain and suffering. Which might be possible to justify on a theoretical level but turns out to be very difficult on the ground, where you're in close contact with the people experiencing the pain and suffering. The people who most need affordable acupuncture are the people least able to pay for it. It might be possible to do some good and make a lot of money with a variation on our model (we're about to find out) but you'd have to focus on a different group of people, ones who didn't need it so badly.

And as an example of social entrepreneurship, the community acupuncture movement is complicated, messy, and full of unsolved questions.

Hmm. Are you sure you're even doing social entrepreneurship? Might there be another term for what you're doing?

The definition of social entrepreneurship is so flexible, I'd have to say yes. But there is another term that also applies and that's *prefigurative intervention*: enacting the world we want to live in.[4]

Using the techniques of entrepreneurship, you can create things that wouldn't otherwise exist in capitalism. You can get outside of capitalism, even if only briefly. Besides providing acupuncture to a lot of people, our clinics and our cooperative also function as anti-capitalist spaces, or maybe head-spaces. I'm going to argue that this is a form of health promotion too.

Not sure we like the sound of anti-capitalism but OK. We have to ask, though: you wouldn't by any chance have an ulterior motive for writing this book?

One or two, yeah.

Even qualified success is complicated. I'm writing this book as the director of the only community acupuncture school in the US (or probably anywhere else). I've come a long way from where I started – so long, in fact, that the distance is creating a new set of problems. If people see you as successful, particularly when it comes to entrepreneurship, they tend to make assumptions not only about what's important to you, but also about what they might expect for themselves if they join you in your endeavors.

Among other things, entrepreneurship implies a tolerance for risk and uncertainty, a willingness to make do with limited resources, and an acceptance that if you want infrastructure you're probably going to have to build it yourself. Lots of people forget this, or try to gloss over it. Coming in to an enterprise that has grown a lot, they may assume that the days of risk, limited resources, and missing infrastructure are ancient history – because otherwise, this enterprise wouldn't look so successful, would it? And if people who are central to the enterprise show joy in their work, or at least you can't hear them complaining, that suggests there's not much to complain about anymore, right?

I've written about community acupuncture in the past,[5] but I tried to keep the focus off myself as much as I could. This time around, I'm doing the opposite. Lately I've had a few interactions that could be summarized as: you've misrepresented your success to me! You led me astray, you deceived me! *What is wrong with you?*

There's plenty, and I'll tell you all about it.

The path of idealism to disillusionment to cynicism is a nice neat familiar arc and people like familiarity. I've discovered that people would like me to locate myself somewhere on that arc, to be idealistic or disillusioned or cynical. Some people would like to enlist me to help them with that arc too, by letting them idealize me so that I can disappoint them and justify their cynicism. The convenient thing about cynicism, of course, is it lets you off the hook from doing anything.

If that's what you want, I can't help you. (Of course, you can do it anyway; lots of people have, without my assistance or consent.) I've never been idealistic or disillusioned or cynical. I've been a lot of other things, though, which I'll explain. If a story about social entrepreneurship that doesn't fit either the template of capitalist success or the template of activist disillusionment is interesting to you, keep reading.

Also, the community acupuncture movement is a work (a pipe?) in progress. It grows only by attracting the right people. An ulterior motive for this book is to find more of the right people, to join our cooperative and to support our school and to become community acupuncturists themselves. But I want to make sure those people know what they're getting into, which means knowing where all this came from.

Candles

1.

Entrepreneurship runs in families, some people say; successful entrepreneurs have examples to learn from. This is the story about entrepreneurship in my family that I heard when I was growing up: in the late 1800s and early 1900s, there were many prosperous German bakeries in Baltimore established by immigrants. And then there was my great-grandfather's. He was often drunk, and when he baked his cherry pies, he forgot to pit the cherries. And so the people who bought his pies ended up breaking their teeth on the pits, and there was one less German bakery in Baltimore.

When he would come home drunk, my great-grandmother would hit him over the head with her rolling pin, which he wouldn't remember the next morning. My mother showed me the rolling pin. It was made of dark wood, worn to a pale shine in some places. I ran my five-year-old fingers over its patina and found a dent, which I imagined was made by my great-grandfather's unfortunate temple. Thwack! That was the first thing I learned about entrepreneurship.

Until I was five and a half, my family lived in my great-grandparents' house. My father had lived with his grandparents; my great-grandmother died when I was a baby. We had all their heavy carved furniture, and the house was full of objects like the rolling pin, things with stories attached: a set of Bavarian china edged in pink and gold, a battered tin filled with buttons, cookie cutters in unrecognizable shapes. The house was at the end of a quiet street in South Baltimore in a neighborhood called Lakeland, not far from Curtis Bay where my father worked in a chemical plant.

When I was old enough to go to school, my family moved across the county line where the public schools were better.

The technical term for that is *white flight*. Like most other German immigrant families in Baltimore, we were Catholic, and my parents would have preferred to send me to Catholic school, but we couldn't afford it. Neither of my parents wanted to move to the suburbs; they were city people. My family had been living in the house in Lakeland since they got off the boat. And in the lower middle class suburb that they found, we stuck out like a sore thumb.

My mother played the violin, which she preferred to things like going to PTA meetings and housekeeping. My father spoke at random intervals in a fake Hungarian accent to confuse people (that's another story); he also liked to dig through their trash, and was unrepentant when caught. He parked a succession of broken down cars on the front lawn, and attached a cowbell to the tail pipe of a battered pick-up truck that he drove particularly to annoy the next-door neighbor. The next-door neighbor called the health department to report the once-neat suburban yard erupting with weeds and junk.

My mother's side of the family was the respectable side, characterized by hard work, decency, and unhappiness. My grandfather had fought in World War I and came home with shell-shock; he would wake up in the middle of the night, sit up straight in bed, and make "ack-ack-ack" noises, reliving the machine gunfire. He left school in the eighth grade, worked as a gas station attendant, and never learned to drive. He fell in love with my grandmother and begged her to marry him. She didn't want to get married; what she wanted was to be an accountant, which wasn't possible for a woman at that time. She refused him. He pined. The neighbors and their families launched a collective campaign of reproach, and wore her down with guilt. Elizabeth, they said, Carl sure looks bad. They kept saying it until she agreed to marry him. She became a housewife, and never forgave him.

* * *

My grandmother's family had their own entrepreneurship story. She was related to the Bruners, who were well-off enough to own a hotel downtown. During the great Baltimore fire of 1904, they watched tragedy approach them in the form of flames racing toward their building, fanned by high winds. Desperate, and being good Catholics, they took a figure of the Virgin Mary up to the roof and prayed the rosary – until the wind changed and the fire went the opposite direction.

My father's side of the family was overshadowed by a gothic awfulness in the person of my grandfather, whom the well-meaning drunken baker and his wife adopted when they couldn't have children. He became a long-distance truck driver, which probably counts as self-employment but nobody remembers him for being enterprising. His legacy has more to do with abandoning my grandmother with four small boys; when mental illness put her in the hospital, my father and his brothers were dispersed to various family members who couldn't afford them and didn't want them. Later on, my grandfather would take up residence in a sprawling, decaying house in rural Maryland surrounded by barking dogs and rusted cars, where he took in foster children. As one of my cousins explained to me when we were adults, everyone knew he wasn't atoning for abandoning his own children; everyone knew he was a pedophile supplying his appetites. I remember him giving me a birthday card when I was nine with a poem inside, written in a loopy cursive hand on scented pale-blue stationery: a romantic poem he had written himself, for me, affirming his love.

You know what they say about rats? If you see one, you can assume there are at least ten more in the general vicinity? In my extended family, that's what sexual abuse was like:

there's what you know about, but there's probably ten times more, that may or may not become visible over time.

My memory seems to be made up of detailed facets, like my grandfather's handwriting curling over the blue paper, or the patina of my great-grandmother's rolling pin, alongside big featureless swaths, like fog, from which nothing can be retrieved at all. But that's what entrepreneurship is about: starting from nothing.

2.

You can't say I was destined for entrepreneurship based on a family legacy of abuse, averted fires and broken teeth, because everybody in Baltimore has stories like that. As John Waters said, It's as if every eccentric in the South decided to move north, ran out of gas in Baltimore, and decided to stay.

You could say I was destined for entrepreneurship because of my friend M. In which case this story starts in the spring of 1980 at a birthday party in another lower middle class suburb of Baltimore, in which everyone was gathered around a girl laughing so hard she was gasping for air. Someone at the party had brought a cowboy hat, she had grabbed it and tried to put it on, but her uncontrollable halo of curly hair was not only sticking out from under the hat in every direction, it was lifting it up off her head. That's M., another girl told me. By then everyone was laughing, but M. was laughing the hardest. We were 12.

We were friends without having the things in common that adolescent girls usually have. We didn't live nearby or go to the same school. We became friends instantly at that birthday party, with no prelude or getting-to-know-you time. It just happened, a done deal, even more improbable for how shy I was and how effusive M. was.

M. was good at loving people, and she loved me in a way I hadn't experienced with anyone else: she was enthusiastic, fierce, always on my side. I remember her running to meet me with her arms thrown out, beaming. She wanted to be an actress and a singer, so I went to a lot of musicals at her high school. She was Jewish, so I learned to say grace in Hebrew. I talked to her about things I didn't talk to anyone else about.

She gave me a copy of Rainer Maria Rilke's *Letters to a*

Young Poet.[6] That's the one with this quote:

Be patient toward all that is unsolved in your heart and try to love the questions themselves, like locked rooms and like books that are now written in a very foreign tongue. Do not now seek the answers, which cannot be given you because you would not be able to live them. And the point is, to live everything. Live the questions now. Perhaps you will then gradually, without noticing it, live along some distant day into the answer.

That was my introduction to prefigurative intervention.

I had skipped a grade so I was a year ahead of her, but we managed to stay in touch after I left for college in Philadelphia. As my mother noted, she was always the first person to call to see if I was home for breaks or holidays. We stayed in touch when she went to college in New York. We saw each other whenever we were both home, and talked on the phone when we could afford the long-distance rates. We wrote letters when she spent a semester abroad in her junior year, studying musical theater in London. She sent me postcards from Amsterdam, murals by Keith Haring; M. and I had similar politics.

I was packing to go home for Christmas break my senior year when the phone rang in my dorm room. It was my mother, and her voice sounded funny. What's wrong? I asked. Is everybody OK?

Everybody in this family is OK, she said, and then she told me. M. was dead.

The plane she was on, coming home from London, blew up. It was a bomb.

* * *

My mother told me that she was coming to pick me up and take me home, even though I had a car at college; later she told me she was afraid I would have driven myself off the Francis Scott Key bridge. At the time, I wasn't thinking that far ahead, but she wasn't wrong, either.

That's a demarcation for me: before the phone rang that day, and after. Before December 21 1988 and the Lockerbie bombing, and after.

In death, M. was no more subtle than she'd been in life. A couple of days after I got home, I got a Christmas card in the mail from her. Being Jewish didn't stop her from sending Christmas cards every year; she went to a liberal Reconstructionist synagogue and she liked Christmas cards. On the front of the card was a picture of a candle, with glitter, and the quote, *It is better to light a single candle than to curse the darkness.* On the inside was a short letter in which she told me how much she loved me, no matter what changes might happen in our lives, and how she knew that the minute we saw each other again (hopefully SOON! – underlined twice) we'd be as close as ever. LOVE ALWAYS, M.

She must have mailed it from the airport.

Four hundred people came to her funeral, and three television crews. Lockerbie would be international news for years. 270 people had died in one of the largest mass murders in British history. I had just learned the lesson that would make me an entrepreneur: there is no safety. You can lose anything you love at any time. So you might as well light all the candles you can.

3.

In the months following M.'s death, I tried hard to avoid the media, and my friends at college tried to help me, but the pictures were everywhere. One of the first ones I saw was in a newspaper, where a photographer had taken a close up of a woman collapsing to the floor of an airport waiting area when she heard the news about Pan Am Flight 103. Later, over and over, there would be the image of the remains of the cockpit, blue and white with the words "Maid of the Seas" printed on crumpled metal, against a winter field.

I was taking a creative writing class, and I had only one thing to write about.

Photograph from Newsweek, 1

Aerial shot: the shaken landscape stilled
to this emerald square with its stand of trees,
its four spared roofs: beyond, the quiet hills
frame the settled ash. Visible echoes
scar the field: cracked window, buckled swath
of metal. It is just dusk: the searchers'
small figures choose their separate slow paths
from each border toward the vacant center
of the page, through strewn rain soaked luggage
to a green glossy blank: the place past shock,
past hope. They move through actuality,
accepting it, into the heart of the wreck –
absence, your absence – as if they could see
in that emptiness something to salvage.

Sycamores in Winter

Stripped to white and still alive
these are trees that have lost

almost everything: the soft
seed-spheres with their tawny
fur; the broad, dusty,
generous leaves;
even their mottled coats of bark
are gone to a few shreds.
In their splayed bleached bones
they stand up straight along
the riverbank. The brown river
slides by beneath them
whispers its sorrow,
and they do not hear. These trees
know nothing of solace.
Hang up in their branches
your particular loss
and move on, move on.

After a few weeks of this kind of thing, and my friends'
urging, I went to see a therapist at the college infirmary. In
the waiting room, there were copies of news magazines with
the cockpit photo on the cover. In the first conversation with
the therapist, it came up that I had been sexually abused, I
had told a few people about one episode, but it was only M.
who fully believed me, who got angry, who worried. It was
only M. who had responded, the therapist said,
appropriately. Given my family's history, it wasn't surprising
that other people didn't react well; but this would explain my
devastation after Lockerbie.

Even at 20 and wrecked by grief, I had an inkling that the
therapist was trying to wrap this up a little too neatly. The
bomb on Pan Am 103 had blown a hole into the center of my
life. It wasn't going to close. Explaining the hole didn't
change it; it was going to change me.

4.

Except for the creative writing class, I had a lot of trouble concentrating on school. My plan for awhile had been to apply to medical school, but first to take a year off after college and do some volunteer work. Alumnae at my college who were in medical school had counseled me to make sure I didn't mind being around sick people.

I applied to the Jesuit Volunteer Corps, a full-time volunteer service program that put Catholic college grads together to live in intentional communities for a year and work in social service agencies. Ruined for life, was the humorous slogan of the program. I figured I had a head start. Looking for program listings that would let me find out if I could handle sick people, I found one for an AIDS service organization in Portland, Oregon. What I knew about AIDS at that time would have fit on the back of the Keith Haring postcards that M. had sent me, but that was OK, the placement organizers told me, I just had to be willing to learn. My best friend in college, Jules, had grown up in the Pacific Northwest, and I had visited her there once; it was a different reality from Baltimore and Philadelphia. A new reality seemed like a good idea, since I was struggling to cope with being evicted from my previous one.

In hindsight, I can almost see the reverberations of the explosion, the shock waves, pushing me off the edge of the map of my known world.

5.

What I didn't tell the therapist at the college infirmary about my relationship with M. was that she also knew I thought I might be a lesbian (she was supportive but doubtful – it was the 80s, neither of us knew any out lesbians) and that I struggled, off and on, with a desire to die.

I had met what would now be called my suicidality a little after I met M.

It wasn't a mood so much as an urge; or, worse than an urge, flashes of what felt like it might be a drive, if it ever fully surfaced. It scared me. I didn't *want* to want to die, but at times, I did, or part of me did. I kept drafts of suicide notes. I had a list in my head of accessible poisons. I had found myself standing much too close to the edge of the subway platform. I had delayed learning to drive because I thought about how easy it would be to swerve into oncoming traffic. I picked up knives and put them down. I felt like something might be waiting for me to let my guard down, and if I ever did, if I ever stopped resisting, I could be in trouble in a heartbeat.

But for whatever inscrutable reason, the murderous part of me didn't seem to see M.'s death as an opportunity. In fact, it backed off. I was so stunned by how much pain I was in, there didn't seem to be room for anything else.

And when the shock began to wear off, what it turned out there was room for besides pain was wonder: at how much I had loved her, how much she had loved me. Both the wonder and the love had a kind of purity that felt like revelation: so this is what's there when it feels like there's nothing left. This is *still there*.

* * *

There was also, for lack of a better term, an awareness of the presence of God. I knew without a shadow of a doubt, God was with me. I would never be the same, but I would never be alone, either. It didn't occur to me to blame God for what had happened – some human being had made that bomb – or for how random and terrifying the world clearly was. God's presence was what made this new, M.-less world bearable. I didn't feel an impulse to ask God why. I didn't care why. No reason was going to change how I felt; nothing short of M. coming back would change that.

Years later, someone asked me if I believed in God and I said no. It's never been a matter of belief for me, only of experience. It's like asking me if I believe in the mailman: I see the mailman every day, he brings me letters, what is there to believe in? I must be intellectually lazy, because I can't seem to be bothered to think about questions of faith. My faith is something that takes care of me, not the other way around.

My experience of God has always felt a lot like solidarity – God offering me solidarity when I needed it. Which is probably why I believe in solidarity.

I don't mean to imply that I was OK because of God, because I wasn't. Before M.'s death, I had tried to be good. Afterwards, I couldn't seem to care much about whether I was good, or about a number of other things that most people seemed to care about. Decades later I would learn the term "foreshortened future" and feel an electric charge of recognition – that was what I was like after Lockerbie. I didn't see myself living very long. I had no expectations. Security, any kind of security, was a bad joke; I couldn't take it seriously.

It was something like fearlessness. The worst thing I could

have imagined had already happened.

6.

I was in great shape to move across the country, live with people I didn't know, and work full-time in an AIDS service organization.

The people in the Jesuit Volunteer Corps were kind and supportive. Nonetheless I had an inkling I might not fit in very well. When we got our tour of the "bad neighborhoods" of Portland where we would be living in our communal houses, all of them looked better than my old neighborhood in Lakeland. Even the worst neighborhoods in Portland had rose gardens, because that's Portland; but there was also something I didn't have language for yet, and that was social class.

I knew I was low class, working class, white trash in fact. I'd learned this in college without being able to articulate it. I'd gone to Bryn Mawr on a scholarship; Bryn Mawr, where the Rockefellers had built dorms so that their daughters would have a nice place to stay. Freshman year, I overheard a conversation between other students talking about their families' cleaning ladies. One of my favorite aunts was a cleaning lady; it was a talent – since she was a little girl she had loved to clean and had done all the cleaning because she was better at it than anybody else. There were lots of jolts like that. Almost all of my friends were other scholarship students, though, so I didn't have to think about it most of the time.

My family, like any immigrant family, was thrilled that I wanted to go to medical school. A year of volunteer work, though, they didn't understand and weren't thrilled about. We weren't the type of people that had the luxury of volunteering.

My fellow Jesuit Volunteers were mostly clean-cut and idealistic. They did believe in volunteering, and in being good. They were good to me, even when I came out to them (by this time I was pretty sure I was queer, though nobody was using that word then), when I flinched at newspapers and the TV, when I cried way more than anyone else. JVC was balm when I was very raw. I could mostly put aside the class differences in the same way I'd learned to do in college, and I got an education in intentional communities.

In the fall of 1989 I went to work as the Assistant Volunteer Coordinator at Cascade AIDS Project. Founded six years before as a grassroots, all-volunteer effort within the gay community of Portland, by the time I arrived CAP had a small paid staff and a suite of offices in a somewhat scruffy building downtown, sharing the second floor with an environmental nonprofit and a coven of goddess worshipers. My position was in the Client Services department, which addressed issues such as housing, getting people on to social security disability once they could no longer work, legal referrals (everything from problems with discrimination to writing wills and powers of attorney) and providing emotional and practical support via a small army of volunteers.

About half of the staff and the volunteers were HIV+, which at that time meant they were probably going to die within a few years. I met one volunteer who had been HIV+ for 10 years: only one.

At that time, CAP was growing as quickly as it could to meet its clients' ever-expanding need for services. When people first got diagnosed, they needed emotional support and legal help; as time went on, they continued to need those things as well as mobility aids, financial support, and all kinds of caregiving. CAP was hovering on the cusp between a small community of friends, lovers, ex-lovers and family members mobilizing to take care of each other and a full-fledged social service agency. It wasn't an easy transition. There wasn't very much support for my volunteer position, which meant I had to figure a lot of things out for myself. In general I felt in the shadow of my predecessor, Kath, the previous year's Jesuit Volunteer. Kath had been fun. Everybody agreed on that. She had been good at using her position to provide social support for clients in the form of organized activities – movie nights, outings, parties with themes. Fun things.

I suspected I wasn't equipped to be fun.

My first month at CAP, my supervisor Paul went on vacation. Paul was CAP's gracious, overworked executive director, recently promoted from being the head of Client Services to running the whole agency. Paul's drag name was Michelle and he occasionally wore a feather boa to work. I saw very little of Paul and tried not to bother him.

Besides the fun activities, I was supposed to be coming up with, the main part of my job was to match volunteers willing to provide practical support with clients who needed it. Most often the practical support involved rides to the doctor, light cleaning, and meal preparation. More than a few of CAP's clients had been rejected by their families for being gay, and they couldn't expect any help from that quarter. I had a little box of index cards on my desk with the names of volunteers, their phone numbers, what they were willing to do and for how many hours a week they were willing to do it. The box was divided into sections for active and inactive volunteers. Sometimes inactive volunteers were simply taking a break, and there would be a note saying when they could be called again; more often, inactive volunteers had become too sick themselves to work. There was a stack of cards at the very back of the box that belonged to volunteers who had died.

* * *

Within two weeks, I learned that my most useful skill set was begging: asking the nice retired lady who sang in the liberal Episcopal church choir and also volunteered for us if she could, just this once, skip choir practice to drive a client to and from his support group; entreating the owner of the auto body shop who donated oil changes to our clients if he could please fix someone's brakes, too; getting prospective volunteers from just thinking about helping to officially signing up.

A few days after Paul left for vacation, I got a call from Philip, whose name I recognized from my inactive volunteer section. Philip was polite and close to panic. He was no longer volunteering because he needed to care for his partner, William. Philip had taken all the time he could take off of work and William had recently gotten much sicker. Philip had to go back to work, next week, and he couldn't leave William alone. Could we help him?

Yes, I said. Tell me your schedule. I'll find people.

I paged through my index cards looking for volunteers who were willing to sit at someone's bedside and also willing to help keep track of medications (William was taking a lot of them) and I started to call. I made a chart with blocks on it: Monday to Friday, 9 to 1 and 1 to 5. I found a couple of people who were willing to take an entire day; the rest had to be arranged piecemeal, sometimes cutting up the blocks into two hours instead of four. I dug through my section of inactive volunteers and found some who could be persuaded to come back, just for this emergency.

When Paul came back from vacation he found me crying at my desk. I'm sorry, I don't think I can do this, I told him. This is too hard.

* * *

Tell me more, he said. What's the part that's too hard? (Paul had a Master's in social work.)

I told him about Philip and William, and all the begging I had done for the last week, and how I was afraid that the volunteers would get tired and stop showing up for William.

Paul said, Wait, how many hours of coverage are we talking about?

Forty, I sniffed. Philip works full-time.

Paul said, Full-time. You put together full-time in-home care for someone? With volunteers?

I nodded. And some meal deliveries on the weekends.

You know, Paul said, that's way beyond the scope of what we expect to be able to do. You don't have to do that. It's too much.

Oh, I said. I didn't realize.

In a different story, the lesson I might have learned from this episode would have been about the need to ask for guidance and help with setting parameters in situations I didn't understand; also, maybe something pithy about the value of self-care. Instead, the lesson I learned was that if you threw yourself at the limits, maybe the limits would give.

Also, fun wasn't my strong point.

7.

Sometime in the fall, my coworker Corey (the mental health therapist on the Client Services team) sat down next to my desk and told me he wanted to talk to me about something. He had set up a program for clients, volunteers and caregivers to learn meditation. It was a brand-new program, twelve weeks of classes on Thursday nights at a local hospital. He was trying to get all the staff in Client Services to go and learn to meditate; he thought we needed it. OK, I said. Sure, I'm game.

I was the only staff person other than Corey in a mixed group of clients and their support people. The teacher handed out Xeroxed manuals and explained that the meditation program was based on the teachings of Eknath Easwaran, an English literature professor at UC Berkeley. As a young man in India, Easwaran had been inspired by Mahatma Gandhi, in particular Gandhi's effort to memorize the Bhagavad Gita in its entirety. Easwaran believed that an effective method of meditation, easily accessible to Americans, was to memorize passages of scripture – any scripture, Easwaran was utterly ecumenical – and to repeat them silently, a word at a time, so that their message would drop deep into the unconscious mind. The plan was to start with ten minutes a day of this "passage meditation", reciting a sacred text slowly and in silence, first thing in the morning, and gradually increasing the time to half an hour. We would all begin by memorizing the first few lines of the peace prayer of St. Francis (Easwaran's choice for beginners) and then practice together– turn to page five in the manual, please.

Lord, make me an instrument of your peace:
where there is hatred, let me sow love;
where there is injury, pardon...

* * *

We all pored over the lines, moving our lips, and then we put the manuals away, sat up straight on our hard chairs under the fluorescent lights in the hospital meeting room, and closed our eyes to try to repeat the words we'd just memorized.

I was instantly hooked.

As I tried to keep track of the words of the passage, something happened in the dark behind my eyes, in my body sitting in the chair. It was like following a rope hand over hand into an enormous, steadying quiet. I was all at once open, and still, and plugged into a current of support and strength. I had had moments like this, every so often, when I prayed; it had never occurred to me that this was a state you could *practice*, something you could decide to make regular in your life.

The teacher emphasized that the point of this kind of meditation wasn't necessarily to relax, though we might feel relaxed; the point was to train our attention. Everyone in that room was encountering a life-threatening illness either for themselves or with people close to them. Trained attention was a resource we needed. And how were we to accomplish this? As it turned out, the gentle professor Easwaran had a ruthless streak. If your mind wandered while you were going slowly through the passage, you had to go back and start over at the beginning. In fact, it was not uncommon to spend your entire period of meditation dragging your mind back to the first few lines of the passage.

Some of the class groaned.

Furthermore, though we would be meditating on passages composed by mystics, the point of this kind of meditation was not to have mystical experiences, to reflect on the meaning of the words we were repeating, or to judge the quality of our own meditation.

It was just. to say. the words. silently, as if. we were. dropping. pearls. one. at a time. into. a quiet. lake.

And then see what happened. The proof would be in our daily lives: were we more patient, more centered, more able to meet challenges?

Over the course of the twelve weeks, it became clear that the project of learning passage meditation had varying levels of appeal for people in the class. During a check-in about how well we were doing keeping up with a daily commitment of fifteen minutes, one client announced that he had discovered that he could meditate for three hours at a time in his hot tub, if he had a glass of wine. Other people found the scriptural passages off-putting; the option of meditating on excerpts from texts that didn't mention God, such as the Twin Verses, didn't make it more pleasant. Attendance dwindled. I kept going.

All that we are is the result of what we have thought: we are formed and molded by our thoughts. Those whose minds are shaped by selfish thoughts cause misery when they speak or act. Sorrows roll over them as the wheels of a cart roll over the tracks of the oxen that draw it.[7]

Whether it was St. Francis or Buddha, the passages were strong stuff, uncompromising, and I didn't mind. Within a couple of weeks, I realized those fifteen minute periods of repeating the same lines over and over gave me a feeling of internal stability, and I was hanging on as if my life depended on it. Possibly it did.

The teacher emphasized that the effects of meditation would

build incrementally over years. Some people were annoyed with the delayed gratification, but I loved the idea; it suggested the possibility of a future. I had already discovered that whether my actual meditation time went well or badly, the sense of connecting to something huge and quiet and solid never varied. I was also beginning to notice a feeling of lightening, as if tension was unwinding from the center of my body, a little at a time. For a long time, I had had a bad secret, the knowledge that part wanted me to die; I was beginning to feel that I had a good secret, a daily arrangement with myself to build resistance to that murderous part. It might try to drag me over the edge, but every day I was quietly tying another knot in a rope that could anchor me.

In twenty-seven years, I think I've missed maybe three days of meditation. I've never wanted to be very far from my rope.

Cut to the Chase, Please #2

Is all this talk about your mental health problems necessary? I mean, we sympathize, OK? But this is supposed to be about entrepreneurship.

Right. There's no polite way to say this but here goes: in my case, I think they might be the same thing, or at least they're very close together.

It's tricky, because it's clear that mental health problems could absolutely interfere with someone's ability to be an entrepreneur in all sorts of ways. I don't want to sound like I'm suggesting that anybody who's struggling with suicidal ideation or PTSD or anxiety should go out and start a social business, or any business for that matter. It's not that simple.

However, I've had a lot of opportunity to watch other people start their own businesses, and I can't avoid the conclusion that my relative success had a lot to do with the level of discomfort I was already prepared to tolerate, and guess what prepared me? I've met a lot of new business owners who gave every indication, at least from the outside, of being happier and more stable or at least a lot less tormented than I was, and I've seen them give up and throw in the towel at points where I kept going. In part, because they felt they deserved to have an easier, more secure life, and entrepreneurship wasn't going to give it to them.

I didn't think I deserved anything, and I didn't care very much what happened to me. My default setting for years and years was: nothing to lose. I'm not saying this is a good way to be, but it gave me a lot of freedom to take risks.

* * *

It was a special advantage in the project of applying entrepreneurial techniques to a social problem – and continuing to apply them for years until they had an effect big enough to be visible to other people. I wasn't expecting, or demanding, to get results that would make me feel good. I had no reason to assume that my feeling good was supposed to be part of the greater scheme of things.

Furthermore, the primary way I found to manage my mental health problems, meditation practice, turned out to have the long-term effects that Eknath Easwaran promised. I developed an enhanced ability to focus. I found a kind of patience (all the more notable for basically being an impatient person). All those years of dragging my attention back to the first line of a passage after it had wandered away gave me the ability to stay with something. When other people got distracted, I stayed on task. These are crucial skills for an entrepreneur, but they were all side effects: I stuck with daily meditation for decades because I was afraid if I didn't, I would kill myself.

Well that's bleak.

Is it? If you're reading this book because you're thinking you might want to be a community acupuncturist, please be advised that a lot of people's inner lives are this bleak (at *least*). Working in a community clinic gives you a window into the enormous amount of hidden suffering just under the surface of any group of ordinary people. This was a good thing for me, because it made me feel a lot less alone. It gave me a sense of solidarity with my patients. It might or might not be that good for you, depending on where you're coming from.

And if you're reading this book for the social entrepreneurship case study aspect, I promise I'll eventually get to the part where I did develop the ability to care about what happened to me (though that's still a work in progress).

8.

During my year in the Jesuit Volunteer Corps, I kept writing poems to M.

In the Rainforest

Some of the roots arch out of the earth; shoulder high,
each is a lean, flexed muscle, black with rain.
In the sprawl of ferns and salmonberry
are hemlocks, spruce, grown in strange straight lines.
This is the reason: a tree falls, by wind,
by lightning, by disease, and on the floor
of the forest its dead length is rich ground
for seedlings. They thrive on the slow disappear-
ance of the nurse log; their roots, reaching down,
encircle its body. Years later these trees
balance above the emptied space on live
flying buttresses. Like them, my heart has grown
to tell your absence; cathedral spaces
steady me, still shaped, without you, by your love.

I also got into my first serious intimate relationship. With a woman (a former JV herself). I left the Catholic Church. And I began to suspect I wasn't going to medical school after all.

Leaving the Church and giving up on medical school were also early lessons in the basics of entrepreneurship. In both cases, it came down to what I could make myself do and what I couldn't. I couldn't be in a relationship with a woman and stay Catholic, not at that point in my life. Being in a relationship, period, was proving to have its challenges; I didn't have the energy to be judged for it every Sunday, or to wonder if I was being judged for it. And now that I had a meditation practice, I had another source of spiritual nourishment.

I didn't have the energy to study for the MCATs, either. I couldn't even make myself register for them. I had left college with all of my prerequisites for medical school completed and letters of recommendation already written. Bryn Mawr had something like a 100% acceptance rate to medical schools – I knew I'd get in. I was a good test-taker, so I wasn't intimidated. There were just a few more straightforward steps to take.

I kept not taking them. I'd think about what I needed to do, and it just wouldn't happen. It was like some kind of stubborn reverse magic.

What I had learned at Cascade AIDS Project was that I was fine with being around sick people, even extremely sick people. I wasn't grossed out by bodily fluids. I didn't get impatient with people with dementia. The whole thing was a non-issue.

What I didn't like, though? Hospitals. I had visited enough clients in hospitals to get a clue that they were not my natural habitat. I couldn't picture myself in scrubs, doing an internship or a residency; I couldn't see myself spending more than a couple of hours in a hospital for any reason at all. To be fair, the AIDS epidemic circa 1989 was not exactly an advertisement for the practice of biomedicine. The few drugs available, AZT and DDI, had horrendous side effects for many patients. Medical procedures were painful, tests were often pointless. Thanks to working with so many people living with HIV, I had an up-close view of the downside of what were supposed to be medical advances in the treatment of a life-threatening condition. Once Paul was out of work for weeks because he'd had a terrible reaction to a routinely prescribed antibiotic; nobody had realized he was allergic.

Palliative medicine was not yet a term in use. What well-intentioned doctors did for our clients seemed to hurt so much and help so little.

I didn't want to do those things. I had to admit that to myself.

I did want to do *something*, though, and CAP was also where I discovered acupuncture. Clients were trying all sorts of alternative therapies. Some of them were bizarre, ill-advised, and associated with side effects almost as bad as those of the AIDS drugs. Acupuncture, though, seemed different from everything else. Everyone who tried it, liked it. It had no side effects; it moderated the side effects of other drugs. I mentioned to one of the volunteers, Micah, that I was thinking about acupuncture school instead of medical school and he said, Oh yes, that's a MUCH better fit for you, kiddo.

I'd given my year of volunteer service the power to veto medical school if that's what had to happen – so there it was, though not for the reasons I'd expected.

Acupuncture school it would be.

9.

To say that I didn't know what I was getting into would be an understatement of epic proportions. All I had was my clients'-eye-view of acupuncture from an AIDS service organization, circa 1990. Here's an overview of what I wish I had known, an abridged people's history of acupuncture in the United States.

Chinese immigrants in the 19th century, fleeing famine at home and seeking work on the railroads and in gold mines, brought acupuncture and Chinese medicine to the US. The oldest recorded practitioner was Doc Ing Hay who settled in John Day, Oregon, about five hours away from Portland. For decades Doc Hay practiced out of the Kam Wah Chung store, a combination community center, general store, and apothecary for the Chinatown in John Day.

Most of the Chinese laborers there lived in tents. Sometimes at night, for entertainment, local cowboys would ride through shooting randomly into the darkness. The Kam Wah Chung store, now a museum in a state park, is a little wooden building reinforced with tin. The windows are narrow and shuttered, and the shutters are pocked with bullet holes. The kitchen in the living quarters of the store has an especially thick floor by the stove, so that Doc Hay and his business partner could chop wood without having to venture outside. Anti-Asian racism at that time was vicious; the Chinese Exclusion Act of 1882 was the only law in the history of the US to prohibit immigration on the basis of race.

Doc Hay, despite being brought up on charges three times for practicing medicine without a license, treated hundreds of patients both within and outside the Chinese community until 1948. In 1910, many of the Chinese laborers moved out of John Day, but Doc Hay stayed, treating local farmers and ranchers for a long list of frontier problems, including blood poisoning, frostbite, typhoid, infertility, and venereal disease. And influenza. When flu broke out within a highway construction crew near John Day in 1919, Doc Hay reportedly arrived on the scene with huge pots of steaming, bitter herbal decoctions. The crew recovered. Long-time John Day residents claimed not one of Doc Hay's patients died during the Spanish Flu epidemic that killed 3,500 people in Oregon alone.

After Doc Hay's death, his family bequeathed the store to the town of John Day. In the process of creating the museum, workers found a box under Doc Hay's bed with $23,000 in uncashed checks, the equivalent of a quarter of a million dollars today. It seems he didn't cash the checks because he knew, especially during the Depression, many of his patients couldn't afford to pay him.

Twenty years after Doc Hay retired, another talented Chinese medicine practitioner (acupuncturist, previously nurse-midwife) named Miriam Lee was working in California, where acupuncture was illegal. She had a day job on a factory assembly line and treated patients out of her house; people lined up on her back staircase until the stairs broke. A sympathetic doctor offered her the use of his office in the mornings, where she treated 80 patients in 7 hours, 5 days a week. Eventually she, too, was charged with practicing medicine without a license, but her patients packed the courtroom and the authorities yielded, first making acupuncture an experimental procedure and eventually legalizing it. Later in her life, Miriam Lee admonished her acupuncture students:

To practice acupuncture, you must be certain of your intention, your purpose in doing so...If the intention is wrong, if you are concentrating on earning money, treating fewer patients and charging higher fees, doing little for much profit, you may get some results from your treatments or you may not. [8]

At the same time Miriam Lee was treating 14-17 patients an hour in California, on the other side of the country the Black Panthers were experimenting with delivering acupuncture as part of their community service work. Also known as Survival Programs, these efforts included free breakfasts for children, health and dental clinics, sickle cell anemia testing, food and housing cooperatives, support for prisoners and their families, even an ambulance service. Besides developing black self-determination and self-organizing, the Survival Programs were intended to provide a model to all oppressed people for taking concrete steps to address their situation.

In the South Bronx, the Young Lords, a Puerto Rican nationalist group, and the Black Panthers took over Lincoln Hospital to protest poor medical care, discrimination, and lack of services, including addiction treatment. During their occupation of the hospital, they established the People's Drug Program, which later became Lincoln Detox and included an acupuncture collective. They learned that a Dr. Wen in Hong Kong was reporting miraculous success in treating opiate addiction by means of auricular acupuncture, and they set out to duplicate it.

Dr. Wen's protocol involved using electrical stimulation on a point in the ear. The acupuncture collective of Lincoln Detox found that this approach got good results, until the electro stim machine broke, and they found out ear acupuncture alone got even better results. It was also cheaper and easier to learn. Eventually, through trial and error, they developed a five-point auricular protocol used for all kinds of addiction. The ear is an acupuncture microsystem, often pictured as an upside-down baby, with points corresponding to internal organs on the inside of the ear, and the toes, fingers, and other extremities on the outer edge. The five-needle protocol includes the points corresponding to the Lung, Liver, Kidney, Sympathetic Nervous System, and a "spirit" point called Shen Men.

In 1979 the authorities dismantled Lincoln Detox by force. The use of acupuncture to treat addiction continued at Lincoln Hospital with the work of NADA, the National Acupuncture Detoxification Association, and the five-point protocol became known as NADA 5NP. NADA has trained over 10,000 health workers, including nurses, social workers and counselors, to use the protocol for what is now known as acu-detox.

Most of the Cascade AIDS Project clients and volunteers I knew who were getting acupuncture were reaping the long-term benefits of the Lincoln Hospital occupation, in the form of acupuncture having a modest role in public health. They didn't know that, and neither did I.

During the same years that the Lincoln Detox acupuncture collective was operating outside the law, a small group of white students of Chinese acupuncturists were working steadily to build what would become the infrastructure of the future acupuncture profession, including schools and standardized curricula. They were mostly professionals, and their priorities reflected their socioeconomic position. They were going to build the acupuncture profession that white upper-middle-class professionals thought the US should have.[2]

It's as if there are two different directions in the development of acupuncture in the US, like separate moving walkways in an airport: marginalized communities using acupuncture and Chinese medicine to take care of themselves, and more privileged individuals working to fence it off with a goal of increasing its status. I was about to get on the walkway moving in the opposite direction of where I belonged.

10.

Acupuncture's weird.

Not just for people who've never had it, people looking at it skeptically from a safe distance, but also for people who've had a lot of it, and for people who practice it. Familiarity doesn't make it un-mysterious. Let me get this out of the way: it's got nothing to do with whether you believe in it or not. Animals both large and small respond to acupuncture in the same ways that people do (though who knows if they think it's weird). Learning facts or theories about acupuncture won't clear up its mysteries because it's not a puzzle to solve. It does what it does, regardless of how you explain it. It's organic, uncanny, ancient.

The first time I got acupuncture, I didn't feel much. I made an appointment with an acupuncturist who worked in a practice that fit the professionalized template: it was in a medical building, there was a well-dressed receptionist to meet me, I was ushered back to a softly-lit cubicle and given a gown to put on. The acupuncturist, a pleasant woman wearing a white coat, was businesslike. I paid about $60 for a first visit, sometime in 1990, an astronomical amount to me.

It wasn't at all like learning to meditate; there was no immediate connection between me and the experience. Like everyone who gets acupuncture in America, I was surprised at how small the needles were. I thought it would be like getting blood drawn in twenty places. (Side note: it's unfortunate we call them needles at all; they're more like delicate pins.) It didn't hurt, but it didn't do much for me, either. I was hoping to relieve some jaw pain that I thought was TMJ but a week later it turned out to be an abscessed tooth; what I needed was antibiotics and a root canal. The acupuncturist forgot a needle on the top of my head; I found it while waiting for the bus afterwards. That didn't freak me out, but since I couldn't afford that acupuncturist, I looked for another one (after I'd gotten the root canal).

By that time, I'd left Cascade AIDS Project, and I had a new job working at a group home for disabled kids. I discovered what most people who work with kids at close quarters find out: there's a lot of opportunity to share germs. I'd been prone to lung problems for a while and I got bronchitis every year. After I'd been in my new job a few months, though, it felt like I barely recovered from one cold before I had another. I wanted to know if acupuncture could help with that. Since my job was minimum wage, I found a clinic, Open Gate, that had a sliding scale. It was in a little storefront in a scruffy part of town; inside was clean and basic, lots of houseplants. My acupuncturist, Greg, was more sympathetic than the expensive one across town, and I was more comfortable. I paid $10 a treatment and I went every week.

This time, the treatments worked like magic. I got over one cold quickly and didn't immediately get another one. Even better, I began to be able to tell when I might be about to come down with something, and if I did the right things – slowing down, drinking fluids – I didn't get sick at all. I was aware of my body in a way I hadn't been before. Winter passed with no bronchitis, and within six months, my immune system was much stronger. I also had more energy and most notably, felt like I'd been given emotional shock absorbers: life seemed to go more smoothly, and if something did go wrong, I had extra patience at my disposal. Clients at CAP had told me that acupuncture reduced their stress; now I knew what they were talking about.

Most people describe getting acupuncture as relaxing, and I experienced that too. Relaxing, though, is generally the tip of the iceberg. Acupuncture often functions like a low-level psychedelic drug. It's common to see colors; some people see whole kaleidoscopes. Once a patient told me he knew his treatment was done when he saw flashing purple lights. It's not uncommon to feel like you're floating, and to have sudden insights about your life. I would lie on the table in the little treatment room at Open Gate and feel like my whole body was dreaming. In a word – weird.

The term self-care wasn't used much in the early 90s, but I was beginning to have an experience of it. Between regular acupuncture and daily meditation, I was putting more energy into my own wellbeing than I ever had. It felt a little strange, but I kept at it.

11.

I enrolled in acupuncture school about a month after my girlfriend and I split up. I wasn't doing well; at 23 I was pretty sure I'd failed at relationships and nobody was ever going to love me again. The first class I attended in acupuncture school was in tui na, Chinese massage. Almost all acupuncture schools are emphatic about acupuncture being only a small part of "the complete system of healing that is Chinese medicine", so students are required to learn bodywork, herbs, qi gong, and Chinese dietary therapy, which serves to both round out their knowledge and increase tuition. I only ever cared about the needles.

The tui na instructor, a severe person with an obvious disdain for first-year students, demonstrated how to roll our wrists back and forth over a little pillow filled with rice. For two hours, most of the class did it badly. Disgusted, he sent us home with our rice pillows to practice. I went home and cried instead, wondering if I'd made a huge mistake.

The best class I had my first year was on the I-Ching – the Book of Changes. It's one of the world's oldest books, both a central text of Chinese literature and a diviner's manual. It's a work of philosophy, but it's also an oracle, and you can ask it questions by means of casting yarrow sticks or coins or – these days – clicking on any of a number of websites.

In her book of essays *The Wave in the Mind*, Ursula Le Guin describes the I-Ching as *a grandmother, wise and mild though sometimes rather dark of counsel...the visionary elder who has outlived fact, the ancestor so old she speaks a different tongue. Her counsel sometimes is appallingly clear, sometimes very obscure indeed.*[10] We learned how to ask questions of the I-Ching using colored beads instead of yarrow stalks. Our teacher, a kind man named Kyle, also urged us to practice, and while my rice pillow sat ignored, my colored beads were a different story. Every day I asked the I-Ching if my girlfriend would change her mind and we would get back together. Every day the I-Ching – appallingly clear – told me no.

There are 64 hexagrams in the I-Ching, each one with a name, an image and a narrative, and each of its six lines has a short oracular text. The lines are either solid (yang) or broken (yin). The lines of the hexagram can be fixed or moving; a moving line changes into its opposite: yang into yin, or yin into yang. This produces a second hexagram. When you ask a question, the oracle will give you either one hexagram with no changing lines, or one hexagram becoming another, with the moving lines describing key elements of the transformation.

It sounds more complicated than it is. Once you get the hang of it, it's like asking someone a question and having them answer you by offering you two elegant, overlapping Chinese landscape paintings. For example: Hexagram 5, Waiting (rain falling from clouds in the heavens) becomes Hexagram 9, Small Accumulation (two piles of grass stacked on top of each other). The changing line of Waiting means, do not lose heart, good fortune comes in strange disguises. That kind of thing.

That's not the answer I got when I asked about my girlfriend. I got Hexagram 23, Splitting Apart. (A house gradually falls into disrepair, its foundations eaten away, until finally the roof disintegrates and the house collapses.) No changing lines.

At the end of the term, Kyle announced he had a present for us. He had found an arcane method of casting the I-Ching that would give us not the answer to a specific question, but a more general description of our fate. It involved a complicated formula of numbers matched to the letters in our name and our birthdate, combined and then broken down in a way I can't remember, creating a pattern of yin and yang lines. I kept the answer in a journal.

My personal hexagram was Hexagram 48, The Well, changing to Hexagram 14, Great Possession. Lines 1, 4, 5 and 6 were moving and are meant to be read in order. What's that in English?

My favorite I-Ching translation, *The Laws of Change* by Jack Balkin, says this:

48: The Well. One can change the town, but one cannot change the well. It neither decreases nor increases...

The theme is the need to replenish yourself and others. A well that is properly tended is inexhaustible. You may think you do not have much to offer. But do not sell yourself short; be willing to dig down deep inside yourself and realize your potential. You do not yet know all the things you are capable of.

Line 1: The well is muddy. Do not neglect yourself.

Line 4: The well is being lined. No blame. To line the well with stone means to take it out of service temporarily to fix it and renew it.

Line 5 (Ruling Line): In the well is a clear, cold spring. Drink.

Line 6: They draw from the well. Do not cover it. There is confidence. Supreme good fortune. A well in working order is available to everyone. Continually fed by a spring, it is dependable and never runs dry, and everyone benefits from it...

changing to:

14: Possession in great measure. This hexagram consists of five yang lines surrounding a single yin line in the fifth position, the place of the ruler. It represents a leader whose receptivity allows him to gather the most talented people around him. As a result, he prospers.[11]

Spoiler alert: those two hexagrams turned out to be the best summary of my career I could have asked for, both in terms of what I'd be doing and what it would feel like.

The primary requirement for a well is a deep hole. Thanks to Lockerbie, I knew I had one of those, I just didn't know there was a spring at the bottom. I didn't know, but the I-Ching did, that a loss that felt bottomless would become a space to be filled. I had room for something very large to come to me, something I didn't know I needed, that would nourish me and (surprisingly) other people too.

And great possession? That's a funny hexagram for a white trash girl to get. But it fit. For most the hexagrams in the I-Ching, the fifth line is the ruling line and the most important; so obviously, the fifth line should be a yang line – strong, positive, masculine – if the hexagram is to be auspicious. In Hexagram 14, there's a yin line, a broken line, in the fifth position – weak, negative, feminine. Yet Hexagram 14 still promises success, because the weakness of the fifth line gathers strength to itself in the form of yang lines in every other position. Weakness attracts support. Brokenness holds the center – and leads.

12.

I was angry in acupuncture school, almost all the time. I couldn't have said why. The distance between what acupuncture school was and where I had come from was too big. The first week my class had a group discussion initiated by someone who felt that the water filter in the student lounge was inadequate, and an hour-long argument about the right brand of water filters followed. Meanwhile, I was still getting invited to funerals of people I'd known at CAP. What is this nonsense, I thought, and who are these people who care so much about water filters? I was 23, a lot of people I knew were dead, and I had no perspective on anything.

Also, something was wrong in my point location classes; there were times when I hated the process of letting other students find points on me. Being palpated, prodded, handled, put me on edge. I found another student who also felt out of place in school; she had enrolled after being a community health worker in El Salvador, and was having a similar sense of culture shock. We paired up for finding points, for needling practice, and for complaining, and that was better. But something was off. I watched some of my classmates all but purr when they were on the receiving end of massage practice, and I wondered why, in an environment where I was being touched so often and with such good intentions, I felt like I wanted to hit somebody.

There were bright spots, like the I-Ching class. And once, in a point functions class, the teacher started out by saying seriously, the reason to learn these things is that you will be able to relieve a lot of suffering. Aha, I thought, that's why I came, maybe there's hope after all.

And then there was observation at Hooper Detox.

* * *

The work of the National Acupuncture Detoxification Association, born at Lincoln Detox, had made it across the country to Portland, which was already progressive in its approach to alcoholism: the detox was named for David Hooper, the last person to die of alcoholism in the Portland city jail in 1971. Instead of arresting intoxicated people, police in Portland brought them in to a residential medical detox program where they could stay for up to two weeks. Hooper primarily took in people who needed to detox from alcohol, a process which could be life-threatening, and heroin, a process which was mostly just miserable. As they say, alcohol detox doesn't feel like it'll kill you, but it can; heroin detox won't kill you, but you wish it would.

Part of the program at Hooper was auricular acupuncture using the NADA protocol. Word was that Hooper staff had found that mandatory daily acupuncture cut the rate of patients leaving detox early, against medical advice, by about 50%; there was a similar reduction in the seizure rate. These statistics were tested when funding for acupuncture was briefly cut – and quickly restored.

Second year acupuncture students had to observe treatments in the school clinic: 150 total hours were required. I discovered I liked observation at the school clinic about as much as I liked tui na. It was a lot of awkward standing around in white lab coats, watching third year students do things we couldn't do yet. I found out I could do some observation hours at Hooper instead, and I hurried to sign up.

At that time, Hooper was located in a big, grim, institutional-looking building with a line of people outside sleeping on the sidewalk; many of its clients were homeless. Inside, the person in charge of acupuncture services, let's call him Alan, was soft-spoken and a natural teacher. He was glad to have an observer, in part because there was plenty to do. I couldn't put in needles, but I could help remove them; there were blood pressure readings to take during intake, and some patients, once they were admitted, wanted as much treatment as they could get. I helped do moxa, which is a heat therapy using compressed mugwort – smoky but very soothing for arthritis. Alan might treat up to 40 patients during a shift, so there was no standing around at Hooper.

Some of the most important things I ever learned about acupuncture I learned at Hooper, within an hour of walking through the door the first day.

1) You don't have to believe in acupuncture for it to work – I mean you really don't have to believe in it. You can actively not want it, you can hate that it's mandatory, you can be cursing your acupuncturist as he's putting the needles in your ears during intake, and it will still work. This will be in evidence first when your blood pressure goes down to normal and you stop cursing and fall asleep with your head on the intake table, and even more so two days later when you're asking for extra head points because the acupuncture you didn't want has made such a difference for your nightmares.

2) Ambience doesn't matter. In school, we were taught that ambience mattered a lot, that our white coats in clinic were crucial props, that acupuncture needed to be presented in a professional setting if anybody was ever going to respect and value it. Alternately, a spa setting with fountains and soothing background music might be OK if the decor was tasteful enough. At Hooper, acupuncture was delivered in hard chairs under fluorescent lights; in the intake room, there was a tape of Brian Eno's Music for Airports, but often enough it was drowned out by the sound of somebody

screaming and banging on the walls down the hall in the
Sobering Station. Alan never wore a white coat or asked his
observers to. Acupuncture worked great at Hooper, better
than it seemed to work in student clinic. I saw it knock out
migraines, stop nausea, and calm agitated people.

3) Treating people in groups with acupuncture is easier than
treating them individually. Between the influence of the
Black Panthers and the Young Lords at the beginning, and of
Alcoholics Anonymous later, it was inevitable that NADA
would reflect the importance of the community. AA
understands addiction as a disease that grows in loneliness
and isolation. NADA believes that people sitting together
with needles in silence is how healing happens. At school I
was studying acupuncture through a lens of individualism –
it's all about the brilliance of the practitioner illuminating
the uniqueness of each patient – but at Hooper I was seeing
something deeply communal at work. Everyone got basically
the same treatment – 5 needles in the ear, give or take some
extra points – but there was a presence and a power in the
group that was missing from individual treatments.

Twenty-four years later, Andrew Zitcer, a scholar studying
our cooperative, would write:

*Acupuncture is inherently and unforgivingly social.
Patients and practitioners are in an intimate, sometimes
ongoing, relationship, body to body...What could be more
path breaking than the idea of communal rest, communal
healing?*[12]

4) Best of all I was learning that whatever soothing and
stabilizing magic took hold under those fluorescent lights, in
that circle of hard chairs, whatever stillness spread outward
from the needles, if I was standing there it reached out to
include me. Years later I would hear Dr. Michael Smith, one

of the founders of NADA, say about treating large groups of people: it will heal you, too.

Hooper was where I saw the healing power of repetition at work. I had already discovered this for myself in meditation: it was the every-day-ness of my practice that gave it power, the repetition of the passages digging grooves in my thought patterns. Perhaps that made it easier to recognize with acupuncture: it was the every-day-ness of the treatments at Hooper that made them work, the incrementalism of each treatment building on the one before, the democracy of everybody getting basically the same treatment, everybody participating in the circle. It was low-key, humble, unthreatening. For someone with destroyed expectations of the world, it was the perfect thing.

13.

But eventually I used up the observation hours I could have at Hooper, and I dragged myself back to the student clinic for observation. And that's where I met S.

At that time, the student clinic had a classroom where everyone gathered when they weren't treating patients in their individual cubicles. The clinical supervisors sat at the front of the room, magisterial, waiting for the interns to bring their treatments and chart notes to be approved. The interns circulated in and out, or lounged around bored when they didn't have patients to treat. The observers waited for interns to invite them to follow them. Everybody wore white coats and looked important. I sat in a corner, kept my head down, and hoped nobody would notice me. Sometimes my strategy worked for entire shifts; it was as if I was so out of place in that environment that I disappeared.

I was busy being invisible one day when a voice said, Hey. You want to come in to my next treatment with me?

I put down my book reluctantly. It was one of the interns, S. In conversations that swirled around the classroom, I'd heard other people refer to him as a troublemaker, and in fact he looked sort of wild: he had a mop of sandy-colored hair, a bushy beard, and his white coat was crumpled and un-ironed. He also looked hopeful; I couldn't think why. OK, I said.

The treatment was a lot more interesting than I expected it to be. My acupuncture school was a TCM school – Traditional Chinese Medicine – which was an identity as well as a description of the curriculum. TCM was the structure that Mao imposed on the vast diversity of Chinese medicine: a bureaucratic committee's interpretation of some very old, very strange ideas and practices. I didn't resonate with TCM, though I tried. But our school had one Japanese teacher, Yoshi, who happened to be visiting for a couple of years; his son wanted to go to high school in the US. Yoshi taught an entirely different, non-TCM way of doing acupuncture, and he had a little group of students who sought him out in clinic and even outside of school to soak up all he had to offer. S. was the foremost of this group; he was working on putting Yoshi's teachings into a pamphlet, titled "Jingei Pulse Diagnosis". I watched S. do a Jingei treatment and cautiously expressed interest. I'll show you, he said, it's easy.

Jingei acupuncture felt natural to me right away, as did working with S. I followed him all the time, and suddenly I was interested in student clinic. Because of schedules, I didn't see much of Yoshi himself, but S. made a point of passing everything he learned on to me. I was grateful.

Over the following months, I learned more about S. himself. Close up, his white coat wasn't just rumpled, it had crayon marks on the lapels and animal crackers in the pockets. He had three little boys, and he took care of them most of the time. He and his wife had recently been teachers in a Quaker boarding school for teenagers in New England; they'd moved to Portland so that he could go to acupuncture school. One day he mentioned casually that he and his wife had an open marriage.

Huh, I said. The word polyamory wasn't widely used at that time, but if it had been and if I'd heard it, I would have accepted it without reservation. One of my coworkers at Cascade AIDS Project had been in a decades-long open relationship. He'd talked about it at work, the upsides and the downsides of him and his boyfriend having other lovers, and it was clear his relationship was joyful and supportive. He and his boyfriend could have been on a billboard for polyamory. Anyway, a year of spending a lot of time with gay men had demolished any ideas I'd previously had about how sex and relationships were supposed to work. So if that was a feature of my new friend's life, that was fine with me.

You know where this is going. *I* should have known where it was going. But I didn't think I liked boys, not in that way. I was dating women, or trying to. It wasn't going all that well; as it turned out, I didn't like dating. When I was lonely, I found myself thinking, well, I can hang out with S. And I'd call him and we'd get together to study and practice needling with the super-thin Japanese needles that Yoshi insisted we learn how to use, or we'd go to the park with the kids.

This book isn't a memoir, it's a case study, and I'm leaving a lot of things out. *On purpose,* so if you came for the gossip, you'll be disappointed. One thing I've learned in writing it is that although I think of it as my story, it's the story of other people: the gifts they gave me, the ways they helped me, the things I learned from them. (A few of those people gave me gifts after, or in the process of, their death.) But there's still a line – I don't want to try to tell anyone else's story.

At the end of the first day I followed S. in clinic, I realized I had a similar feeling about him as I'd had about M. the first time I met her: an immediate recognition alongside a sense of bone-deep relief. Something like, oh, it's *you* – thank God, you're here.

S. was also going to love me in a way that kept me off ledges.

But six months later, it was clear that S.'s marriage wasn't just open, it was also in the process of ending, and things were about to get very, very complicated. By the time I was 26, I had an instant family: S. and the kids, who were 5, 6, and 9. My underlying attitude that I had nothing to lose continued to serve me well in taking risks. And that's all I'm going to say about that.

14.

When I graduated from acupuncture school there were, relatively speaking, a lot of opportunities to do acupuncture in public health settings in Portland. One way or another, almost all of these were the work of an acupuncturist whom I'll call Daniel, a former social worker who had trained under a Chinese teacher and who had worked with NADA in its early days at Lincoln Hospital. Daniel had a big energetic New York personality, and he had approached a Portland social service agency, Central City Concern (CCC), about incorporating acu-detox into its programs. CCC ran Hooper Detox. Acupuncture was so effective there that it soon expanded to other parts of CCC.

I picked up a few shifts, first as a sub and then as a regular, doing acupuncture at a residential alcohol and drug treatment program for women with children. Two days a week I went to a huge old house in a leafy residential neighborhood in Portland and set up in a room off the attic or the kitchen, and the women would file in, some of them holding babies, for ear acupuncture. Public health acupuncture in the 1990s meant reusable rather than disposable needles; the used ones went through a dental autoclave and came back sterilized, and Central City Concern employed one person whose job was just to autoclave needles, all day long. Funding was never abundant, and so the needles had seen a lot of use. In fact, they were old and dull and some had burrs on the ends; sometimes they made a faint but audible crunching noise when they sank into the cartilage of someone's ear. I'm making this point because my sojourn in the women's program taught me a few more important things about acupuncture:

1) If people like acupuncture, they'll put up with a lot to get it.

Needles with burrs on the ends, uncomfortable chairs or even just a hard floor to lie down on, acupuncturists who don't know enough about the challenges of their lives to provide good support. (I wish I had done a better job.)

2) Acupuncture doesn't work the way it sounds in the textbooks.

A number of the women in the program were pregnant, some hugely so. When I mentioned that acupuncture was supposed to be able to induce labor, their eyes lit up with hope. So I unwrapped another gauze packet of longer (but equally dull) needles, got ready to insert them into the labor induction points (the points that in school we were forbidden ever to use on pregnant women), and inwardly braced myself for my patients to double over with intense contractions.

Nothing happened.

I tried stronger stimulation, twisting and thrusting the needles the way I'd been taught (and now cringe to remember). My patients winced but didn't go into labor. A few of them reported that afterwards, the chronic back pain that went along with being hugely pregnant felt quite a bit better, but that was all.

When I came back the next week, they were still pregnant and still hopeful, ready for me to try again. With my packet of thick, old, dull needles, strong stimulation, and treatments twice a week, I got exactly nobody to go into labor. They all ended up being medically induced when they got too far past their due date. I was puzzled. I had followed the directions in the books, why didn't it work?

Twenty years later, having treated a lot more pregnant

women (one of whom did have to get up from a treatment to call her midwife because contractions kicked in with a vengeance) I know that it's more complicated. All kinds of factors affect someone's readiness to go into labor: their relationships, their living situation, their mental and emotional state, really their entire life. All the acupuncturist can control is what goes into giving the treatment; the outcome is out of our hands. And this turns out to be true of treating any condition, not just trying to induce labor. Whether it's the acupuncture textbooks themselves or a generally reductive approach to medicine in our society, most people who learn acupuncture start out with an exaggerated sense of their own importance to the healing process and a lack of awareness about how many factors beyond their *or their patients'* control affect the results.

3) Acupuncture jobs weren't like other jobs.

After a year in the Jesuit Volunteer Corps and three years of acupuncture school, I had begun to get a clue that my perspective on jobs was different from the perspective of the people around me. I had figured out that most of them looked at any individual job as one piece of the much larger whole they thought of as their career. Jobs were things that you weighed, considered, tried on for a good fit, stepped on sequentially like rungs on a ladder, left behind when they weren't to your liking.

This was news to me.

My father had had the same job for almost his entire life, working for W.R. Grace in a chemical plant that manufactured the ingredients for catalytic converters. He had a high school diploma (years later he got an AA degree from the local community college). It was a good job, like blue collar jobs could be at that time: there were pensions and health insurance and security. As far as my family was concerned, the Grace plant in Curtis Bay might as well have been the sun because our whole world orbited around it.

Which is not to say that we took it for granted. My extended family included not only working class people and lower middle class people (and one uncle who was moving into the professional class thanks to the Navy) but underclass people – meaning they lacked basic stability in terms of consistent housing, regular income, and being able to avoid periodic intrusion of the state into their personal lives. Where I came from, you could see the edge of the socioeconomic cliff and it wasn't far away; people I knew had gone over it. One bad choice, like getting into a car with the wrong person, could start the downward slide. In college, I listened to various friends and acquaintances talk about struggling with their parents' expectations for them, and I realized that the only firm expectation that ever came my way was that I was not to end up on welfare. Because that was bad, that was really bad.

There was a period when I was in high school when the W.R. Grace sun wobbled in the sky, and it was terrifying. There were rumors of layoffs at the plant. Neither of my parents talked to me about it directly, but they didn't have to: I knew that our world might end. It wasn't just the paycheck; my father's job represented the larger part of his dignity and self-respect, and it was entirely in Grace's power to take that away.

These friends I had now who surveyed jobs with a speculative eye to their career potential – without having words for it, I knew we weren't the same species. I felt like I did the one time at college when I ended up at a dinner where there were three different forks in my place setting; I watched to see how other people handled the situation, and hoped I didn't betray that I had no understanding of how this was all supposed to work.

But jobs in the acupuncture profession – this was a few standards beyond what I already didn't grasp. It had never occurred to me that there might be a profession where there were no jobs to speak of. I had grown up knowing there were jobs I might have to do even though I hated them, there were jobs I couldn't get because I wasn't qualified for them, there were jobs that could vanish in the catastrophe of a whole factory shutting down – but I had never encountered jobs that just weren't there.

Being a part-time/substitute acupuncturist for Central City Concern in the 90s meant that you had to attend periodic acupuncturists' meetings at the main treatment center downtown, which was housed in a renovated old hotel. The top floors were single-room housing for people newly in recovery, while what had been the old coffee shop was the acupuncture treatment room. It was a beautiful space with huge windows and shining hard wood floors, and specially designed acupuncture chairs (upholstered, with good armrests and headrests) arranged in a big circle. Twice a day, fifty to a hundred people filed in for the NADA 5 Needle Protocol. During our meetings – which happened in the middle of the day, between treatment sessions –we acupuncturists pulled the chairs into a smaller circle. Then the lucky ones who had regular hours would announce shifts that they needed someone to cover, and the unlucky hour-less substitutes would shout out their availability and hope to be called on. The sun streamed down through the big windows on to a feeding frenzy for the underemployed.

I hated it. There were so many of us who wanted work, and so little work to go around. Like all group processes, though, it involved an element of transparency which helped me in the long run, because I could see that it wasn't just me who was desperate. There was a handful of acupuncturists who had full-time work at Central City Concern, and then there was a rotating cast of frantic new graduates hoping to pick up their scraps. Over time, the ones who didn't get any shifts drifted away.

When I went to acupuncture school, the extent of our preparation for our future careers was a one-term class in practice management. By then I had established a routine of sitting in the back of the room, reading novels under the table, and scowling, so nobody made much effort to ensure that I was absorbing the material – not that I can blame them. It was an upbeat class: in 1994, leaders in the acupuncture profession were convinced that wide-spread insurance reimbursement for acupuncture was just around the corner, along with acceptance from the healthcare establishment and prosperity for any acupuncturist willing to take a seat at the table.

I hear they were equally convinced of that ten years earlier. In 2017, they're still convinced, and they're still telling acupuncture students: acceptance into the mainstream and the accompanying professional-level salaries for acupuncturists are just around the corner. They'll be here any minute now.

It's like a thirty-year production of "Waiting for Godot".[13]

Practice management classes in acupuncture school have a reputation for being vague and glossing over some uncomfortable trends. The conventional estimate is that there's a fifty or maybe even eighty percent attrition rate for acupuncturists in their first five years. Graduates quit because they simply can't make a living. I didn't know this when I went to acupuncture school. If someone had told me, though, I probably wouldn't have been able to wrap my working-class brain around it: it's a *profession* – how can it be a profession if so many people can't work? Surely a hard-earned credential couldn't lead to – nothing at all?

The term "practice management" contributes to the vagueness by implying that if you're an acupuncturist, you will of course have a practice to manage. It skirts around the prospect of having to build a practice from scratch *before* you can manage it, and the long list of entrepreneurial skills and techniques required to do so.

All of us new graduates who showed up at the CCC acupuncturists' meetings, hoping to pick up a few hours of paid work here and there, were in theory building our own practices at the same time. Most of us didn't have the faintest idea of how to go about that. I was lucky, though, because I had someone who was teaching me the foundations of creating a job for myself.

15.

Donzel was one of my regular patients in student clinic. He had started out as one of Yoshi's patients, and he liked getting treatments from student interns who practiced Yoshi's style. This was something I learned about Donzel before I knew anything else: he liked to collect interesting things. In a school clinic dedicated to teaching a Chinese style of acupuncture, he found the interns who did Japanese style treatments and stuck with them. By the time I graduated, I'd been seeing Donzel once a week for almost a year. He let me know he'd be following me after school.

I would have one patient at least; that made me hopeful.

Donzel was physically striking: lean, graceful and over six feet tall, he swam butterfly for exercise at the community pool, arcing his long body through the water lap after lap. He was black with close-cropped graying hair, a melodious voice, and perfect manners. He had been in the Army in Germany and liked that I came from German immigrants.

Donzel was charming, and he used his charm to run an improbable business. He was a bookseller who built libraries for private collectors. He didn't have a bookstore or even an office; he shared a small house with his brother. He ran his business mostly out of his car. In the pre-internet era, Donzel simply knew people: people who owned books, sold books, liked books, wanted more books, and people who knew those people. The breadth and variety of his social network was, like Donzel himself, grand.

Right before I graduated, during one of our regular appointments, I confessed that I didn't know anything about setting up a business (our practice management class had been sketchy on the basics) and that I was nervous. Don't worry, he said. I'll show you. You can do it. And so a few months later, I was sitting at Donzel's kitchen table with a cup of tea and a blank copy of the IRS's Schedule C (Form 1040), Profit or Loss from Business.

Donzel was a lot more like the people I'd grown up around, and a lot less like the people I went to acupuncture school with, and so I *could* learn business from him. He knew I was intimidated by the bureaucracy of self-employment and he was on my side. He came from a big African American Catholic family and told me stories about his siblings and cousins that made me nod my head in recognition. He made himself a bridge between where I was coming from and the uncharted territory of entrepreneurship. I was learning that a lot of people in Portland got by in a stubbornly bad economy by doing a little of this, a little of that – and many more people than I would have expected were self-employed somehow. Besides his book business, Donzel always had one or two other projects in development. This kind of life was a very long way from W.R. Grace and Curtis Bay; I couldn't have figured out how to enter this world on my own. I'm sure without Donzel's encouragement, I would have given up.

He also gave me a copy of Paul Hawken's *Growing a Business*.[14] Reading that, plus the session at his kitchen table with Schedule C, constitutes all the useful business training I ever got. Twenty-two years later, handing out blank copies of Schedule C to a classroom full of acupuncture students, I found myself saying out loud that marginalized people often approach the process of starting a business very differently from, say, white upper-middle-class men with savings in the bank. Donzel never suggested I write a business plan, and I'm not sure he had one himself. I didn't know enough about what I was doing to write a business plan, and trying would have only intimidated me further. What I needed were the basics: how to think through profit and loss, and how to be myself while being an entrepreneur. Donzel was a great role model.

Because the basic demands of being an entrepreneur are so intense, if you're also trying to pretend to be someone else, you won't make it. Once I told Donzel that I was frustrated because it seemed like I was never able to finish a to-do list for my business: I would get maybe 70% of my tasks checked off, and then I'd have to make a whole new one, and there were always things I never got to at all. He threw back his head and laughed: I was cracking him up. 70%! he said. That's pretty good! As a general rule, you're lucky to get 50%. Some days, it's 25%.

Donzel lent his considerable social capital to my fledgling practice: for years, I got a steady flow of new clients who came to me directly or indirectly through him. It was a master class in how word-of-mouth marketing worked. After his butterfly workout, he would sit in the hot tub at the community center and give impromptu lectures about the benefits of acupuncture; I got three long term regulars that way. At an estate sale with a collection of books, somebody overheard him talking about acupuncture and started asking him questions; he gave them my card. He sent me his cousin; his cousin sent a friend; the friend sent her hairdresser. Once, I asked a new patient how he'd found me, and he scratched his head. You know it was funny, he said. I was in the grocery store. I was standing in line and my knees were bothering me so I was complaining about my arthritis. And there was this guy standing behind me, real tall black dude, sounded like a radio announcer.

Donzel? I said.

Didn't get *his* name, my new patient said, but he gave me yours.

Years later, when I was having a conversation with someone knowledgeable about the acupuncture profession, regarding how I had become persona non-grata among most of my peers, they commented, you know you just don't fit. You're not like them at all. And you've never treated the kind of people they're treating – your patients aren't anything like their patients.

I thought of Donzel. Yeah, I said, I'm lucky.

Ally

16.

From 1994 when I graduated until 2002, my life as an acupuncturist fell into a predictable Portland pattern: a little of this, a little of that. (Not an uncommon pattern for acupuncturists in many cities.) I couldn't get enough hours at CCC to make up a full-time job; despite Donzel's help, I couldn't attract enough patients to have a full-time private practice but I never gave up either; and I was desperate enough to pick up some teaching assistant hours at the school. S.'s work life looked very similar. We were barely scraping by.

Later on, I would joke that I developed a different business model for acupuncture because S. and I couldn't make use of the prevailing business model for acupuncture success: not the conventional private practice model, the one that people think of as predominant, but the truly prevailing one at the time. That would be the Sugar Daddy business model, in which an acupuncturist asserts that they're successful in their practice, because in reality they don't need to earn a living, since their partner/husband/wife has a real job and supports their household. Plenty of acupuncturists, regardless of gender, have claimed this kind of success. The difficulty for me and S. was that both of us wanted to be acupuncturists. Neither of us was willing to quit acupuncture and get a real job in order to be the Sugar Daddy.

When S. and I and the kids first began living together, we rented the bottom floor of a duplex. Technically it had two bedrooms, but the smaller one was more like a large closet directly off the larger one. The walls were made of particle board and the carpet was thin and grimy. There were little piles of broken glass all over the tiny backyard, so the kids could only play outside on the front steps and the sidewalk. They attached a rope to a five-foot high crabapple tree and pretended it was a swing. We didn't have room for storage, so toys and projects tended to spill out everywhere, and there was always a layer of Legos on the floor waiting to be stepped on. Everything about that place was makeshift, and it smelled damp even in the summer. I loved living with S. and the kids; I was happy there. But it was just too small.

Eventually we qualified for the services of a low-income housing nonprofit, because being two acupuncturists with three kids, our income was very low indeed. We moved a few miles away to a rental house, and it was a real house with a real backyard and a big sequoia with a tire swing in the front. It had three actual bedrooms and even a hallway. We had tried to get a house with four bedrooms so that we could treat patients out of a spare room, but that was against the housing nonprofit's rules. We were grateful to get the house that we got. It was less than half a block away from a sizable park in a quiet low-income neighborhood. When the kids were at school or with their mom, sometimes we would set up a massage table in the largest bedroom and treat one of our few regular private patients. (Mostly Donzel and people referred by him.)

One of our neighbors, whom I met while walking in the park, was a diminutive white-haired blue-eyed lady named Betty. She was a retired secretary who lived alone with her dogs, two rescued Pomeranian mixes and a poodle. One day I looked up from my walk to see Betty hobbling with a cane across the park as fast as she could go, trailing her dogs, waving frantically at me.

WHAT was it you said you did? she gasped when she got close enough.

Um – acupuncture, I responded. Why? Are you OK?

* * *

73

My sciatica is just killing me! I'm all but crippled and the doctor wants to give me another one of those shots, well I don't want another shot because they don't do a damn thing, pardon my French. I don't know what I'm going to do, I can barely get around, I saw you and I just – can you help me? I'm about at the end of my rope.

The little dogs had caught up and they were looking back and forth from Betty to me with bright eyes. I'll try, I said.

In acupuncture school, we had been taught that the way to treat back pain was by inserting needles into the back, in conjunction with manual therapies such as vigorous tui na massage and cupping. I still wasn't a fan of manual therapies, and treating back pain had never been my favorite thing; it seemed like it was often frustrating for me as well as the patient. Recently, though, S. had learned of an acupuncture teacher who espoused what he described as "the Balance Method". This was the charismatic Richard Tan, and in 1997 he was just beginning his career of persuading acupuncturists that it was possible to treat pain effectively by using "distal" points, in other words, putting needles in places other than where the pain was.

When students in his workshops expressed disbelief, he would wave his arms at the overhead lights. You see those lights? he demanded. Do you turn them off by smashing them? No, you turn them off by using the switch! And where is the switch? It's across the room on the wall! To treat pain, you must find the switch!

S. had just picked up Richard Tan's first two books, in which he detailed his favorite switches. For sciatica, that was three points on the back of the hand: two points between the thumb and first finger, and one at the juncture of the fourth and fifth metacarpals, used in combination with a point on the inside of the ankle whose function was to support the kidney energy (and thus the low back). When Betty appeared later that day in our living room, we led her to a battered reclining chair with crayon marks on the upholstery and we treated her there, putting in only those points in her hands and her ankles. Like many people who are desperate for relief from pain, she didn't have time to be skeptical or even interested in acupuncture, let alone our particular techniques. She didn't ask why we didn't try to put points in her back. After a few minutes, she nodded off in the recliner.

Being on a fixed income, Betty was worried about paying for treatment. I told her that working in public health clinics had taught us that getting good results often required much more treatment than people in America thought they needed, and she should try to come every day for a week; could she afford $5 for treatment if she came that often? She could, she said, and since she got up from her first treatment feeling marginally better, she was willing to try.

After a week of daily treatments – just those points on her hands and ankles, sitting in our living room – Betty's sciatica pain was about 50% reduced. She started coming every other day, and within a month, the pain was gone. Having Betty asleep in our living room for an hour or so on a regular basis wasn't onerous, and watching her gratified surprise as she began to feel better was kind of addicting. The first time she got up out of the chair without pain, relief washed over her face, and then something like joy. It was easy to see how much it meant to her to be able to walk without pain.

And so when she asked if she could bring along her sister, who was having neck pain, we said yes. We got another reclining chair, but it was beginning to look like we might need a bigger living room.

Cut to the Chase, Please #3

Are you ever going to explain how acupuncture works?

Yes and no.

No, if what you mean by that is *show me the biomedical mechanism for acupuncture.* I don't know about that, and I don't think anybody else does either. There are various theories floating around but nothing has been proven. My personal take is that acupuncture is a gentle psychedelic that reduces inflammation throughout the body, regulates the nervous system, and speeds up healing processes. I don't have personal experience with using any other psychedelics myself so that might not be an appropriate comparison, but it's what comes to mind after providing 50,000+ treatments over the course of 20+ years as an acupuncturist. Research on psychedelics is limited because they're illegal, but my hunch is that if we knew more about psychedelics we'd probably know more about acupuncture too.

But yes, if what you mean is, how does acupuncture work in the lives of ordinary people. I have a lot to say about that. But first I'd like to bring up something I learned while preparing to teach a class of second year acupuncture students: we don't have a good definition of the word "health".

In 1948, the World Health Organization declared: Health is a state of complete physical, mental and social wellbeing and not merely the absence of disease or infirmity.

I can't think of anyone I know who lives in a state of *complete* physical, mental and social wellbeing, not if you look closely enough.

In 1986, the WHO amended their definition of health as: a resource for everyday life, not the objective of living. Health is a positive concept emphasizing social and personal resources, as well as physical capacities. In 2009, an article in the *Lancet* challenged the WHO's definition of health as inadequate in light of our current understanding of the complexity of disease.[15]

Despite calling ourselves healthcare providers, we struggle to define exactly what we're providing. This might sound abstract, but I'm bringing it up because treating a high volume of patients with acupuncture is likely to make you question the usefulness of the health/disease binary. It's not that simple. Most people are somewhere on a spectrum, trying to manage various problems related to their physical, mental, and social wellbeing. Acupuncture tends to offer incremental improvements and relief in all of those areas, though not necessarily right away or for the problem that led the person to try acupuncture in the first place. It's very common, for example, for someone who tries acupuncture for chronic pain to notice that they're sleeping better before they notice that their pain is reduced. In real life, this can translate into the difference between hope and despair.

Sometimes what acupuncture shifts is the person's relationship to their pain or their illness. Patients will say things like, the pain is still there but it doesn't bother me as much, I'm able to do more things. When it comes to chronic conditions that have to be managed rather than cured, having a more positive relationship to the problem itself can mean significant improvements in overall quality of life. And incremental improvements tend to add up over time.[16]

So it could be a placebo.

77

* * *

Maybe. There's a lot of discussion recently about whether antidepressants and sleep medications are placebos as well.[17] The people who get relief from them typically don't care.

Here's something else about acupuncture: it's got some frustratingly recursive terminology. Guess what the definition of an acupuncture point is, according to most textbooks? The place where you put an acupuncture needle.

The Chinese term for an acupuncture point, xuéwèi, can also be translated as hole, cavity, or cave.

One of the things a good acupuncturist does is to hold space for their patients. Once you put the needles in, you step back and let them work, which means getting yourself out of the way and not fussing or hovering or interfering too much. However, holding space doesn't mean doing nothing. It means being present as a supportive, compassionate witness to the healing that happens within each person. Acupuncture points are holes, empty spaces where something can happen.

17.

I might have continued to muddle along in the acupuncturist mode of a little of this, a little of that indefinitely, but circa 2000 things started to come apart for me. There were four distinct components of the coming apart:

1) I was gearing up to a full-fledged mental health crisis. More about this shortly.

2) During some of my hours at Central City Concern, I worked alongside a recovery mentor named David, who was like a skinny tattooed lightning bolt of personal integrity.[18]

3) I began treating Chico and Bobette, two more charming self-employed patients who were going to destroy any remaining faith I had in how both acupuncture and the acupuncture profession worked.

4) The kids kept growing and we needed a bigger house. The housing nonprofit we rented from didn't have one for us. Renting from commercial landlords when you have three kids, a large dog, two cats and a limited income is a scary undertaking. We needed to buy a house, which we seemed ill-equipped to do, but there it was.

I signed up for a first-time homebuyer's program and went to an all-day Saturday class. Coming back from the lunch break, I had a few extra minutes so I decided to sit quietly in my car. My intuition decided to ambush me. I've had this happen more than once (more often while getting acupuncture than in the car) and sometimes it feels like a jolting shift of perspective, like abruptly finding myself in a helicopter with a birds-eye view of my life. It's more like a view, or just *knowing*, than actual words, but if it were translated into words it might have sounded like this (in a tone not unlike Micah the volunteer's when he encouraged me to go to acupuncture school):

Your life as it involves your job and money in general isn't working the way it's supposed to. You've been letting things happen to you and accepting situations that you shouldn't accept. You're downstream from the action, and you need to be upstream, IN the action. Time to start MAKING things happen, kiddo. You might think it won't work out, but it will.

OK, I thought, if you say so. I went back in to the home buying class. Two months later, we'd bought a house in another marginal neighborhood a couple of miles west, called Cully. We could just barely afford it. It was only about 1500 square feet but it somehow had five bedrooms: one for each kid, and one left over to treat patients.

18.

There was a fifth thing that was threatening to fall apart around this same time: funding for my public health job at Central City Concern. This wasn't anything personal, it was just how funding for public health acupuncture tends to go.

At this point, S. and I mostly worked at the main treatment center downtown, in the renovated hotel, only occasionally going out to Hooper to sub. After 5 years, we'd become some of the lucky ones with regular part-time hours. In addition to providing acupuncture to CCC's clients who were in outpatient treatment, our program also had something called general medical acupuncture. This meant that anyone from the community could come in during acupuncture hours and pay on a sliding scale of $5 to $30 to get a treatment. I treated everyone from recent graduates of the outpatient program, getting acupuncture to support their hard-won sobriety, to college students stressing out over exams, to actors in rehearsal, to a sympathetic state senator. This program funded itself with no advertising or marketing whatsoever.

It was CCC's contracts with the state and county that paid the bills, though, and these had nothing to do with general medical acupuncture for the community, only with the acupuncture treatments for recovery (NADA 5 Needle Protocol) that the clients in the drug treatment program were required to get. As far as we could tell from our vantage point as employees, this funding ran on a nerve-wracking boom-bust cycle. We'd get a new contract, and there'd be more hours for everybody; even some of the substitutes would get hired for awhile. Then the contract would end and there would be cutbacks, people getting laid off. S. and I had survived a few rounds of this already. Sometime around 2000, there was general jubilation because we'd gotten our biggest contract yet. The acupuncture department had money to burn.

When this was announced, S. and I caught each other's eye. We were both thinking: shit. This is the top of the rollercoaster and we've never been this high. Looks like a long way down from here.

My first pass at social entrepreneurship consisted in trying to talk my boss, Daniel, into putting some serious energy into building up the general medical program. I was convinced that with some work, the cash fees from those patients could become a way to cushion the ups and downs of contracts and grants. The idea of earned income for nonprofits was just becoming a topic of discussion; in fact, CCC had created a painting crew of treatment program graduates, both to provide them with sorely needed job experience and to experiment with an earned income project. Daniel heard me out but wasn't interested.

I loved the general medical program. I loved the cross-class mix of people I got to treat. And because treatments were so inexpensive, we had regulars who came in with the frequency approaching that of clients in the later stages of the outpatient program: sometimes two and three times a week. Without a doubt, they got better results than the patients in my vestigial private practice (except for Betty and her sister, that is) who tended to struggle with paying me $40 a treatment or whatever it was I was trying to charge, especially people with chronic problems that had been around for years and didn't improve enough after one or two treatments to justify the ongoing expense.

Speaking of Betty, I had tried to get her to come downtown and enroll in the general medical program. It would have made my life a little easier. But she wouldn't go. Downtown was too far, she said, she didn't want to deal with the parking. I got the sense, though, that she was spooked by the idea of getting acupuncture onsite at a drug treatment program, and a little offended by the idea that she might qualify for a charity program. She wasn't a charity case, she just didn't have any money: there was a big difference.

I had another on-again-off-again patient I'd met doing house calls; her friend on hospice had passed away, but she still wanted acupuncture. She lived in Northwest Portland, quite close to the treatment program downtown. My house in Northeast was too far, and I didn't want to do a house call for her if I didn't have to. Come see me downtown, I said, and she agreed.

When she showed up during general medical hours, all the private rooms with treatment tables were busy with other general medical patients, so I led her into the big sunny space where the drug treatment patients got their NADA 5NP. The morning rush was just ending. She got settled into one of the upholstered acupuncture chairs and put her feet up on a stool. I put her needles in and she seemed to be sinking into relaxation when I walked away. After about ten minutes, though, she waved me back.

I'm sorry, I'm just not comfortable here, she said. I think I need to go.

What is it? I asked. Can I adjust your needles? Is that stool not working for your knees?

She shook her head and then motioned me to come closer, so she could whisper in my ear: It's that man sitting across from me. I recognize him. This morning I caught him going through my trash.

* * *

The cross-class mixing I liked so much had some limits. Working class or lower middle class people often didn't want to come into spaces designated for underclass people. I remembered my family living in fear of getting too close to the socioeconomic edge. I was disappointed but not ready to give up.

My intuition, though, was waving at me from the periphery of my vision, mouthing the words:

Hey, kiddo, you're not going to be able to stay here much longer. You're trying to make this job more stable than it's ever going to get. Remember where you're supposed to be: upstream.

I ignored it for as long as I could.

19.

As its experiment with acupuncture suggests, CCC is an innovative organization. While I was working there, another new idea was in the development stage – the Mentor Program. It emerged from the realization that clients in very early recovery often needed somebody to hold their hand and walk them through the first steps of a sober life: getting settled in drug-free housing, attending support groups, showing up at the right place at the right time to get the process of outpatient treatment going. People getting off of heroin particularly struggled with these first steps, and too often they succumbed to overdoses. A mentor might be the difference between life and death. David was one of CCC's first mentors.

Before he was a mentor, David was a UA technician downtown (meaning he collected urinalysis samples) and once a week our shifts overlapped. He was very quiet at first, and always wore long sleeved shirts and high collars to cover up the tattoos he'd gotten in prison. I thought he was shy. As time went on, I noticed him talking more; he would check in with clients, see how they were doing, make time to have brief, supportive conversations.

After awhile, I realized that despite his apparent reserve, he missed *nothing*. He had an eagle eye for the smallest details that showed somebody might be struggling with their recovery: they were 10 minutes late to group, they looked upset after they got off a phone call, they lingered a little too long in a conversation where people were telling war stories about their addictions. He paid attention with a laser focus to the difference between what people said they wanted to do and what they did – but with no judgement whatsoever. Without making a big deal out of it, and while being paid close to minimum wage, David established himself as a still point amid the howling internal chaos that most people in the program were trying to survive. He was there for them in a low-key but absolute way, with the authority of someone who knows exactly what they're going through.

If ever someone was doing what they were supposed to be doing in life, it was David. He was engaged body and soul in the project of giving people a chance at sobriety. He was a walking example of what vocation looks like.

If I was honest with myself, I was at CCC because, like a lot of other acupuncturists, I needed a paycheck. The contrast with David's passion wasn't comfortable or reassuring.

People in early recovery could be irritable, and irritating. One morning I got into it with a client over something stupid that I can't remember, and I stalked back to the employee area, rolling my eyes. David was filling out paperwork. He'd heard the whole thing; he looked at me. I threw up my hands and said something like, Sometimes I don't know why I bother.

He didn't nod sympathetically, the way the other acupuncturists would have. He was quiet, letting my words hang in the air. Then he said, What you do matters, even if they can't tell you that. You're doing a good job. You're trying.

I was ashamed of myself.

I made a mental note: Figure out why you're not more like him.

20.

One of the components of my little of this, little of that work life was providing acupuncture to hospice patients. I'd started out volunteering in an AIDS hospice which eventually turned into a part time job, picked up a couple of private patients who needed regular house calls, and finally, ended up doing a pilot study with a large health maintenance organization.

One of my first visits was with a woman who had never had acupuncture before. She was lying on a couch in her living room. I put the needles in and sat down in an armchair to read the book I'd brought. After a few minutes, she said, Ohhhh!

I jumped up. What is it, what do you need?

She looked at me, her eyes shining. Nothing, she said. I don't need anything. I feel *wonderful*. In fact, I can't remember when I've felt this good.

I sat back down and thought, I don't understand acupuncture at all.

My time at CAP had left me with an awareness of the often-overlooked needs of caregivers, so I'd developed a firm conviction that if I was in a room and I had enough acupuncture needles (and I always had enough needles) I should treat whoever was there and wanted treatment, not just the hospice patient. At the beginning of the pilot project, I insisted that I had to be able to treat caregivers and family members, and the organizers agreed. It always worked out well. One of my favorite examples was the visit I made to a Hmong patient, who was lying on a mattress on the floor of a big room with at least a dozen of his family members in attendance; they were holding his hands, massaging his feet, stroking his hair – someone was constantly touching him. About half of the people in that room wanted to get acupuncture too. The result felt something like what I imagine the inside of a beehive might be like if all the bees were dreaming: darkness humming with connectedness and peace.

My policy about treating caregivers was what led me to Chico and Bobette in 1999. Chico, who had stage four lung cancer, didn't like acupuncture and didn't want it. But his wife, Bobette, did, so he signed up.

The first time I went to their house he explained this to me. He was a big man who looked like a slightly sardonic Santa Claus. He'd been through a lot; he'd had radiation and brain surgery, and he was tired. He didn't have time for any nonsense. Of course, I said. I can do just a couple of needles for you so we can say we've done it, and I'll go treat Bobette.

He agreed, and silently I thanked God that I had had Yoshi as a teacher. In school, we had been given the impression that the bigger the needles, the more effective the treatment; Japanese acupuncture took the exact opposite approach, so I had some truly tiny needles and I was good at slipping them in with minimal sensation. Chico closed his eyes and off I went to Bobette.

Chico and Bobette had been an upper middle class couple in Southern California, with Chico being a member of the Young Republicans. One day they experienced a change of heart which led to them to leave that life behind, move to Oregon to raise their kids and become hippies in the little town of Mist, in the Coast Range. They were experts at a little of this, a little of that. They made furniture, then leather clothing that they sold at Portland's Saturday Market. Their friends were jazz musicians and artists. One year on Chico's birthday, they had such a big party that the guests of honor, the Flying Karamazov Brothers, had ended up sleeping on the ping-pong table. When I met them, they were living in a little white Victorian house on the outskirts of Portland with a huge meandering garden, both the house and the garden full of their friends' artwork. Bobette was sewing handbags on commission.

She loved acupuncture; it helped her stress as a caregiver. After a couple of visits, Chico allowed as how it wasn't so bad, and possibly he felt a little more energy after the treatments, so that was all right.

We used up the treatments allotted by the pilot project, and to my surprise, both wanted to continue. Chico said in general he was feeling better. I asked Daniel at CCC if they could come to the general medical part of the acupuncture program and pay $5 a treatment; he said yes. They started coming downtown to see me and getting treated once a week, sometimes twice.

I had done enough hospice work by now that I knew how the next part of the story went. Chico might feel a little better for awhile, but soon he would start to decline and they'd stop coming. If you were admitted to a hospice program, you were expected to live no more than 6 months. When Chico said he was having a bad week, I thought, OK, this is it.

But he just had a cold, and he got better.

Then one day he said he was feeling deeply exhausted, just wrecked, and I thought, OK, this is it. I made some sympathetic noises and he elaborated: he'd been feeling terrible ever since he'd mowed the lawn. The size of their yard flashed into my mind's eye and I demanded, Wait, you mowed the whole lawn?

Took me two hours. Big mistake, he said, lying back and closing his eyes.

He felt better the next week. The next time he felt terrible, it was because he'd gone out fishing with his son and stayed all day. He kept *not dying,* which his hospice nurses couldn't fail to notice. Six months was long gone so they terminated him from the hospice program; he was back to being a regular late-stage cancer patient.

After a few months, we could all see a pattern: when he got regular acupuncture, he stopped coughing up blood and he had more energy, a *lot* more energy. If he missed a treatment, he started coughing up blood again and his energy started to decline.

I'm going to take some writerly liberties here and fast forward this narrative to a morning about three years later. I'm standing in my office when the phone rings. It's Chico's doctor, who is also the head of pulmonology at the local hospital, and he wants to know if I have a minute to talk. Chico's yearly chest x-ray just came back. This is the only form of monitoring he gets anymore; since his illness is terminal and late-stage, there isn't any point in doing much. Chico's doctor clears his throat and said, The x-ray shows that the cancer has stopped growing. It hasn't moved in a year. The only thing that's different is that Chico's been getting a lot of acupuncture. From you. Can you explain what's going on?

Uh, I said. No, I can't, I'm sorry.

The pulmonologist sighed. OK, he said, In that case, I have a request. Can you do something about getting him off the morphine? If his cancer isn't progressing, I can't justify continuing to prescribe so much morphine.

I'll try, I said.

Chico passed away in 2004. According to Bobette, acupuncture allowed him to reduce his total narcotic use by 70% and added 5 years to his life.

Here's the thing, though: he never liked it. He would let me do hardly any needles. When I treated him, I wasn't doing Jingei acupuncture and I wasn't doing TCM acupuncture either. I was just putting in the few needles he permitted, and those were mostly in his chest. Most of the useful acupuncture points I'd learned were in the hands and feet; he wouldn't let me anywhere near them. After years, I negotiated my way down to just below his elbows and knees. When he came in he would unbutton the Hawaiian shirt he always wore, get out his Bible (somewhere along the line he had become an evangelical Christian) and settle in for an hour of scripture reading, prayer, and putting up with the acupuncture. That was our routine twice a week, and for a few years, it stopped his cancer in its tracks. He wouldn't take herbs, wouldn't change his diet, wouldn't let me practice any other part of Chinese medicine the way I'd been told I had to if I wanted to see any results.

I was just putting in a few needles twice a week; let me see if I can explain to non-acupuncturists what heresy that is, in the US acupuncture profession.

Acupuncture is so old and has been practiced in so many locations around the globe (China, Japan, Korea, Vietnam, and yes, in India Ayurvedic practitioners claim they invented it) that there are probably thousands of ways to do it. Each of these ways has a theoretical framework explaining why it's effective. The theoretical frameworks sometimes directly contradict each other.

Not long after those early white students of Chinese acupuncturists got busy professionalizing acupuncture in the US, they began to argue passionately about which theoretical framework was the right one. Complicating the discussion was the arrival on the scene of an Englishman, J.R. Worsley, who claimed to have learned (in Asia, under shadowy circumstances) the truest form of traditional acupuncture, which he called Five Element Acupuncture. When I was in acupuncture school, a bitter war between the Five Element acupuncturists and the Traditional Chinese Medicine acupuncturists had already been in full swing for years. Both these systems, of course, are products of the twentieth century while claiming to be the reflection of millennia of tradition.

What the warring devotees would all agree on, though, is that there is nothing worse than *just putting in needles*, using *no* theoretical framework at all. That's what arrogant, undertrained MDs and chiropractors and physical therapists do when they're trying to steal and corrupt acupuncture. That's what ignorant Westerners do, who want quick fixes without getting to the root of the energetic imbalance underneath. There is nothing lazier, more impure, and more degrading to the refined nature of Chinese medicine. If healing were food, *just putting in needles* would be Velveeta. And Spam.

What a surprise, that my white trash soul would wing like a homing pigeon to the debased and worthless end of this particular professional spectrum.

I had tried, in acupuncture school, to care about the arguments over whether TCM or Five Element or Japanese acupuncture was better. If I was honest with myself, though, I liked Jingei because it was simple and straightforward. Now I had found something even simpler. It wasn't supposed to work, of course, but there was Chico, mowing his lawn and going fishing and *not dead*. It worked fine from his perspective.

This was the upshot of my experience with Chico: everything I thought I knew about the right way to do acupuncture was wrong.

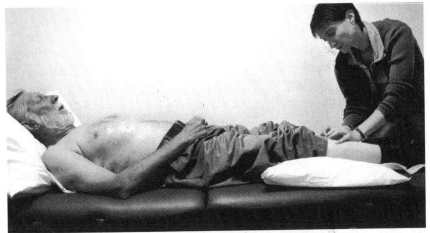

Me and Chico, circa 2001
Photo by Benjamin Brink, *The Oregonian*

21.

Some of what I thought I knew about myself was also wrong.

While I was in acupuncture school I had picked up the expectation that *working on myself* was something I needed to do if I was going to be an acupuncturist. This had a lot to do with being in close proximity to various strains of New Age spirituality. However, I didn't need a qi gong master to reveal what I already knew: there was something wrong with me. In my late twenties and early thirties, I still didn't *want* to want to die, but there still were too many times when I did. Meditation helped, but it didn't make the basic problem go away. Working on myself seemed logical and also gave me an outlet for my anxiety. And since I considered myself an ex-Catholic, why not explore other forms of spirituality?

My college roommate, who became a professor of religion, would point out to me later that all of American society, New Age spirituality not excepted, owed a lot to the Puritans. Despite inhabiting an airy subculture of alternative medicine, there was a grim Protestant work ethic undergirding my efforts to improve myself. By 2000, I had been at it for years, mostly feeling terrible at my failure to *be in my body*, as various helpers kept trying to get me to do, to *feel things deeply* and *open myself up*. I was always somehow disconnected, guarded. There was no compassion in the work I tried to do on myself. I was driven by self-hatred and fear.

To be honest, if I could leave this part out of this book altogether, I would.

Instead I'll let one five-minute interval stand in for a couple of years' worth of similar stuff. I had taken up yoga with the hope that it would help me get into my body. One day, I was practicing at home, lying on my back on the floor trying a new pose, stretching my right leg out in a way I'd never done before. Something shifted in my hips and low back, and a kind of visceral knowing clicked into place, like a dislocated joint sliding back where it belonged: when I was a child, I was in an ongoing sexual relationship with an adult.

Not an incident or two of sexual abuse like the ones I had always known about, but an ongoing relationship, for years. There were no conscious memories and there weren't going to be any. But I knew. Every part of me knew.

And then the rage and grief broke through, like a river through a dynamited dam.

I was feeling things deeply, all right. No longer disconnected. I wanted to murder every healer who had coaxed me to get into my body; I wanted to strangle them with their diaphanous scarves. I wanted to kill a few people I was related to; also, myself.

I fell apart. The acute period, when I could barely function, went on for about a month. I felt like I'd been flayed. My boss suggested psychiatric disability because I couldn't get through a shift at work without crying, but I was too scared to follow through. This peaked during the time we were supposed to be moving into our new house; a team of friends helped S. pack, because I couldn't do anything. It was like the aftermath of Lockerbie, only worse.

One day when I dragged myself to work downtown, I was letting myself into the building when I glanced through the plate glass front door at the patients in the drug treatment program, filing in for acupuncture, and I felt that same sliding sensation of a dislocated joint going back into place. Here I am, I thought, for all these years believing these people are so much worse off than I am. I thought they were the ones in trouble and I was here to help them. What a joke.

It wasn't long after that I realized, paycheck or no paycheck, I couldn't work there much longer. I was too raw to be around people in early recovery; there was just too much chaos, outside me and inside me. I wasn't strong enough. And that was the first green tendril of compassion curling up through a crack in the concrete of my self-hatred: a genuine urge to take care of myself.

22.

The concrete kept cracking and the new growth kept coming.

A mini-round of layoffs had arrived at the acupuncture department downtown – just a little dip on the rollercoaster of public health funding, a little foreshadowing of what was coming next – and I volunteered. I had to get out, and I thought being on unemployment for a little while would let me build up my private practice. But my private practice had taken a shape that was going to make that difficult.

By now Betty was regularly bringing both her sister and her nephew as well as occasionally one of her neighbors for acupuncture, and even though our new living room was bigger than the old one, it wasn't ideal because the kids were bigger too, and they took up more room. I got tired of nagging them to keep the living room clean. I would have preferred to treat Betty and her entourage anywhere else, but the living room was the only place that could accommodate three or four people at once.

When Chico and Bobette came for acupuncture, I'd put Chico in the little treatment room and Bobette on my and S.'s bed, which would've been weird with anybody else, but the rest of the house was covered with kid-related debris and it seemed logical. The real problem with treating them was money. We all knew that I was trying to build up my business, and we all knew there was no way they could afford even the modest private rates I was trying to charge. Chico needed to come twice a week or he would start coughing up blood.

My practice management teacher in acupuncture school would have said: Refer them all back to the general medical program downtown. *You* don't have to treat them.

* * *

But I did. Betty wouldn't go downtown. Chico and Bobette wouldn't see anybody else and I didn't want them to, either. Cutting ties with the patients who were defeating my attempts to have a normal private practice was unthinkable for three reasons: first, I was attached to them; second, I knew what their lives would be like without regular acupuncture; and third, when I was working I forgot myself in the best possible way. To be in the practitioner role, I had to put myself aside; it was like a vacation. Everybody I treated was offering me small, regular doses of peace and sanity. I needed them all, whether they could pay me or not.

Now that I knew what was wrong with me, in some ways my emotional life was a lot better and in some ways, a lot worse. When the desire to hurt myself arose, it was so strong that I learned that the only way to respond was to hold physically still until it passed. I was too scared to move, I didn't know what I might do. Sometimes I couldn't meditate, either; the passages I'd been reciting for years were too much effort. So I spent a fair amount of time sitting still, silently repeating: Help. Help, help, help.

During one of those times, I felt my long-standing urge to work on myself, to improve myself, drop away. I understood that I couldn't afford it anymore. If I wanted to survive, I had to stop treating myself like a project. Any kind of seeking or spiritual growth was beyond me. God wasn't someone I could reach for; I was too hurt to reach. God was someone to fall back on.

So I fell back. Once again, God was right there, and God didn't care if I was working on myself or not.

I wasn't ready to go back to church, but I picked up my old Catholic habits. I started saying rosaries, in part because they always calmed me down. And sometime in January 2002, I lit a candle to St. Jude, patron saint of hopeless cases and things despaired of. I whispered, show me what to do about money.

23.

When I would go to take the bus downtown, I would walk past a nondescript building three blocks from my house that always had a For Rent sign in the window. I remembered that building when I realized the only possible solution to my private practice conundrum was to rent a space outside my house that would allow me to treat multiple people at once. If I had enough room, I thought, maybe I could charge normal rates to the people who could afford it, and I could treat Chico and Bobette at the same time for what they could afford, and I might be able to earn a living. It would take the pressure off all of us.

The new problem, of course, would be paying rent. But I had to do *something*.

In the 7 1/2 years since I graduated, I'd done what most struggling acupuncturists do and rented a single room in a variety of different healing centers, each time hoping my practice would take off. It never did. Donzel and his referrals followed me to every new address, but I couldn't seem to expand my patient base much beyond that. Eventually I realized it was because I was participating in a business model where more established practitioners made their own healing practices viable by subletting to a revolving cast of hopeful new graduates. So no healing centers this time; I needed something else. What, I had no idea. I had never seen anything that looked like what I needed at this point in my troubled career.

I walked the three blocks to the bus stop and wrote down the number on the sign in the window of the nondescript building, mostly because it was something to do.

The landlord who called me back was friendly, and I agreed

to meet him at the space.

When I got there, I found that he was a retired teacher, social and talkative. As he was letting me in to the space, he told me a little about the history: it had most recently been a TV repair shop, then somebody had tried to run a thrift store out of it. They went broke and disappeared, leaving most of their wares behind. That was three years ago. The space was in the middle of a rambling building almost the size of a city block; it had started out as a couple of smaller buildings that merged over time, with an alley roofed over here, a connecting hallway put in there. Inside it had staircases that went nowhere, hidden rooms nobody had been in for years, and places where the floors were still dirt. We're still tunneling our way into the middle, he joked.

Just through the door off the street was what looked like a little waiting room. I could use a waiting room, I thought. This looks pretty good. Then he led me through another door, down a short hallway, and into the space itself.

It was cavernous and filled with broken furniture. It was more than 2,000 square feet, bigger than my house. By acupuncture professional standards, it was ugly, uninviting, ridiculous.

This is, um, more space than I was thinking of, I admitted.

Oh? the landlord said. Well, I could be flexible.

In general, writing this book is interesting because I remember things that happened and realize I have explanations for them now that I didn't at the time. It's satisfying, to have understandings emerge. But what happened at this point in the story, I don't understand and I have no explanation for. I didn't then and I don't now.

* * *

I knew the space was unsuitable. I knew I couldn't afford it. I prepared to thank the landlord for his time and politely extricate myself from the conversation. I was about to say the words, Thank you, but –

I opened my mouth and that's not what came out at all. Instead I said something like, Thanks, this looks great. I'm very interested. Can I think about it and write up a proposal?

Sure, he said.

Of course, the proposal I wrote was as ridiculous as the space itself. Since I had no money, I proposed paying a percentage of whatever I could earn, until I got to something approximating rent. Also, I asked to use only about half of the space; I judged the rest of it to be a lost cause, just too hideous to use, but I'd put a curtain over the doorway to that part. Ever since I told the landlord I was interested, I'd been buoyed by a weird electric hopefulness.

The landlord called me to discuss the proposal. You know, he said, if you earn nothing, I'll be getting a percentage of nothing.

I know, I said, but that won't happen.

He was silent for a minute. Then he said, everything in my experience as a businessman tells me no. I should say no to you. But my gut says yes. So – okay. Yes.

When I went to pick up the keys, he made me promise I wouldn't tell any other potential renters what he'd done for me, because he didn't want every inexperienced business owner in Portland coming to him with their hands out. I had never rented commercial space before, so I had no clue about the improbable extent of his generosity. I didn't realize that a miracle had just occurred. But I gave him my word that I wouldn't let on that he was prone to fateful acts of kindness.

24.

S. was alarmed. I'm not going to help you with this, he warned. This doesn't make sense. If you want to do it, it's all yours.

Then he amended: I'll help you paint it. The boys and I will help you paint it. But that's ALL.

Spoiler alert: it wasn't all.

25.

Three weeks later, when my landlord came by to see how things were going, he stopped at the end of the little hallway and said: Wow. You have an imagination, don't you? Did you SEE this?

I shook my head. I'm not very visual, I said. It just kind of...happened.

I had ended up buying as much of the abandoned thrift store furniture from him as I thought I could use, and after a number of trips to Goodwill, a painting party with S. and the boys, and some decorating consultations with Bobette (she sewed all the curtains), what we had was:

- A little waiting room in the front with a big desk (the landlord admitted that he wasn't looking forward to getting that desk out the front door, so he gave it to me) and some acupuncture charts on the walls for decoration;

- The hallway with a closet-like little bathroom;

- A space off to the side, where I imagined I'd put my massage table and keep giving private treatments, and

- The main space, which is what my landlord was looking at in disbelief.

I don't quite remember how it happened, but at some point, S. and I had decided what we needed to do was make it look like a 700-square foot version of our living room, so if one day Betty showed up with 10 relatives in tow, there would be no problem. We'd bought or scavenged 10 recliners and arranged them in groups of 3 or 4. From my previous attempts at private practice, I had some Japanese paper screens. In one corner, we'd put a futon couch across from a long built in shelf, which Donzel had agreed to stock with books to create a little library. It was dark and the windows didn't open, so we'd put second-hand lamps all around (it's a law of the universe that all thrift stores have more lamps and end tables than anyone could ever need, so we had found plenty amid the abandoned furniture). There were throw rugs on the cement floors, gauzy curtains over the windows, and a heavy curtain over the doorway to the part of the space I didn't want to use. It was cozy and shabby, but somehow managed to look bigger than it had when it was empty. It looked like it was ready for something. And it felt good, really good.

A few years later, a visiting acupuncturist from Texas would walk in to this dimly lit space, full of patients asleep with needles in the recliners, and burst out laughing. This is crazy. It's like performance art, he said.

If acupuncture was weird and uncanny, this space on Cully Boulevard was even weirder and more uncanny. It came together like something assembling itself, with our help but with its own plans. From the beginning, it was obvious there was something at work that wasn't me.

Cut to the Chase, Please #4

Enough about thrift store furniture. What's the business model?

This is probably a logical point in the story to break off the linear approach, because the details of how we arrived at the model, the tiny tweaks here and the little adjustments there, are not all that interesting. So this is a summary of what coalesced over a couple of years.

Within another year, S. got laid off too. A couple of years after that, almost every acupuncturist we'd worked with lost their jobs; the funding rollercoaster rocketed down to the bottom and for awhile public health acupuncture in Portland was a shadow of its former self. The space on Cully Boulevard was the only way we were going to make a living as acupuncturists so we had to make it work.

We had inherited a strict binary from the acupuncture profession: there was public health acupuncture, which was for poor, homeless, and addicted people, and it was funded via grants and government subsidies; and then there was private practice acupuncture, which was in theory for everyone else, and it was funded via insurance or cash payments. At the time we first opened the clinic that would become Working Class Acupuncture, the going rate for a single acupuncture treatment was about $65. Public health acupuncture meant NADA 5NP in a group; private practice acupuncture meant lying down on a table in a room by yourself.

It went without saying that private acupuncture was superior in every way.

* * *

And there was nothing for people like Betty, Chico and their families, no acupuncture funded by government subsidies and also no acupuncture they could afford. If acupuncture providers were restaurants, there were soup kitchens on one hand and five-star bistros on the other, and well, I guess everybody else didn't need to eat.

We broke the binary. We decided to charge $15 to $35 per treatment sliding scale, pay what you feel you can afford, for anybody who wanted to come and sit in one of our recliners in our cavernous, shabby space. Cash, no insurance. No matter what you paid on the scale, you got the treatment the acupuncturist determined you needed, based on your chief complaint; the amount you paid didn't relate to the number of needles you got. It was *from each according to his ability, to each according to his needs,* all the way. We set up our appointments so that we could see 4-6 people an hour, reasoning that if we got 4 people paying $15 a treatment, that was close enough to seeing one person an hour for $65.

We still thought we might want to give private treatments to people who wanted to pay more and who wanted more individual time, but that didn't last long. We soon realized that people didn't get better results when they paid more and lay down by themselves on a table for an hour in a private space, compared to the people who paid less and sat in a recliner around the corner in the open space. Also, when we treated people in the recliners, we could let them stay as long as they wanted. We had enough recliners that we never needed to kick anybody out; not so with the private space and the one table. We discovered that some people would fall asleep for hours with needles if they had that option. The people who started out thinking they wanted private acupuncture tended to realize that there were a lot of advantages to the recliners.

* * *

We also had our previous patients, Betty and her family and Chico and Bobette, who had been paying less than $15. It turned out this was fine too; as long as we had enough chairs, we were likely to make enough money anyway.

The first acupuncturist outside Portland to take up the model, somewhere around 2004, dubbed it community acupuncture. Which stuck (no pun intended).

Later on, when I was talking to other acupuncturists frustrated with their private practice and wanting to break out of the binary, I would summarize the process:

- Lower your prices
- Simplify your treatments
- Build community

Later still, the People's Organization of Community Acupuncture, our international multi-stakeholder cooperative, would define community acupuncture as the practice of offering acupuncture:

1) in a setting where multiple patients receive treatments at the same time;

2) by financially sustainable and accountable means;

3) within a context of accessibility created by consistent hours, frequent treatments, affordable services, and lowering all the barriers to treatment that we possibly can, for as many people as possible, while continuing to be financially self-sustaining; and

4) with a commitment to social justice in health care.

If you want exhaustive detail on the business model, via

wikis, videos, and forums, that's a good reason to join the POCA Cooperative: https://www.pocacoop.com/join-page

26.

There's a quote by herbalist Susun Weed that I love:

Every problem, each pain, disability, disease, is understood, in the Wise Woman way, as a hole for the entry of wholeness, a portal for the arrival of an ally. An ally who opens doorways of transformation. An ally who can protect you. An ally who brings you gifts. An ally who returns your missing pieces. An ally who guides you toward integration, through disintegration. An ally of wholeness, who accepts all of you. An ally who reminds you of your mortality and your immortality.

My limited understanding is that in Wise Woman herbalism, the ally is usually a plant. For me, though, the space on Cully Boulevard was the portal that materialized out of my breakdown, and the model of community acupuncture was my ally.

27.

Capitalism and I had a pretty nice honeymoon for a couple of years.

I was relieved to be out of public health work and I swore I'd never go back. I was high on the fumes of a new kind of self-sufficiency, a little giddy with the responsibility for my own economic fate, with no one to blame if I couldn't earn a living. I loved working only for myself, and for awhile I loved capitalism for making it possible.

I was delighted with all the inventing, tinkering, scavenging and improvising that went into being self-employed at this new scale. My previous work hadn't offered that kind of creativity; I had mostly felt helpless, at the mercy of public health funding – money was never anything I could do anything about. Now *everything* that happened was a result of what I did. It was exhilarating.

I found *Banker to the Poor* sometime in 2004 when one of my patients said, hey, you should read this book – it reminds me of what you're trying to do. I read it cover to cover in about two days, crying. Years of encouragement from Donzel hadn't fully convinced me that I was a business owner, but somehow Muhammad Yunus did, by being explicit that low income people could be entrepreneurs. Low income *women* could be entrepreneurs. I had company.

I felt empowered and free and I wondered how I'd ever worked for anyone else. I vowed I never would again.

I was less aware at the time that I, like Betty when she balked at getting acupuncture in a drug treatment program for homeless people, was recoiling from my proximity to the deprivations and restrictions associated with underclass life.

I was done with public health. I wanted to stop treating people who hated acupuncture but had to get it because their parole officers required it. I wanted to put a planter outside my clinic door and not worry that the patients would kill the plants when they used it as an ashtray and a toilet. I was tired of hanging out on the edge of the socioeconomic cliff and I wanted to forget, at least for awhile, that it was there. (Some people think entrepreneurship is a socioeconomic cliff in its own right, but I wonder how much time those people have spent in the company of people who live on the streets, people who have fallen through all the safety nets. Or whatever safety nets are left in this society, but that's another topic.) Capitalism let me do all the things I wanted to do, and let me make a job for myself besides. I didn't feel like asking too many questions about our relationship.

I wanted to believe Muhammad Yunus' suggestion that capitalism and I had a long and peaceful future together. It was only a matter, he wrote, of motivation:

I profoundly believe, as Grameen's experience over twenty years has shown, that personal gain is not the only possible fuel for free enterprise. Social goals can replace greed as a powerful motivational force. Social-consciousness-driven enterprises can be formidable competitors for the greed-based enterprises. I believe that if we play our cards right, social-consciousness-driven enterprises can do very well in the marketplace.[19]

If anybody had warned me it just wasn't going to be that simple, I wouldn't have listened.

28.

At the same time, I couldn't forget David the recovery mentor. It took me awhile, but I eventually figured out one reason at least that I wasn't more like him: he was practicing solidarity with his own kind, every minute of every day. He was demonstrating with his entire being that people like him were worth caring for even though almost all the rest of society said the opposite. While I was collecting a paycheck at CCC, he was remaking the order of the universe, placing marginalized people right at the center.

Once he got clean, there was nothing to stop him from moving onward and upward, as they say. He didn't have to take all that energy and personal power back where he came from, to the people society didn't care about. He chose to, and I saw what that looked like. (You could probably see David's commitment from outer space.) In any case, what he was doing was what I wanted more than anything else, I just didn't know it until I saw it in him.

That's the big thing about the community acupuncture model: it allowed me to treat people like myself. Like my family. To organize my work life as if they mattered.

And that's one thing that gets lost in discussions of social entrepreneurship when you only measure success in terms of capitalism. For me, it wasn't about competing with greed-based enterprises, or competing with anybody at all. The enduring benefit of my experiment with the techniques of entrepreneurship was that my life changed: a barred door flew off its hinges and a sturdy bridge appeared over a chasm. I gathered up the skills I'd picked up in the world and I took them home. To my own kind. I'm white trash and I got to take care of people like me, to put them at the center instead of at the margins.

No amount of therapy was going to offer me that level of repair. No amount of conventional success could outweigh its value to me. The long list of healers who'd been worried about how disconnected I was had never noticed I was cut off from myself in more than one way: not just from my feelings and my memories, but from my own people. Once I wasn't disconnected anymore, though, once again the first thing that came pouring through the link was rage. This time the object was the acupuncture profession, all the institutions that had built the framework in which people like me weren't even visible, let alone worth treating.

29.

And thus a new era began in my life: in which my relationships with other acupuncturists got a lot more interesting. Some of them mistook me for a humanitarian, and I resisted the impulse to snarl at them.

It's *so wonderful,* one acupuncturist gushed, what you're doing for *those people.*

I smiled through clenched teeth. You mean, my neighbors? My friends?

You're so *inspiring,* another enthused. So *progressive.*

No, I said, I'm just angry.

I was better equipped to deal with the opposite side of the coin: the acupuncturists who spotted a traitor. They were mad too. At first there were a few quasi-polite inquiries. You know, an acupuncturist reminded me, it is all about people's *priorities.* People need to *prioritize* their health. It's sad when people don't do that, but it's *very concerning* that you would lower your prices in response.

The next email, more direct, said:
If working class people didn't spend all their money on beer, cigarettes, and cable TV, they wouldn't have any problem paying for acupuncture.

Eventually, the howling started:
You are devaluing this ancient and honorable profession! You are demeaning your colleagues and risking everyone's reputation! It's an insult to those of us who have invested thousands of hours in learning this art! It's deplorable! (These are quotes.)

* * *

In general, these kinds of interactions just fueled my fire. Though it would have helped, back then, if I'd had a copy of this book. I could have given it to them and said, I'm sorry but you see, I'm coming from the bottom of a deep, dark well. Trying to shame someone like me is a waste of your time.

There was a third category, though, that more than made up for the other two, acupuncturists who saw in my work what I'd seen in David's: hope, integrity, and a freedom they wanted.

30.

But before I get to my soon-to-be-comrades, I'm going to take some more writerly liberties and quote a discussion from a decade later to try to explain what at least some of the fuss was about, from the perspective of the acupuncture profession. Because over 10 years, the fuss didn't change much. By 2012, community acupuncture was a thing, not just in the US, but in other Western countries as well. In the UK, they called it multibed acupuncture; they didn't like the recliners, but they liked other aspects of the model.

It will surprise nobody that I got into it with a British acupuncture luminary. He wrote on a blog:

The hardest thing is to get a rewarding (emotionally and financially) practice. So many new practitioners never get a practice off the ground – at least one that can give them a decent living. In my mind, there are two answers. The first is the work being done in the field of community acupuncture ... matching patients who simply can't afford high fees with practitioners happy to work in multibed clinics. The other is the development of the highest level of skill and knowledge allied with a degree of specialisation. I think these two strands can find a way to co-exist.

There is a buzz about multibeds right now, and lots of patients benefit from the affordability, the communal atmosphere and the ability to have more frequent treatments. They are a pragmatic solution to a particular problem. However, I don't think they represent best practice and I feel very strongly that best practice (which is almost inevitably more time consuming) risks being diminished by the need to offer quick treatment.

In fact, I think that lots of practitioners need to raise their game – continuously studying to build on their initial education. How many practitioners for example know the diagnostic tests, natural progression and prognosis of the hundreds of different musculoskeletal disorders the human body can suffer from? This despite the fact that musculoskeletal problems probably form the majority of the cases we treat.

I also feel that acupuncture – having its roots in the Chinese medical tradition – has a lot to offer patients in terms of understanding cause of disease and what are helpful and unhelpful behaviors. The way I was taught, this was part of the job and Chinese medicine has extraordinary wisdom in this respect.

When community acupuncture offers three-minute consultations and tacitly or overtly expects 'the needles to do all the work' I think this is a betrayal of acupuncture as medicine. After all, much dismay accompanied the transition from the old-style GP who lived in a community, knew their patients and their lives, relationships, strengths and weaknesses, to the modern rushed GP whose main preoccupation is to find a way to stop their patient talking so as not to exceed the few minutes allotted to each consultation.

Yet even they spend considerably longer than three minutes.

I responded on the co-op's blog:

Isn't it interesting that Mr. Luminary, like any number of acupuncturists and scholars before and since, has no qualms about glancing over the vast historical diversity of acupuncture practice and choosing (coincidentally?) its "best practice" as something which the majority of patients will never be able to afford? There are thousands of ways to practice acupuncture, some of them quick, some of them slow; there is no objective evidence that any of those ways work better clinically than any others, and yet the best way to do acupuncture, the right way to do acupuncture according to these scholars, is a way which inevitably puts it out of reach for millions of people who could otherwise benefit from it.

I was thinking about Mr. Luminary's comments during my first hour in clinic this morning and how "best practices" might apply to the first 6 people I treated. My first patient – let's call him Joe – is a security guard who has worked the graveyard shift for the last 20 years. He has a variety of health problems related to diabetes. His most acute problem right now is neuropathy in his feet, and it's acute not just because it hurts, but because he has to take a physical fitness test tomorrow and if he doesn't pass, he'll lose his job. There are all sorts of lifestyle changes he'd like to make to address his diabetes, such as exercising more and eating better, but he hasn't been able to make them because he's in so much pain that he can barely get through the day (or rather, night) and also, his sleep is wrecked. He's now in love with acupuncture because, since he started treatment earlier this week, he's had several pain-free hours in a row and also, he's sleeping much better. (He slept in the clinic yesterday, with his needles in, for 6 1/2 hours.) I learned all of this in 3 minutes as I was putting in his needles – he could only stay for an hour today so I needed to get them in quickly. He's counting on this treatment to help him get through the physical fitness test and keep his job. The last thing he told me before he fell asleep was that the relief he's getting from acupuncture gives him hope that he'll be able to start an exercise routine.

He knows the lifestyle changes he needs to make. I know where to put the needles to give him relief. He needs a nap and he needs to keep his job. What good would it do him – or me – to spend any more time talking? I don't need to palpate, I don't need to take his pulses in three positions, I know what to do and I know it will work. It's been working all week.

My second patient, let's call her Lydia, started crying right after she said hello to me. She's crying because she had an entire day of pain relief for the first time in about five years after her last treatment. Lydia is in her 70s with a history of depression and excruciating knee pain. Her doctor sent her to acupuncture 3 weeks ago, and we've treated her 10 times since then. She told me that both her doctor and her grown children can see the change in her and they're thrilled. Her mood is much better, and she's able to do more for herself. "For the first time in years I have hope." Her goal is to start exercising and to reduce her pain medication; she's started reading books about nutrition. As with Joe, my conversation with her took about 3 minutes, and there's nothing more to say. We both just have to keep plugging away, on opposite ends of the needle.

My next two patients, Jennifer and Cindy, both have allergies that make them miserable. The lovely Willamette Valley in which we all live is one of the worst places in the world for spring allergies. My car had what appeared to be a quarter-inch of yellow pollen on the windshield this morning. I have a protocol for allergies and I know it works, not only because my patients tell me that it does, but because I receive it myself. Jennifer tells me she's gotten off Zyrtec and she's very happy about it. What is there to talk about? They both are very clear about their treatment plans: come in at least once a week until the pollen count goes down.

My fifth patient, Daniel, is a new patient so I have, in theory, a luxurious 20 minutes to talk to him and treat him. Except that I don't, because he's late and he hasn't filled out his paperwork. In the 7 minutes I end up with, I learn that he has had a lot of acupuncture because he has had HIV for almost 20 years. He's here because his partner of 30 years died of cancer in March. This set a series of events in motion: he can no longer go to the public health clinic where he's been getting acupuncture because his partner left him just enough money to make him ineligible, but not enough money to afford a conventional acupuncturist; the HIV medications he'd been taking for years mysteriously made his liver, in his words, "suddenly just go flat" so he had to stop taking them; and he completely lost his appetite. The chief complaint he wrote on the intake is "grief". His doctor, like Lydia's, wants him to get acupuncture, and in fact sent him directly to us. Daniel says he mostly just wants to stop thinking.

OK, I say, how about we also work on supporting your liver and getting your appetite back?

Great, he says. I used to get acupuncture three times a week at the other clinic, I was thinking I'd like to do the same here.

Sure, I say, let's start with that.

Daniel also tells me that he always knows when his body's done with the treatment and he prefers to have the needles in about 45 minutes. Better and better, I tell him, we like for all of our patients to tell us when they're done instead of the other way around. He's so thin that he has no problem rolling his pants all the way up to the top of his thigh so that I can needle Tung points on his Liver meridian. Daniel falls asleep immediately after I put in a cautious (for me) 15 needles. Again, there's not much to say, and the treatment's pretty obvious. In our 7-minute conversation, Daniel told me that he knows he needs to eat, and in fact, he knows what he should be eating; the problem is wanting to eat.

So I'm on time for my sixth patient, which is good, because my sixth patient is two patients in one slot: Juan and Rigoberto, the teenage Ramirez brothers. Three weeks ago, Juan, who is 16, came in with his father, Juan Sr. Though Juan Jr.'s English was much better than his father's, Juan Sr. did all the talking while Juan Jr. hung his head: Juan Jr. has terrible headaches every day, his father said. He is depressed and angry, having a hard time in school. Juan Sr. also has headaches; his wife Elena has headaches and a swollen leg. The whole family is very stressed because they own a taqueria and business has not been good lately. On the first visit, I told Juan Sr. frankly that Juan Jr. would probably need a series of treatments, and his face fell. They couldn't afford it, he said. I took a deep breath, looked into the eyes of my fellow small-business owner and fellow parent, and said, How about $25 for 10 treatments? He brightened – they could afford that. I explained to him how to buy a punch card for Juan Jr. The next thing I knew, Juan Sr. had bought punch cards for everyone in the family, including Rigoberto, who was the only one who doesn't have headaches. Rigoberto just has stress because he is in an accelerated college program, he is only 18, and of course he has to work in the taqueria. We see quite a lot of the Ramirez family. They bring us burritos. The best part of treating them, though, is not the burritos (which are delicious), it's the change in Juan Jr. He no longer has headaches every day, he smiles at me, he volunteers some information about his stress level. (Way down, he said.) Treating all of the Ramirez family members is quick and mostly not very verbal: Juan Sr. and Elena don't speak much English, and Juan Jr. and Rigoberto are teenage boys, they don't talk to adults in any language. But they all love acupuncture. And they're all getting better, sometimes dramatically. Elena's leg isn't swollen anymore, and she's delighted.

* * *

Why not define "best practice" as that which produces the best results for the most people? Or at least acknowledge that how you define "best practice" is profoundly influenced by your personal class lens and the class of the patients you want to treat? To do so, of course, would require admitting that for acupuncture to work, people have to be able to receive it. Expensive, time consuming ways of delivering acupuncture, regardless of the skill and knowledge associated with them, are utterly worthless to people who aren't going to receive them because of outright cost or any of the other subtle class barriers that the acupuncture profession has put up around itself.

I'm not attacking the kind of acupuncture practice that Mr. Luminary is promoting; I'm just saying it has no value to the people I want to treat, to all the Joes and Lydias and Daniels and Juans Jr. and Sr. Certain practices may have value to people who have more resources than my patients, but I'm sorry, I'm not going to accept those practices as "best" when they are no good at all to the people I saw this morning. Wouldn't that be kind of like saying that Joe, Lydia, Daniel and the Ramirez family don't count, that their needs don't deserve to be considered? I would have no issue with Mr. Luminary's comments if he framed them in a less classist way: if he simply specified, for example, that he is discussing "best practice" for a set of patients who have abundant disposable income, plenty of time to spend in one-on-one consultations with a practitioner, and no cultural or class barriers to the way that acupuncture is conventionally practiced in the West. If acupuncturists who want to treat those people in that way accept it as best practice for their limited circumstances, that's fine with me, I have no problem co-existing politely with that strand.

I'll even acknowledge that there are situations for some

practitioners and some patients where it could be useful to know the diagnostic tests, natural progression and prognosis of the hundreds of different musculoskeletal disorders the human body can suffer from. There are situations for some practitioners and some patients in some socio-economic environments where I'm sure it's helpful to do back points, and maybe even to give lifestyle advice. Mr. Luminary thinks that lots of practitioners need to raise their game – continuously studying to build on their initial education. But no matter how much you raise your game as a private-room acupuncturist, you are never going to be able to get the results I get with the Ramirez family. All the back points and all the continuous studying in the world will not get you Lydia crying with *hope*. Because you are never going to be able to treat these people at all unless you can treat six people an hour and let the needles do the work.

I do have a big problem co-existing politely with a strand that tells me that I diminish the profession by treating Joe, Lydia, Jennifer, Cindy, Daniel, and the Ramirez brothers all in the same room, in the same hour, in a way that gets good clinical results, that works for them and works for me. Statements like this don't make me feel like coexisting politely, either: *When community acupuncture offers three-minute consultations and tacitly or overtly expects 'the needles to do all the work' I think this is a betrayal of acupuncture as medicine.* If you put it like that, OK, I'll gladly betray acupuncture as a medicine. If I have to choose between being loyal to that and being loyal to my patients, the Ramirez family is going to win every time. Also, doesn't it occur to the critics of community acupuncture that statements like that are insulting to our patients? If their relief, their hope, their clinical improvements require their practitioners to betray acupuncture as a medicine – what does that mean about them? Is acupuncture not medicine when it works for people who are poor? On their own terms? [20]

31.

Implicit in the idea of entrepreneurship is the quality of striving, aspiration, continually reaching for something better. In terms of Chinese philosophy, entrepreneurship is about as yang as you can get: bright, energetic, upward moving. Social entrepreneurship adds some more yang attributes to the list: virtuous, high-minded, transformative. My experience of entrepreneurship was mostly the opposite, which is to say, yin. It had everything to do with brokenness, collapse and letting go of progress. This might seem like quibbling over abstractions but the lack of distinction about it has caused any number of real world problems for me.

Pretty much from the beginning, a lot of people have wanted community acupuncture to reflect only the positive. They've wanted to see it as an expression of humanitarian aspiration. However, social entrepreneurship for me wasn't an optimistic upward climb, step by step into the sun. Social entrepreneurship for me was a torrent of creativity powered by rage and grief, filling a space opened up by the breakdown of denial. It was largely about the rejection of aspiration; it was all about accepting the bottom of the well rather than trying to climb out.

Why, you're probably wondering, am I so determined to the record straight about that?

Starting in the 1970s, those white students of Chinese acupuncturists had lofty, professional aspirations for the practice of Chinese medicine in the US. Acupuncturists would wear white coats and receive the same respect as doctors. They would all be scholar-physicians, a long way from the bad old days in China when some acupuncturists were peasants, at the same level as itinerant tooth-pullers and worm-expellers. (During our argument, the British acupuncture luminary suggested that community acupuncturists were a contemporary version of the worm-expellers. I thanked him.) What these professional aspirations have meant, over the course of my career as an acupuncturist, was that both acupuncture itself and acupuncture education became so expensive that ordinary people couldn't afford them.

The profession wanted to go up the ladder of status; I've only ever wanted to go down. But professionalism isn't the only form of aspiration I'm allergic to.

Not long after I started writing about the community acupuncture model, I started receiving a steady stream of admonitions that I should be more like Gandhi and/or Mother Teresa; I should try harder to get along with all my colleagues; I should work to unify rather than polarize acupuncturists. More than once, other acupuncturists have scolded me that I fall short of my ideals.

The thing is, I don't have any ideals. People keep being shocked and disappointed when they find this out. Maybe I should say, a lot of middle and upper middle class people have been shocked and disappointed to find out I don't have ideals; a lot of working class people seem to understand that ideals can be a form of luxury goods. Nonetheless it seems like a good idea to go on the record about it to try to avoid causing further dismay.

It's like the Thomas Merton quote:

Do not depend on the hope of results. When you are doing the sort of work you have taken on... you may have to face the fact that your work will be apparently worthless and even achieve no result at all, if not perhaps results opposite to what you expect. As you get used to this idea, you start more and more to concentrate not on the results but on the value, the rightness, the truth of the work itself. And there too a great deal has to be gone through as gradually you struggle less and less for an idea and more and more for specific people.[21]

Except that I didn't start out by struggling for an idea. I've always oriented myself in relationship to specific people as opposed to abstract ideas or ideals. Specific people are real to me in a way that ideals aren't. And it wasn't ideals that created the community acupuncture model, it was a collision of real world needs of people with limited resources: my need to pay my mortgage, Chico's need to stop coughing up blood, Betty's need to be able to walk her dogs. This model didn't come from a lofty place.

It's probably similar to my faith: I wouldn't say I believe in God, but that I have a concrete and practical relationship with God in which God does all the care taking and I'm just grateful. It's also related to what I learned during my breakdown: that striving to improve myself as opposed to practicing compassion toward myself was probably going to kill me. I had to accept my limits. It takes energy to get along with acupuncturists who think I'm a traitor or who wish I was a humanitarian; it takes effort to try to be good and polite and not angry. If I made those efforts, on the one hand some people would feel more comfortable, but on the other, I wouldn't be doing much else.

There were a lot of other things I wanted to do, so I did them instead, using the energy I saved by not making peace with the acupuncture profession and not trying to be a better person.

Here's a question: now that we're looking at the community acupuncture model itself —low cost, high volume, simplified, community-based – it's obvious it isn't rocket science. So the question is, why am I the social entrepreneur writing this book? Why didn't dozens of other acupuncturists do it first?

There were acupuncturists, especially Asian acupuncturists, for whom the low cost high volume aspect wasn't unfamiliar at all. Once I got a friendly email from a newly arrived Chinese acupuncturist thanking me for affirming that he could practice this way in the US, after so many people had told him that he couldn't because it wouldn't work here. The specific focus on community as a positive benefit, though, as opposed to something people had to put up with in order to get bargain acupuncture, that was new for the US. But it still isn't rocket science, so why didn't the idealistic acupuncturists, the ones who are like Gandhi and Mother Teresa, why didn't they do this instead of me?

I'm sure you're getting my drift here: I'm suggesting that a combination of anger, desperation, and destroyed expectations broke the binary that had to be broken in order to give the community acupuncture model space to form. And when it formed, it was out of concrete needs rather than aspirations. I'm suggesting that idealism isn't a prerequisite for social entrepreneurship. Just like you can do social entrepreneurship without aiming for capitalist success, you can do it without striving for anything. You can do it as part of falling back to where you belong, as part of having mercy on yourself. You can do it while you're broken.

You might even get more done that way. People will probably complain that what you're doing isn't good enough and you're not doing it right according to their standards, but you'll still get more done than they do. As Rebecca Solnit says:

Perfection is a stick with which to beat the possible.[22]

32.

In the early aughts, there wasn't a lot written about acupuncture and business. In fact, when I first tried discussing the community model, a prominent acupuncturist warned me that I should never talk about pricing. I shouldn't post my prices (I should make patients *ask* about them) and I should never, ever tell another acupuncturist what I charged or why, because anyone who participated in the conversation could be accused of price-*fixing*. I think this demonstrates a general aversion, at the time, to looking at the economic nuts and bolts of acupuncture practices. For awhile, I'm pretty sure I was one of the only acupuncturists in Portland who posted her prices (possibly the only one). Working class people learn early not to get interested in something before they know they can afford it.

I had the sense that I was engaged with something that was supposed to be larger than my own practice, and so I kept trying to talk to other acupuncturists, even when I didn't know exactly where I was going with it, or when someone scolded me that the conversation shouldn't be happening at all.

In 2005, S. and I went away for a weekend with our laptops and pounded out a zine. A couple of disgusted colleagues had already called us communists, so we entertained ourselves by titling it, *The Little Red Book of Working Class Acupuncture*. We printed up copies at Kinko's and mailed them to any acupuncturist who expressed curiosity about what we were doing. Around the same time, I discovered that someone who called himself, let's say, the acu-practice-guru was promoting himself as a business coach for acupuncturists. There are a lot of those now, but he was the only one then. He put out a free eBook about how to grow your practice with integrity. It contained such gems as:

- move your office to the best part of town – people will expect you to be expensive
- raise your fees, because it puts you in the exclusive box and you'll improve the type of patients you'll get
    - upgrade your patients: identify who your ideal patients are and make sure they're people of means; ditch the ones who aren't, because they just drain you

I was so angry I wrote my own version of a marketing eBook for acupuncturists. There's a copy in the appendices, a souvenir from my honeymoon with capitalism. Paul Hawken's influence, via *Growing a Business*, is clear: your success is a function of being yourself. I took that message and filtered it through the lens of acupuncture. Reading it 11 years later, it sounds annoyingly chirpy; I can't believe I was ever so cheerful. But there's the evidence in print – I was. And I wasn't constantly polarizing, either. There were times when I earnestly tried to coexist with other acupuncturists and even encourage them.

They just didn't last long.

The most productive period of trying to reach out to other acupuncturists started in 2005 when I read that one of the only industry publications, let's call it Acupuncture A La Mode, was looking for new columnists. I offered to write a column on social entrepreneurship and to my surprise, they accepted.

Spoiler alert: this was not exactly a competitive gig to get, but even so it would be short-lived. After I'd been writing about what I was doing for a year or so, six columns' worth, I got an email from the editor that said, in closing: *After several conversations with my publisher and others, we are concerned about continuing your column under its current "theme", for lack of a better word. While the concept of social entrepreneurship, particularly the "pay according to what you can afford" aspect, is admirable, it has dangerous potential from the perspective of professional advancement.*

Translation: we'd hate to promote the concept that acupuncture could be affordable to ordinary people.

In the days before widespread social media, though, this column and its comment section gave the community acupuncture model a platform. By the time Acupuncture A La Mode cancelled the column, word had gotten out. The online comments section for the social entrepreneurship articles turned out to be an effective petri dish, and a new culture was already growing.

Cut to the Chase, Please: #5

You had a model that worked and other acupuncturists were interested in it. Please tell us you had the sense to trademark it, franchise it and capitalize off it before somebody else did. Oh God, you didn't, did you?

See what I mean? I keep disappointing people.

Dropping the price for acupuncture and adjusting the delivery model to make it much more patient-centered did, in fact, open it up to more people, to a dramatic degree. *In Growing a Business,* Paul Hawken suggests that's one strategy for carving out your individuality in the business world. He says, *be the low-cost provider...then get out of the way, for if you have done it right, you will be mobbed.*[23]

Relative to most other acupuncturists, who were seeing maybe 10-15 patients a week, I was indeed getting mobbed. I wasn't so busy that cash flow was no problem, but I was able to support myself and my family, which was a refreshing change. However, I learned quickly that the bottom end of my sliding scale, $15, was still a lot for some people relative to how many treatments they needed. This is mind boggling to certain capitalists, so here are some examples.

Ray works for a landscaper, making just over minimum wage. He strained some tendons in his shoulder moving rocks. He has no savings and no short-term disability insurance. His goal for acupuncture treatment is to get back to work as soon as possible. The most appropriate treatment plan is acupuncture daily for 10 days. He won't have any money until he gets back to work. Charlotte was a CNA for many years until she suffered a brain injury; now she's on disability, which means her income is fixed and very low. She struggles with blurred vision, chronic joint pain, and depression. Acupuncture twice a week dramatically improves her quality of life in terms of mood and pain relief, but it's not going to cure the long-term effects of a brain injury. Her income isn't going to change, either. Sheila is a single mom and works full time as a grocery cashier. She lives with her parents, which is very stressful; she sought acupuncture when she started having panic attacks. Acupuncture relieves her stress and has eliminated her panic attacks but of course what would help the most would be to move out and get a place of her own, which requires saving up for rental deposits. Cutting acupuncture out of her budget would help with the savings, but not if she's immobilized by panic attacks.

I could go on and on with this list, but the point is, acupuncture works best in large and/or regular doses, and the lower you are on the socioeconomic ladder, the more likely you are to suffer from conditions that acupuncture can substantially relieve. How neat is that?

In order to get the results I wanted to get, I dropped the low end of the scale whenever it was clinically indicated to do so. In return I got to see acupuncture work like magic for people who had few, or maybe no other, options for relief. I couldn't resist. When my practice was big enough to hire acupuncturist employees, they couldn't resist either. And the more clinical experience we all got, the more confident we became about acupuncture's effectiveness in large quantities, and the more invested we got in being able to be flexible with fees. To be able to offer the treatment that you want, constrained by nothing other than the patients' willingness to show up, is an addictive rush of freedom. It made the business run on thin (OK, skeletal) margins, but I couldn't imagine the model without it.

* * *

It won't surprise you to hear that capitalists could and did imagine the model without it.

In order for me to franchise the model, the margins would have had to be wider than I could stand. There would have had to be a little bit of comfortable padding, and it would have come from turning people away when they needed more treatment than they could afford. Fees I received from franchise owners would have come at the expense of their clinical freedom as acupuncturists, their ability to tell patients to come in as often as they needed and don't worry about the scale. Furthermore, any acupuncturist who was interested in the model was probably as broke as I was when I found it. You can't get blood from a turnip. Franchise fees would increase the start-up costs, which would have to be passed on to patients. Purpose: defeated.

The model worked. It worked *in capitalism*. It just didn't work *as capitalism*, not the way I was using it. Franchising wasn't going to lead to anything I wanted.

So you just gave it away?

I gave it away with a vengeance.

But before you get apoplectic, impatient capitalists, let's return to the discussion of acupuncture points as holes and an acupuncturist's job as holding space – because that's a crucial part of the model, and I'm not sure even you can fault me for giving away empty space.

33.

The community acupuncture model is a set of systems, refined and codified by the POCA Cooperative.[24] That's the quantifiable stuff. The unquantifiable stuff is in the empty spaces; a clinic can't run without it. An acupuncturist has to be able to hold space for patients before the patients will show up.

About a year or so into trying out the model and seeing my patient base grow steadily, I met with an experienced owner of another affordable acupuncture clinic. This person, let's call him Dev, was not an acupuncturist himself but employed a few in order to provide a set of services that he had identified a need for. His clinic had started out by offering Chinese herbs, shiatsu, and acupuncture to AIDS patients; more recently he had expanded access to patients with other chronic and/or life-threatening illnesses. I told him I was excited about making acupuncture available to many more people. He was polite but skeptical.

Affordable acupuncture practices don't grow, he told me. My clinic hasn't grown in 11 years. You could offer free acupuncture with the best acupuncturist in Portland and people wouldn't take you up on it.

After considering for a moment, he added: though it might make a difference if the practitioners at my clinic were more...charismatic.

I don't think that's quite right. Charisma doesn't hurt, but it's not an essential ingredient for holding space. Passion and a sense of urgency are. I'd met the acupuncturists who worked for Dev. Like many acupuncturists who were drawn to public health type environments, they were kind people but they weren't on fire with vocation. David the recovery mentor was my role model for that. He was like an illustration of the John Wesley quote: *If you set yourself on fire, people will come from miles around to see you burn.*

Or, as David himself said in the documentary trailer: *What you need to understand? I give a fuck.*

In a discussion a few years back with other community acupuncturists about how challenging our businesses are to run, I wrote:

I have a theory about our product. Small business is hard, no matter what kind of product you've got; it demands a lot from you. But if you're running a small business that sells plumbing fixtures, people know what plumbing fixtures are and why they might need them. It's not a leap into the unknown to go buy some. If you're running a coffee shop or a microbrewery, even if not everybody is familiar with locally roasted coffee or handcrafted sour beer, your products in a sense offer people an escape. Coffee and beer make people feel good. They don't have to admit they were feeling tired or stressed out in order to use them to feel better. Anyone can just wander into a coffee shop or a brewery and sit down and nobody has to know anything about them. If you're running a coffee shop or a brewery or a plumbing store, your business can slip into a groove that thousands of coffee shops or pubs or plumbing stores have dug for you.

Our product, on the other hand, is unfamiliar to most people; if that weren't bad enough, to use it you need to admit on some level that you are feeling bad and need help. Not only that, you need to TELL somebody else you feel bad and need help, and the first time you go in, that person is a stranger.

The implicit risk level for our customers is sky-high. (Not to mention there are sharp objects involved!) It's testament to the amazing power of acupuncture that we have any customers at all. The reason that we have businesses while a lot of other acupuncturists don't is that we didn't decide to make our product unaffordable on top of its other challenges.

Bottom line is, at this point in our society, the only thing that can draw people in to community acupuncture past the unfamiliarity and the implicit vulnerability and risk is somebody standing there with their heart wide open, aching to help. That's the necessary magic. If it's not fully present, because the acupuncturist isn't fully present in the waiting, the readiness, and the urgent desire to help, then the unfamiliarity wins out and the clinic doesn't attract any patients. (POCA Forums)

If you hold back and refuse to show up until you have patients to show up for – which is what a lot of acupuncturists do because they don't want to hang out alone in an empty space, both literally and figuratively – you won't have a practice. You have to show up first, when there's nobody there. And you have to burn.

This seems like a good time to revisit my desperation and traumatic history as a key ingredient to my entrepreneurial success. In 11 years, Dev's affordable acupuncture clinic didn't grow at all; mine grew something like 2000%. Dev was sane, well-capitalized, and experienced in running a business; in fact, he had another successful business that supported the acupuncture clinic. I, on the other hand, needed to put food on the table and needed someplace to put my rage. What I had going for me was that I didn't need to set myself on fire, I was already burning.

Also, I was fine with the void. Thanks to Lockerbie, I'd had my entire adult life to adjust to it. Thanks to passage meditation, I'd had almost as long to practice one-pointed attention, so I was able to stay focused on holding space. I could go into the emptiness of my clinic and stay there, body and soul, until patients showed up, and when they showed up I was delighted to see them. I didn't get distracted, I didn't complain, I didn't worry about what else I might be missing. I wasn't ever resentful that I had to show up first.

Probably because I didn't know the difference between the void and normal life, or what passes for normal life in this society.

Since then, a lot of people have gotten angry at me because they saw me burning, they were fascinated and came closer, and they ended up meeting the void. When everything wasn't neatly laid out for them, when everything they needed wasn't provided, when they didn't feel supported and affirmed, they got mad. I've never known what to say to that except, look, if I insisted on any of those things the way you do, I wouldn't be here at all. (And neither would you.) It didn't occur to me that I needed to explain why I have a sky-high tolerance for empty space – a mistake I'm trying to correct with this book.

But even so, it's never seemed like a good idea to try to *sell* the model to anyone.

Fractal

34.

The online comments for my column at Acupuncture A La Mode attracted so many acupuncturists trying out the model in one form or another and needing to talk about it, that it seemed like we should have something more sophisticated than a set of comment threads on a forum that after all, didn't belong to us. (This hunch was confirmed when Acupuncture A La Mode fired me as a columnist and we lost that platform altogether.) The budding online community evolved into a 501c6 nonprofit membership organization for acupuncturists called the Community Acupuncture Network. By that time, blogs were a thing and so CAN had its own blog and its own member forums where we could discuss the model in detail. We called the blog "Prick, Prod and Provoke" (synonyms of the verb *to needle)*. We were clearly getting on other acupuncturists' nerves so we might as well have some fun with it.

It turned out the dominant practice model wasn't working for a lot of people, but only CAN would say so in public. The culture of the acupuncture profession at that time was competitive, secretive, and status-conscious. We were breaching a taboo by being open about what we charged and how many patients we treated, and we were breaking new ground by encouraging each other to share information. We were cooperating instead of competing, though it didn't occur to us to use the word cooperation. It just seemed like common sense.

I had been annoyed by my cursory practice management class in acupuncture school; I found out I'd been lucky because it could have been way worse. For a number of acupuncturists, practice management classes included being told to buy a Jaguar and learn to play golf so that they could connect with the kind of people they should have as patients (and if they were female, they should also be sure that their manicures were impeccable). Other acupuncture practice management advice included urging students to start an online retail business for custom herbal formulas, scented candles or exercise balls, because they shouldn't expect to make any money by just doing acupuncture. The implication was that if you didn't want to invest in a fancy car and an online business, you didn't deserve to have a real practice. Many graduates were so overwhelmed or alienated that they never practiced at all. More than a few CAN members said they cried when they first read the CAN forums and realized they could ask basic questions of their peers about business without being made to feel a) ridiculous, and b) like failures. Not to mention, they could expect straight answers.

People who were drawn to the community acupuncture model were attracted by its authenticity, its commitment to providing acupuncture as opposed to selling scented candles, and the promise of being able to connect to their own communities. Not everybody was working class, not by a long shot, but everybody was aware that in their private practices, they were charging prices that they themselves couldn't afford, let alone their friends and neighbors, and the pretense was wearing them down. Many were trying to get by with their own version of a little of this, a little of that, and were feeling discouraged and scattered. The prospect of being able to do one thing, wholeheartedly and without affectation, was compelling.

We were a motley conglomerate. There was the working-class bartender who told me that acupuncture school was where he learned he was supposed to hate his family for their unhealthy lifestyles. There was the woman who could fix anything, an expert pickle-maker who spent years working on organic farms. There was the Canadian skateboarder from East Jesus Nowhere, who had gone to acupuncture school in order to treat his own skating injuries since he couldn't afford the going rate for acupuncture. There was the second-generation Chinese acupuncturist who had been helping out in her parents' clinic since she was a kid. There was the woman who built her own house in the New Mexico desert, who said she had a sensitive bullshit-meter that kept going off during acupuncture school, until one night she typed "acupuncture community" into a search engine and found us. There was the Russian immigrant juggling three different part-time acupuncture jobs. There were bewildered new graduates and conventionally successful private room acupuncturists who were too burned out and miserable to continue. And there were nerds of breathtaking variety: queer theory nerds, science fiction nerds, electronic music nerds, and lucky for us, organizational nerds for when we started to get serious about building organizations beyond a loose online association.

My role began to resemble that of the kid in the story of the Emperor's New Clothes, with the acupuncture profession being the emperor. One way or another I kept saying, hey, this doesn't look like it's working so well. Other acupuncturists in the past who thought the same thing had been silenced by the fear that voicing their doubts in public would prove they were unfit to be in business. I didn't care who thought I was unfit, plus I was making a living, so I kept talking about how naked the emperor looked from the vantage point of people who couldn't afford $50+ for an acupuncture treatment. On some level the truth is always a relief, right? I found comrades who agreed. (He's not only naked, he has a hairy ass! crowed one disillusioned veteran of the acupuncture professional wars.)

We were often perceived by the rest of the acupuncture profession as fiery militants or just bad mannered thugs, but that's not what drew us together. We had all found out that the rigid binary of the acupuncture profession – subsidized acupuncture for poor people and expensive acupuncture for people of means – didn't work for us or more accurately, didn't allow us to work.

And we all needed to work, not only for financial reasons. We were looking for our vocation.

Muhammad Yunus writes about social businesses having dividends other than profits. One of the dividends of community acupuncture as a social business was salvaged acupuncturists. Without the model, a lot of us would have ended up bitter, underutilized, and marginalized. We would have stayed on the sidelines of the acupuncture profession – that is, if we didn't give up on it entirely – contributing nothing more than occasional snark.

With the model, we were still snarky, but we were also useful, engaged and productive. We discovered an important role in our own communities and meaningful work for ourselves. *I am a machete in the jungle of pain,*[25] one woman wrote, and most of us felt the same. A sense of being at a loss in the world is not an uncommon motivation to become an acupuncturist. Acupuncture schools attract seekers. Unfortunately, plenty of them stay lost after graduation, when they can't put their education to any tangible use or find their place in society. Our conglomerate might be motley, but we shared an intense, newfound sense of purpose and belonging.

We had a lot of work to do. In a profession where so many people were underemployed, having work to do didn't feel like a burden; it felt liberating. We were about to build a new organization out of scraps, gleanings, odds and ends. The scraps were us.

35.

Remember my personal hexagram, possession in great measure? A weak leader who prospers through attracting strength and talent by being receptive? At Cascade AIDS Project I learned I had a talent for begging; once I had the model to work with, I learned I was even better at delegating. Some small business owners can't delegate to save their lives: they're sole proprietors because they don't want anybody else's interference. I didn't have that problem; I had the reverse of that problem.

I remember once reading a description of abused kids who join gangs. They have so little self-esteem, the author wrote, it's like they're not there. If they're the only person in the room and you ask them a question, they look around for who you're talking to. Oh shit, I thought, that's me, that's what I do. Not exactly that way, but I have a lot of trouble remembering I'm here sometimes, and that's been both an asset and a liability.

Hence the truth of my hexagram. If you're skilled at begging, you've got a worthwhile project, and you're not sure you're there, you won't have any trouble attracting talented people to help you and you won't get in their way when they do. The upside is, when you're not good at one of the many tasks that are part of running a business or an organization, it's easy to find someone who's better at it and let them do their job. Those people will be happy, because people love being useful, the cause is noble and your gratitude is heartfelt.

The downside is...well. I've got more than a decade's worth of examples of the downside. Sometimes making space for other people to do their jobs is just making space, and sometimes it's abdicating.

* * *

I'll let one example stand in for the upside, though: Ilse, the first person I hired, who at 86 still works for Working Class Acupuncture. A few months after opening the space on Cully Boulevard, I was giving about 30 treatments a week – 3 times more than any other acupuncturist I knew. I was hitting a wall. I needed help. Once the phone rang and I picked it up and snapped, What? What do YOU want?

Ilse lived across the street from me and I had been treating her and her husband, Oreste, at home for about a year. They were retired, both immigrants who had come to the US after World War II. Oreste, a big good-looking Ukrainian who spoke five languages, would occasionally express polite skepticism that I would survive in business. When I told him I was having a grand opening party, he said, And when is grand closing party? (His accent made it sound charming.) One day he joked that I should get Ilse to help me organize my office. Ilse's German. No disorder could stand in her way.

Then Oreste died of a heart attack. They had been married 45 years. A week later, I impulsively asked Ilse if she would come and help me get my office in order. She said yes. I don't think she had any serious goals beyond getting out of the house. She's a natural extrovert and sitting at the front desk was a kind of tonic for her. I was relieved that someone else was answering the phone, because that meant that I didn't have to scurry between patients in the back and a ringing phone in the front.

Pretty soon she started making suggestions. She noticed that after acupuncture, people were so relaxed that they often had trouble making their next appointment, as well as writing a check for the treatment they just had. They were likely to drift out the door without paying, so Ilse instituted a policy that patients pay and schedule their next session before their treatment. It worked like magic. A month after Ilse started I made twice as much as I had in any previous month. More people were scheduling because the phone was being answered by a live person (not to mention a warm, friendly, non-harried one) and income was up. It turned out I had been forgetting to collect payment from about half of my patients.

Ilse wouldn't let me pay her at first. She insisted I was just humoring her, and that I didn't need help. She couldn't keep that up once she saw the state of my office, but she still maintained that since she had never been a receptionist she wasn't qualified for a paying job. I was giving her acupuncture, so we sort of had a trade. After a few months, she admitted that she was experiencing an unexpected drop in income. There was a difference between what Oreste's pension paid while he was alive and what it would pay her after his death, and that amount equaled her entire food budget.

By this time, it was pretty clear that Ilse's presence in my office was consistently bringing in more business; I was up to 50+ visits a week from 30. We made an arrangement that I would pay her a percentage of whatever I brought in. Initially, that percentage added up to groceries, but eventually, it wasn't very different from putting her on payroll. With Ilse, it worked out well for her to be good at things I wasn't good at. Together we created a kind of interdependence that benefited both of us and the patients too.

I probably have enough material for a whole other book on all the ways the dynamic of my personal hexagram has gone wrong: the times I've attracted people whose vision eventually diverged from mine so that the working relationship fell apart; people who thought they'd gotten lucky and found a fixer-upper, who harbored fantasies of improving me and the model and who got resentful when I or the model resisted being improved; people who got angry when they met the void at close quarters (manifesting as uncertainty, lack of validation, and sudden change); people who needed things I couldn't give them.

I had no particular ability to organize an office. I didn't figure out how to create payroll, hire acupuncturists, have an HR department, start a 501c6 nonprofit or build a website. I didn't figure out how to hold conferences for acupuncturists, take our workshops on the road, or provide continuing education credits. I didn't figure out how to make t-shirts with our logo and I didn't draw up the logo, either. (S. and I can't remember whose idea the logo was; I only remember idly scribbling on a napkin in a bar after work one night, both of us tipsy, when one of us said, RED FIST and the other said YES. I went home and called a friend who's a graphic designer.) Other people made all those things happen, and more. I was just good at asking for help.

I'm leaving a lot out here. But it does get us to the next two important topics – fractals and infrastructure.

36.

My friend Cris, the pickle-maker who could fix anything (and the founder of Providence Community Acupuncture), was the one who pointed out we had a fractal.

A fractal is a pattern that repeats itself, also called an expanding symmetry. Nature is full of fractals: think of frost crystals spreading over a window. Also ferns, broccoli, pineapple, trees, river networks, lightning bolts, and peacock feathers. The human body has fractals in lungs, blood vessels and heart sounds.

The community acupuncture movement is a fractal because the same patterns appear repeatedly at different levels of organization – or rather, self-organization. Community acupuncture is a self-organizing thing. Around the time I started noticing this was around the time I realized capitalism and I weren't getting along so well and might even have some irreconcilable differences. This isn't the place for a discussion of the history of capitalism: I think it's enough to say that there was a lot of planning and collusion involved in the emergence of capitalism and it's not a natural, self-organizing system.

The community acupuncture model felt like my ally; it also felt like it wanted things from me. Specifically, it wanted the next level of organization to emerge so it could repeat its patterns. In social entrepreneurship that's called scaling up. In capitalism, scaling up is fueled by profits. We didn't have those.

One thing I loved about the model was that it provided stability. All along, S. and I had in the back of our minds that we wanted to create the stable jobs that public health had almost, but not quite, been able to give us. We liked the predictability of regular hours and regular paychecks; we had learned the hard way that these things were luxuries for acupuncturists. Our goal on the one hand was to charge our patients as little as possible, so that they could come as much as they needed to get optimal results, and on the other to pay the acupuncturists (including ourselves) a living wage so that they could commit themselves to the clinic. This proved to be a stretch, but it worked by creating a neat self-reinforcing loop: low prices meant lots of people trying acupuncture, and enough of them getting good results to stick with it; a steady stream of patients meant we could keep regular hours; regular hours for patients and acupuncturists created consistency and reliability; since our services were easy to use, easy to describe, and we were open a lot, patients readily referred their friends. As acupuncturists, our perspective was that if we all worked to cultivate a big shared patient base by being consistent, reliable, and accessible, then we would all have stable jobs. It didn't take us long to learn that there was almost no money left over to pay for management, and so we were going to have to learn how to manage ourselves.

As a social business, the dividends of community acupuncture were affordable treatments for patients and living wage jobs for acupuncturists. There were no other dividends. It was obvious, though, that the better we could organize ourselves, the more stable we would be. The purpose of scaling up for community acupuncture would be to provide more acupuncture, create more jobs, and secure more stability for everyone.

Let's look at the levels of self-organization in community acupuncture.

The basic unit of low-cost, high volume community treatment – people sitting in a circle of chairs receiving acupuncture – had been self-organized by patients, whether you traced that back to the Black Panthers and Young Lords occupying Lincoln Hospital in order to create the services their community needed, or more recently back to Betty showing up in my living room first with her sister, then with her nephew, and then with her neighbor. (I have to think that something about acupuncture encourages self-organization.)

The next level of the fractal was the individual clinic, an acupuncturist figuring out how to make a job out of a configuration of cheap rental space, recycled recliners, and simple treatments. In hindsight, it's amazing to me that community acupuncture managed to establish itself on the precarious foundation of so many people being willing to start their own clinics, given that most of us had no previous experience in running a business.

At that level, more self-organization naturally occurred if the acupuncturist was invested enough: more patients began to show up and they brought their skills with them. In the early days of my clinic, patients built bike racks, designed flyers, did the bookkeeping, scavenged furniture we needed, and got us on TV. Eventually this steady flow of contributions could lead to the clinic establishing formal employment or a formal volunteer program, but it also tended to go on at an informal level regardless, because people are generous.

And this is the point where capitalism stops supporting the self-organizing pattern of the community acupuncture fractal, and even becomes a deterrent. Here's where the need for infrastructure arrives. Capitalism won't fund or reward the investment in infrastructure because in our fractal, the return on that investment comes to the collective and not to the individual. Let me explain.

If the clinic owner is balancing the need to provide

treatments to people who don't have much disposable income with the need to create living wage jobs for the people giving the treatments, the owner isn't going to make any money off of having more acupuncturist employees. The owner may create more stability by securing a larger patient base for the clinic as a whole, but they won't make a profit – and they will create more stress for themselves by becoming an employer and a manager in addition to being a regular community acupuncturist. With additional jobs, the clinic needs more infrastructure and someone to tend the infrastructure, because infrastructure can't take care of itself. (Ask me how I know.) The value of the infrastructure is that it stabilizes the clinic at a level where more people are involved – more people getting treatments, more people working. It's good for everybody in general but it's not *better* for anybody individually.

But for narrative purposes, let's just say that the clinic owner has accepted that her relationship with capitalism just isn't working out like Muhammad Yunus implied that it would, but now she's obsessed with the fractal itself and determined to see the symmetry continue to expand. She wants to know what this particular window will look like when it's completely covered with frost crystals, so she makes some anti-capitalist choices, including borrowing money to fund the creation of necessary infrastructure. In my own case, this included both infrastructure for more jobs at my own clinic and infrastructure for the next level of organization for the movement itself. (Pro tip for budding social entrepreneurs: nobody will give you a 501c6 for free.) So with capitalism sidelined for the moment by rebellious personal choices, the frost crystals keep spreading over the window and the pattern gets bigger: both more visible to other people and more identifiable in its elements.

If there's enough infrastructure – a membership

154

organization and a website sophisticated enough to archive information in a useful way – then community acupuncturists self-organize to support each other in a cooperative context. They recognize that everyone's biggest obstacle to making a living is the unfamiliarity of Chinese medicine in the US. The more people get acupuncture, the more people *get* acupuncture – and so we're *better together*, we're better off rooting for each other's success instead of competing. Like the patients who have found a community clinic that meets their needs, community acupuncturists are motivated to bring their contributions to the organization. They share their clinic forms, their marketing materials, their treatment strategies, their numbers. The fractal is big enough now that certain crucial elements are easy to identify: transparency, simplicity, solidarity.

If this were a science fiction movie, right about now is when somebody should rush out of a laboratory waving their arms and screaming, Oh my God, it's alive!

What brought this particular fractal to life are acupuncturists' and patients' innately social inclinations. It's like what Rebecca Solnit says in *Hope in the Dark*:

To live entirely for oneself in private is a huge luxury, a luxury countless aspects of this society encourage, but like a diet of pure foie gras it clogs and narrows the arteries of the heart. This is what we're encouraged to crave in this country, but most of us crave more deeply something with more grit, more substance.[26]

The community acupuncture fractal came alive in people's cravings to share rather than hoard, to include rather than exclude.

Once the fractal was alive, though, it began to take on the

characteristics of other life forms: it became increasingly complex, which meant it began to demand more complex infrastructure; and it wanted to reproduce. This would involve the mind-bending exercise of building a multi-stakeholder cooperative, and it would also create more conflicts. In the long run, the fractal would make me break up with capitalism.

37·

But before we get into that, I'd like to spend just a little more time on the share-rather-than-hoard theme. This is a blog post I wrote in 2013:

Stone Soup and Social Business, a Confession.

A poor soldier is traveling home from the wars, somewhere in Europe or Russia. There's been a famine, and nobody he meets wants to share their food with him. He arrives in a village, and the villagers look over his ragged clothes and battered wagon and tell him that he should move on, they've got nothing for him. I have everything I need, he tells them cheerfully. In fact, I was planning to share my food with you.

He gets out a big iron pot, fills it with water, makes a fire, and when the water is boiling, he takes from his pocket a velvet bag and with great ceremony, opens the bag and drops an ordinary-looking rock into the pot. You see, I am very fortunate, he says to them. I have this magic stone, which makes delicious soup out of nothing at all. And he closes his eyes blissfully, inhaling the steam. I love stone soup, he murmurs.

The villagers look at him like he's crazy, but he keeps sitting there, looking rapturous and periodically licking his lips. After a little while he says happily, this is going to be an especially fine batch, I can tell. But you know what would make it even more delicious? Some carrots. Stone soup with carrots is an incomparable delight.

His happiness is hard to resist. A villager approaches him and cautiously offers him some carrots from her secret hoard. The ragged soldier is overjoyed and makes a huge performance out of lovingly cutting up the carrots and adding them to the soup. When he's done, he inhales deeply and says, It's perfect! The only thing that could make it more perfect would be a cabbage...

So of course, someone else goes and gets a cabbage out of their stash. The soldier couldn't be more enthusiastic. It's contagious; before long, everyone in the village has opened up their hoard and contributed something they were previously determined not to share: mushrooms, onions, potatoes, beef, fragrant herbs. The atmosphere is so festive that soon people are getting their guitars out and singing. It's a party. The soup turns out to be the best meal anybody's had in ages, and there is indeed plenty for everyone. By the end of the night, the villagers are offering the soldier outrageous amounts of money for his magic stone, but of course it's not for sale at any price.

Stone Soup is a fable about social business and multi-stakeholder cooperatives, at least the way we do those things in the community acupuncture movement. Like a lot of fables, it revolves around a trickster. In this case, it's about tricking people to act for the common good instead for their own selfish interests. In Stone Soup, everybody wins, but they were tricked into winning.

Stone Soup is a comedy; its opposite is called "the tragedy of the commons". According to Wikipedia, "the tragedy of the commons is the depletion of a shared resource by individuals, acting independently and rationally according to each one's self-interest, despite their understanding that depleting the common resource is contrary to the group's long-term best interests." In the tragedy of the commons, there's no trick involved. Everybody knows exactly what's going on, and everyone ends up losing instead of winning. The idea originally referred to farmers in England sharing a parcel of land for grazing. Each individual farmer benefited personally if he let his animals overgraze the commons, but the result was that the commons were ruined and nobody benefited. You could say, for lack of vision; or for lack of a trick in service of a vision.

It's very hard for people to look past their own self-interest and see something bigger, something that includes both their own self-interest and other people's too. It's especially hard in the context of business, and even worse when the business in question is healthcare. OK, I confess: POCA is based on a Stone Soup trick. WCA before it too. I tricked you. Some of you don't need me to confess to this; you figured it out a long time ago, and you've been making soup with the exact same technique for years now. But I think it's time to explain the technique to everybody. If you're a POCA volunteer – and we need a lot of POCA volunteers – you must understand how to make Stone Soup.

Let's start by looking at WCA as an example. WCA benefits possibly thousands of people, but it can't benefit any of them without benefiting all of them. The nature of a low-cost, high-volume social business is that it needs a lot of people to support it; and if they do support it, for the most part they'll benefit proportionally to what they put into it. This is different than a conventional capitalist business, whose focus is on extracting profit disproportionately for the owners, and from a charity, whose focus is on benefiting people who are not necessarily contributing anything to the organization. Stone Soup feeds the people who make it, and so it's a great approach for people who don't have a lot of resources.

Stone Soup is a poor person's trick. The scariest and most difficult part of it is the time after you've dropped your "magic" stone in the water and before anybody else has put anything in the pot. This is the part where you have to believe in something that nobody else can see, and you have to believe in it so hard that you can get other people to change their attitudes and help you make it. You wouldn't attempt this unless you were desperate. You wouldn't try it if you had other resources and other options. The part where there is nothing in the pot except a rock, and everybody's looking at you skeptically, is not something you do for kicks. (Ask anybody who was on the original POCA Steering Committee.)

Even some people who are into social business don't want to go through this to make Stone Soup. Their idea of social business is that you somehow make a bunch of money in a conventional capitalist way, but at some point, you find a way to use that money to "give back". Maybe you figure out how to have a "triple bottom line" of "people, planet, profits". In the Stone Soup model, you're not even thinking about profits, you're thinking about survival. You don't have anything to give back, because you're not starting with anything. You just need to eat, and you know that other people need to eat too, but for some reason everybody's gotten paralyzed and nobody's eating. Somebody needs to start somewhere, even if it's only you and all you've got is a rock.

When I started WCA, I needed to eat and I needed to work, and I realized that other people needed acupuncture. Eleven years later, WCA is a lot bigger, but it's still about people's need to eat, work, and get acupuncture. Profit isn't part of the equation. This is true for almost all of the other POCA clinics. The best part about WCA being much bigger, and about all these other POCA clinics, is that nobody quite has to go through the part about the empty pot and the rock in the same way anymore. You don't have to sit there totally alone with your boiling water and the skeptical crowd; you've got a community of other people cheering you on. And enough people have tasted Stone Soup that they know what it is and they know that it's good, and it's worth putting their carrots and cabbages into the pot. Maybe they haven't put their cabbages in your pot yet, but their sister in another city has been putting her cabbages into the pot that is the POCA clinic in her town, and she swears by it – so they'll try it. The pot that is POCA as a whole is so big and so full of good things these days, that you have to look hard to see that down at the bottom, under all the ingredients, there's a rock. But if you're going to successfully keep the pot going, you can't ever forget about that rock.

The great satisfaction of Stone Soup is that you are simultaneously nourishing yourself and other people at the same time. That is what working in a POCA clinic, whether as a staff member or as a volunteer, should feel like: nourishing and also, creative. But in order to keep it feeling that way, there are a few important cautions. You can't be too picky; you can't be a control freak; you have to be aware and responsible; and you have to take risks. Momentum is important.

Stone Soup is perhaps not your favorite kind of soup. If you had a choice, maybe you'd prefer to eat a soup that came from a recipe in a book that a real chef had carefully followed in a nice kitchen – a soup made from ingredients that you had personally selected from a lovely farmer's market. Maybe instead of the chaotic mélange that is Stone Soup, you'd prefer something somewhat more artful and elegant, like cream of heirloom tomato soup.

However, cream of heirloom tomato soup is not on the menu. In fact, there is no menu. We're not even in a restaurant. From the perspective of conventional capitalism, you're always supposed to be in a restaurant, and the point of everything is to order what you want, and the more of it, the better: The Restaurant of the Haves. Where we are, is the

Lisa Rohleder

Campfire of the Resourceful Have-Nots. There are not many Restaurants of the Haves in the acupuncture world, and the few that there are don't seat many people. You can stand outside one of those in the cold for a very long time, or you can come sit down with us at our fire – the company is better, I promise.

But you can't be too picky. The cabbage that someone wants to put in the soup is perhaps not the kind of cabbage that you would have chosen. That does not matter as much as the fact that they are putting something in the soup. Smile and say, "Thank you so much!" You can't be a control freak. If you try to line people up in the alphabetical order of their donated vegetables and require them to drop them in the pot at timed intervals, you're going to lose their support (and your dinner). Just go with it and have some faith. You have to be aware and responsible. For quite a while, everyone else's attitude about the process of soup-making is going to depend on your attitude. Eventually they'll develop their own relationship to the soup, but at first, you set the tone. If you don't believe first, nobody else will. If you get tense and start complaining, other people will too, and there goes your soup. You have to take risks. See all previous advice about the wrong kind of cabbage, people dropping vegetables in at irregular intervals, and you believing first: these are all risks.

Making Stone Soup does not involve much security. If you had security, you wouldn't need a magic rock.

Finally, momentum is important, momentum is everything. For people to contribute, they have to believe that this thing is going somewhere, and if not enough people contribute and the soup doesn't come together fast enough, it won't go anywhere and you won't be able to trick them into altruism. Conversely, the more people are contributing, the more people will want to contribute. That's why it's so important not to get hung up on trying to make your soup perfect. If a lot of people are contributing, it will definitely not be perfect; it will be deliciously imperfect...

It can be disconcerting to realize that there's a rock at the bottom of your soup. Maybe you didn't want to know that the clinic where you love to get acupuncture has nothing in its savings account, or that the co-op that inspires you is sometimes only barely strung together by extremely tired volunteers. There's an art to letting people know how precarious our soup-making enterprise is without scaring them off. Maybe the best way to say it is that we need EVERYTHING. Regardless of how full the pot looks, we still need everything. We need all sorts of skills; we need word of mouth marketing; we need goodwill; we need money; we need encouragement; we need enthusiasm and imagination. Whatever you have to give, we need it, even if it seems to you like a negligible amount. That's the beauty of making

something out of nothing: everything that you give counts. [27]

Cut to the Chase, Please #6

OK, let's talk about the POCA Cooperative. We don't mean to hurt your feelings, but that's one weird-looking co-op. Are you sure it's even a co-op? Seriously, is THAT what you broke up with capitalism for?

Yeah, I get that POCA requires some explaining. To me it's one of the most interesting parts of this narrative, but the technicalities make some people's eyes glaze over. I'll try to keep it simple.

But first, a key to understanding this story is 1) noticing that we were starting with nothing, and 2) that being the case, anything we made (and continue to make) is both a step in the right direction and cause for celebration. I've learned that these premises are very challenging for a lot of people. They want the acupuncture profession as a whole to be in better shape than it is and also, for some benign authority to take responsibility for acupuncturists being able to earn a living. The idea that acupuncturists might have to take on that responsibility themselves, and that acupuncturists and patients together might have to take responsibility for making acupuncture accessible, is hard to swallow. That we might all have to do this with limited resources, as self-taught organizers, is even less appealing. That no one is going to hand us the perfect solution, but that we'll have to cobble together our own imperfect solution, is enough to make some people throw up their hands in disgust.

But if you can wrap your heads around those premises, POCA makes a lot of sense.

Though in truth we weren't starting POCA completely from

nothing: we had CAN, our 501c6 nonprofit membership organization for acupuncturists and we needed to tinker with it. No, that's not quite right either: we didn't need to *tinker* with it, we needed to strip it down to the studs and rebuild it with a different floor plan. Just like I don't have a good explanation for why I wanted to rent the space on Cully Boulevard, I don't have a good explanation for wanting to make a co-op. I was noodling around online one day and came across the Mondragon Corporation, a set of interlocking cooperatives in Basque Spain, and my intuition ambushed me again. It wasn't offering any detailed directions, it was just yelling YES, YES, YES THIS IS IT at the top of its incorporeal lungs. Right away I called a dozen or so of my CAN comrades. If I couldn't get them on the phone, I left incoherent messages on their clinics' voicemail to the effect of, I know what to do! We have to make ourselves into a co-op!

I didn't know anything about co-ops. If you do, you know that the co-op universe is a rabbit hole in its own right, and only somebody desperate would just dive in headfirst. I dove. Eventually I found *Solidarity as a Business Model, a Multi-Stakeholder Cooperatives Manual* by Margaret Lund (blessedly free online).[28] Nora of Detroit Community Acupuncture won our naming competition for the co-op by suggesting the People's Organization of Community Acupuncture, and a few of us became the POCA Steering Committee in order to figure out how to set it up. Margaret Lund describes multi-stakeholder cooperatives as transformational rather than transactional; they're most useful in economically dysfunctional settings (looking at you, acupuncture profession).

We had some problems which required a structural solution. First, CAN was a professional organization for acupuncturists, and yet the emergence of the community acupuncture model had depended entirely on patients. I would never have had a practice at all if Donzel hadn't offered to teach me how to be self-employed; Betty and her family self-organized in my living room; and Chico and Bobette showed me that access to acupuncture could be a matter of life and death, providing the urgency to break the binary. Almost all new community acupuncture clinics relied heavily on the contributions of patients in the form of donated time, skills, used furniture and word of mouth marketing. In the co-op universe, that's called practicing mutualism. We were doing it all over the place, it was the essence of the fractal, and yet our organizational structure didn't reflect it.

Second, CAN had been operating long enough to acquire some competing visions and priorities. A 501c6 is not just a nonprofit, it's also a business league, and CAN was attracting a lot of people who were primarily interested in the community acupuncture model as a key to creating a lucrative business. The low-cost high-volume idea just made sense. One of my friends confessed to me that his first reaction to community acupuncture had been aversion, because the practitioner who introduced him to it seemed like such a hustler. CAN had the potential to become hard and shiny and competitive, a club for superstar entrepreneurs and their acolytes, with just a sprinkling of social consciousness to increase our self-congratulation and improve our advertising. On the other side, some CAN members saw our mission more like a twelve-step program: to foster honesty and support and talk each other off ledges as needed. A fellowship of the broken.

Bonus points for guessing which camp I'd gravitate towards.

Third, pretty much from CAN's inception, people had been asking about whether we could figure out how to offer micro loans to start up new community acupuncture clinics. The structural solution there was about as neat as it could get: simply by becoming a cooperative we would become a micro-lender for our members.

From a big picture perspective, though, what we needed was a foundation and a framework to develop the idea of community acupuncture as part of the commons. A 501c6 nonprofit/business league wasn't going to give it to us. Here's a useful description of the commons, excerpted from the book *Toward a New Common School Movement*:

When land, labor, and other social and natural resources necessary to sustain life are held and valued as collective property they can be said to form a commons.[29]

As Nobel economist Elinor Ostrum has detailed:

Communities have historically developed ingenious strategies for governing access and usage of common property resources in order to maintain their collective value and benefit over time. Commons cannot be separated from the notion of enclosure, which signals efforts to transfer aspects of the commons from collective management for common benefit to private ownership for private gain...

From the natural world to the social world, the commons appear everywhere in peril. The all-encompassing drive for profit and endless commodification is despoiling the shared basis of life on the planet, and as a set of global crises widen and deepen, demands for authentic democracy and community become the minimal demands for the survival of humanity...

The common can be built and expanded, and it can never be

fully enclosed because there are parts of human experience that cannot be turned into property and have to be held in common. Compassion, ideas, social relationships, and the planet itself must be held in common.[30]

We needed an organizational structure that reflected the truth that sharing rather than hoarding made acupuncture more valuable. Neither acupuncturists nor patients benefit when acupuncture is too expensive to be widely used. One notable thing about POCA as a cooperative is that it doesn't offer any financial dividends to its members. POCA's dividends are collective: you become a member of POCA not because you want a better deal for yourself, but because you believe everybody benefits from the existence of community acupuncture clinics. In that sense POCA is a social business according to Muhammad Yunus's definition: *non-loss, non-dividend, created to solve a social problem.*

POCA's mission is: to work cooperatively to increase accessibility to and availability of affordable group acupuncture treatments. POCA, as a multi-stakeholder co-op, is designed to build a long-term, stable economic relationship based on fair treatment for everybody. Multi-stakeholder cooperatives recognize that producers and consumers are mutually dependent on one another, and that the health of the relationship between these groups is connected to the health of the larger community and economy.

Because POCA doesn't offer any financial dividends, some co-op experts did question whether we were indeed a co-op. The general consensus, though, was that we were practicing mutualism quite successfully, so if it acts like a co-op and it's incorporated as a co-op and it files its taxes as a co-op (which, by the way, isn't cheap), then it's a co-op.

* * *

It sounds like a lot of trouble to set up and to maintain, for no financial dividends. Are you sure it was worth it?

During the time when we slogging through the hardest parts of the setup, a famous acupuncturist publicly asked the rhetorical question, *What is the significance of helping an individual feel better when the human species is threatened with extinction?* and I decided to answer him. That answer applies to your question too. Here's what I wrote in a blog post:

My own clinic was born out of my need to take care of myself. Interestingly enough, as I kept trying to take care of myself, and that kept working out better than NOT taking care of myself, it also became clear that taking care of myself was not separate from taking care of my neighbors. The only way to integrate myself as a working-class person and an acupuncturist was to take care of working-class patients. Like a lot of other things about the community acupuncture movement, it took an awfully long time to recognize the obvious. The only way for me to manage my history was to live in a different kind of present, one that I had to create, and one which allowed me to be connected to my community instead of separated from it – that was part of the healing.

I know that plenty of people out there don't believe in oppression, or think it's some completely abstract dimension of political correctness, and I'm not going to try to convince you, but I am going to say that looking at oppression helped me reconstruct and integrate myself in a way that was based on truth instead of denial. Society doesn't treat poor people or working-class people well, or women and children, or immigrants or people with mental illness – it's one thing to think about that abstractly in college, and it's another to admit what it means, concretely and without denial, in your own history and your family's history. I realized I had a choice: I could continue to treat myself the way society had taught me I deserved to be treated; I could perpetuate various subtle forms of violence against myself for the rest of my life, because that was familiar, or I could stop. I could refuse to be my own oppressor. Maybe I had no control over how society or any other person treated me, but I didn't have to participate. That was just the negative part – deciding that I won't hurt myself, no matter how subtly; the positive part was more powerful. The bravest and most radical thing I could do was to take care of myself, to approach my own wellbeing like a serious project that deserved time and thought and attention and effort. As Audre Lorde said: *Caring for myself is not self-indulgence, it is self-preservation, and that is an act of political warfare.* [31]

And every time I took care of a patient who was like me in some way – a working-class person, a woman, someone who had experienced violence or lost someone they loved, someone with chronic physical or mental illness in her family – I was building a new world for myself, a world in which people like me were valuable.

I find myself thinking about these themes as I'm working on the development of our cooperative, POCA. It's so technical, there's so much detail, it's so much time and trouble to set up a cooperative, that I catch myself thinking, oh God, is this worth it? What if this doesn't work out? And that's exactly the point. It IS a lot of time and trouble, and that's why nothing like it exists for us and our patients already. Creating it requires making a decision – and making it over and over – that we deserve that much time and thought and attention and effort from ourselves. We deserve something complex and well-designed that meets our collective needs. This is just as true of creating a clinic as it is of creating a cooperative. Acting like people like *US* deserve something like *THAT* requires courage.[32]

What I would say now, in 2017, having gotten this far in my case study of myself, is that investing so much time and energy in POCA as a foundation for community acupuncture is what I needed to do to challenge my sense of a foreshortened future, which I recognize (and you probably do too) is a symptom of PTSD. I had spent a couple of decades believing I wasn't going to live very long. Making POCA required me to act as though I would. I like to think I took all the intricate legal and financial details of making a co-op and mixed them with my pain and anger and suicidality, the way people used to mix blood into mortar to make it stronger, and I helped build something useful. For my own kind. And that worked for me like nothing else ever had. Maybe individual healing does it for some people, but I needed to be part of healing at a collective level.

So yes. It was worth it.

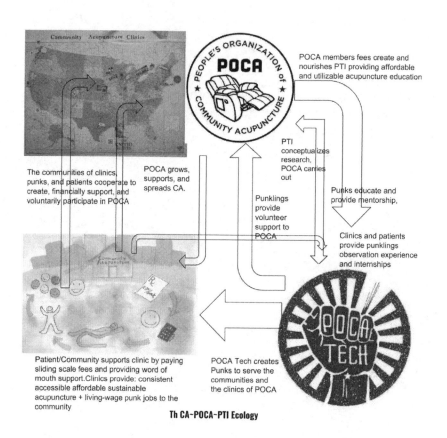

POCA members fees create and nourishes PTI providing affordable and utilizable acupuncture education

PTI conceptualizes research, POCA carries out

Punks educate and provide mentorship,

POCA grows, supports, and spreads CA.

The communities of clinics, punks, and patients cooperate to create, financially support, and voluntarily participate in POCA

Punklings provide volunteer support to POCA

Clinics and patients provide punklings observation experience and internships

Patient/Community supports clinic by paying sliding scale fees and providing word of mouth support.Clinics provide: consistent accessible affordable sustainable acupuncture + living-wage punk jobs to the community

POCA Tech creates Punks to serve the communities and the clinics of POCA

Th CA~POCA~PTI Ecology

POCA Ecology

by James Lorr of Urbana Acupuncture

38.

In terms of my personal hexagram and how it relates to social entrepreneurship, we're making our way through the changing lines of 48, The Well.

Line 1: The well is muddy. Do not neglect yourself.

I learned how not to neglect myself; it required not neglecting people like me. Self-care in my case was meaningless without a collective, structural element.

Line 4: The well is being lined. No blame. To line the well with stone means to take it out of service temporarily to fix it and renew it.

By lining the well, I think the I Ching meant building, fixing, and renewing infrastructure for community acupuncture. Or to go back to the introduction: The dominant model for providing acupuncture involves doling it out in tiny, expensive increments to a limited number of privileged individuals. Acupuncture works better when you deliver it by means of clinics that function less like boutiques, or even hospitals, and more like public libraries or public utilities: high volume, a diverse group of users, community-supported. Instead of trying to sell acupuncture in limited quantities like fancy bottled water, try pouring it out through a big pipe, and let people take as much as they need. This is about building the pipe.

Pipe building and well-lining aren't glamorous activities. They're grueling and tedious and frustrating at times. They're also not individual projects; there's too much work for any one person.

Healing, especially alternative healing, is framed in

capitalism as both an individual project and as a commodity. Self-care is big business these days. By the time I was on the team that built POCA, I had figured out that no amount of individual healing was going to fix me. It wasn't a question of observing the world from some idealistic perch and deciding that collective healing was a more worthy effort than individual healing, which seems to be what some people think, so let's be clear about that; it was a grim personal conclusion that individual healing just didn't do it for me. The big holes in my life were never going to be anything other than big holes. I wasn't going to be able to fill them in and dance victoriously on top and take smiling selfies of the process. The holes were going to remain deep and dark, but they could be meaningful (and tolerable and useful) as wells.

And so I learned to love building infrastructure. Well-lining might not be glamorous, but it was always more compelling than the alternative. This is one of the things that bothers me about people mistaking me for some kind of humanitarian; it implies I had a range of options when I didn't. Think about it: wouldn't *you* rather have a well in your life instead of a hole?

The same acupuncturist who asked, what is the significance of helping an individual feel better when the human species is threatened with extinction, also wrote:

It seems to me that the minimal requirement for being a healer ought to be having come to a place in one's own life where no more time is being taken to overcome one's past and all attention and effort is placed on creating a more wholesome future.

I wrote:
Huh. It sounds like my past and this acupuncturist's were considerably different. Can I have his? Also, how can you

"overcome" your past when people you care about are still living it? My clinic IS me overcoming my past, and also creating my future. I don't get how you separate those, or

how you separate them from your community. [33]

From the beginning, the big question about POCA has been, why should anybody bother to join it? In the early days, there was a lot of discussion about why patients would be interested in membership at all; lots of people were sure the whole idea was a non-starter. (The irony is there are more patient members than acupuncturists in POCA these days.) As for the practitioners, now that community acupuncture is relatively well-accepted by conventional acupuncturists, you can figure out the model by looking at other clinics' websites or joining one of many groups on Facebook – so why should acupuncturists join POCA? And circa 2017, if you want a seriously shiny version of the model for a wealthier demographic than the one that created it, there's an honest-to-God capitalist franchise to give it to you.

So who cares if there's a co-op dedicated to promoting community acupuncture?

POCA, being a non-dividend co-op, is mostly a way of holding space for community acupuncture. The elements that line the well, so to speak, are a set of relationships among practitioners and patients, and the intellectual property associated with the model that POCA has painstakingly accumulated over the years. Because patients are members, it means that the well and the infrastructure belong to patients as much as they belong to acupuncturists. I'll have a lot more to say about why that's important when we get to POCA's school, but in the meantime, it's a good way of acknowledging that community acupuncture originated with self-organizing by patients.

* * *

These relationships and this intellectual property allow
POCA to support acupuncturists in opening new community
clinics and maintaining existing ones, by means of
continuing education in the form of regular conferences
(POCAfests) and online videos, wikis and forums. POCA
provides free peer mentors to acupuncturists who are
working in or starting up POCA clinics. POCA also offers
micro loans for starting new clinics, expanding existing
clinics, and for employee relocation. Most of all, though,
POCA is the foundation for a shared patient base that has the
potential to be big enough to support acupuncturists having
stable jobs and patients having reliable access to
acupuncture. That's how a multi-stakeholder co-op is
supposed to work – by recognizing that producers and
consumers have common interests, and so building a
foundation to support those common interests is good for
everyone.

We're all socialized to be consumers, and that means people
will approach community acupuncture wanting to know,
what's in it for me, right this moment? All co-ops have to
have a transactional element; none survives without
members being able to point to some way that their
membership fees pay for themselves, and POCA was
designed so that basic math works out.[34] I'm not going to say
that approaching community acupuncture with the attitude
of, what's in it for me? is wrong. I am going to say, though,
that I don't get it. What's in it for me and what's in it for
everybody else have always been the same. Not because I'm
an idealist, but because I only ever had a choice between
holes and wells.

39.

Returning to the social entrepreneurship case study in a more direct way: in general, the topic of infrastructure has been difficult for POCA because capitalism doesn't reward building it. The peak capitalist return on the model is if you're an acupuncturist who's a sole proprietor of a space where you can keep your overhead down, you don't hire any acupuncturist employees, and you don't put any resources into POCA in the form of membership or volunteering; you can make the low-cost high-volume aspect relatively lucrative. If you want support from other community acupuncturists, you get it on social media and it doesn't have to be POCA's social media. (Starting a Facebook group requires no investment.) You've still got a social business, because if you're using the model you're solving the problem of ordinary people in your community not being able to afford acupuncture.

One of the unresolved questions of community acupuncture is: why isn't that enough, all by itself?

I don't know, maybe it is. It just wasn't enough for me. If it were, I would never have bothered to tell anybody about what I was doing in the space on Cully Boulevard. There was a little while, before S. got laid off and before I hired Ilse, that I was alone with the model. Just it with its fractal tendrils wrapping around the space, and me inching back from my breakdown, trying to return to the world. Maybe I could have stayed like that, especially since I don't tend to get along with many other acupuncturists, and also the model by itself is quite a lot of company. But as I said, I felt like it wanted things from me. I wanted to give it what it wanted, because I've always felt like it saved me.

I guess that's the crux of at least some of my problems: other people feel the model owes them something, while I feel like I owe the model. A lot.

Anyway, capitalism being what it is, people have gotten angry at POCA for promoting anything outside of what creates peak capitalist returns for individual acupuncturists, and especially for prioritizing building infrastructure. That debate keeps resurfacing. I wrote this a couple of years ago, and I think it still applies:

The acupuncture profession is a harsh environment: it can't support much life, especially not in complex forms. Professionally, we're the equivalent of a bunch of single-celled organisms competing for scarce nutrients, bumping around, unable to do much for each other. CAN could have helped a few people be the biggest, best amoeba in their corner of the wasteland, but that's not what we wanted. The point of POCA was to organize. To become a complex organism. To have a spine and a heart and a brain, not just a mouth.

And over time I've observed that many of the superstar entrepreneurs, the ones who can succeed in our harsh professional environment, are not especially interested in helping with that kind of project. They don't tend to share or reach out. They're fine on their own. If you give them enough ego strokes, they'll help for awhile, but in the long run what POCA needed was a bunch of patient, self-motivated geeks who didn't need strokes in order to work, because they just thought building infrastructure was cool. If POCA was going to be organized enough to provide the stuff we knew people needed, then POCA needed people who liked doing that work for its own sake. What we needed to get where we are now was many small leaders, doing many small unglamorous things – not a handful of individual superstars for everyone else to look up to.

* * *

And here's the kicker: none of the many small leaders who stepped up to build POCA and stuck with it over time were particularly interested in maximizing their income. Some weren't even that interested in their personal financial security. All were lit up by the cooperative aspect of what we do. So if you are asking, why hasn't POCA enthusiastically gotten behind the superstar entrepreneurs who want high incomes, it's partly for strategic reasons. We didn't think we could get any real cooperative work out of those people, and as it turned out we were right. (POCA Forums)

40.

This seems like a good place to put the text of a keynote speech I gave at our second POCAfest.

Welcome everybody.

Within the acupuncture profession, POCA stands out as being effective. We get a lot done, especially considering how lean our budget is. That's unusual. Over the years, I've heard a lot of people say that organizing acupuncturists is like herding cats. And that's why most acupuncture organizations can't get anything done, because of course you can't herd cats. Well, if organizing acupuncturists is like herding cats, then creating a multi-stakeholder cooperative with acupuncturists and patients and acupuncture clinic staff, and getting acupuncturists to participate in it – that's more like, I don't know, organizing cats to play instruments in a rock band?

There is a real cat rock band. There are three cats and they play drums, guitar and keyboard. It's kind of a punk rock sound, or maybe experimental music. They travel around in a tour bus, doing shows. They're called Tuna and the Rock Cats – and we've booked them for the coffeehouse tomorrow night. No, we haven't. But you can look them up on the internet and see that it's possible, it can be done. You can teach cats to play instruments in an ensemble.

You can teach cats, and other animals, to do all sorts of complex tasks, by using clicker training and what they call behavioral shaping. Behavioral shaping was originally introduced by the psychologist BF Skinner; he trained pigeons to pull levers, which is easier than teaching cats to play drums. But the principles are the same. Let me read you something that he wrote about behavioral shaping:

* * *

"We first give the bird food when it turns slightly in the direction of the spot from any part of the cage. This increases the frequency of such behavior. We then withhold reinforcement until a slight movement is made toward the spot. This again alters the general distribution of behavior without producing a new unit. We continue by reinforcing positions successively closer to the spot, then by reinforcing only when the head is moved slightly forward, and finally only when the beak makes contact with the spot. ... The original probability of the response in its final form is very low; in some cases, it may even be zero." Note: pigeons don't go around pulling levers on their own. "In this way, we can build complicated operants which would never appear in the repertoire of the organism otherwise. By reinforcing a series of successive approximations, we bring a rare response to a very high probability in a short time. ... The total act of turning toward the spot from any point in the box, walking toward it, raising the head, and striking the spot may seem to be a functionally coherent unit of behavior; but it is constructed by a continual process of differential reinforcement from undifferentiated behavior, just as the sculptor shapes his figure from a lump of clay."[35]

So if you want a cat to play the drums, the first thing you have to do is to just to get the cat to look at the drum set. Whatever the complicated end performance that you want – pigeons pulling levers, cats playing drums, acupuncturists and patients working together in a cooperative to build economic infrastructure for a profession that doesn't quite exist yet – you have to break it down into the tiniest components. And the first step is, literally, just to turn and look in the right direction.

I thought about this when we had some visitors at WCA from another multi stakeholder cooperative. We spent all this time trying to explain how POCA works, the different member categories, all the projects we're working on, how our governance structure is set up – and when we finally gave them a tour of the clinic, the first thing they commented on was, wow, so people don't mind being treated in the same room together?? That's amazing. I would have thought you'd have a lot of problems with that.

So it was good for me to have this perspective on the stages of cooperative behavior with regards to community acupuncture. It's very hard, in this culture, for people to get past thinking of themselves solely as isolated individuals, especially with regards to health care, and even more especially if they are acupuncturists. With POCA, we're trying to think of ourselves as a collective, we're trying to behave like a collective, and the very first step in that process was just to get people to receive acupuncture in a room together. To turn towards cooperation.

As everybody knows by now, I believe that POCA's a fractal. An elegant, self-organizing pattern. I also believe that POCA's an intelligent fractal – that the fractal knows more about itself and how it works than we know about it, and it's teaching us to understand it. To embody it. It's patiently shaping our behavior. If POCA weren't such a lovely thing, I would probably feel kind of disturbed about having it go all BF Skinner on me.

But at this point, I've had a decade or so to get used to it, and I have to admit that I like how the fractal has shaped my behavior. My life – especially my life as an acupuncturist – is a lot better now, being part of the community acupuncture fractal –than it was before. I didn't used to have any other cats to play drums with. Anyway, it's not like the fractal is standing off at a distance somewhere, holding a clicker, rewarding me when I turn in the direction of cooperation.

We are the fractal and we're teaching each other. Turning in the direction of cooperation feels good. The experience of people getting acupuncture together in a space is inherently rewarding, for the acupuncturists and the patients – which is what I said to the folks from the other co-op. No, we didn't have a lot of problems with getting people to have acupuncture in the same space, because they LIKE it. We need each other, and we're starting to understand how much we need each other, and every time we turn toward each other, it feels good. Click.

There was an article in the New York Times awhile back titled, "What Shamu Taught Me About Life, Love and a Happy Marriage".[36] The author was researching a book on training exotic animals, and she encountered the practice of behavioral shaping, and naturally, she decided to try it out on her husband. He was driving her crazy with a variety of behaviors, like leaving his socks on the floor, and so she started using what she learned from dolphin trainers to get him to put his socks in the hamper. This article was the most viewed and emailed of the New York Times online for the entire year. And of course, some of the response online was not altogether positive; if you google the title, you'll find some horrified blog posts. When the author joked about feeling like she should toss her husband a mackerel, some people did not find it funny. And yeah, tossing your mate a mackerel is perhaps not the most romantic vision of married love.

Anyway, I thought of that article too when we were talking to the folks from the other co-op. I thought about how far we've come in our experiment with cooperation. And I remembered, a couple of years ago, talking with someone who's been in the acupuncture profession a very long time, with a lot of experience with acupuncture organizations. I was talking about how much fun we were having with CAN, getting so much done, and he kind of sighed and said, yes, Lisa, that's because you all like each other right now. Let me tell you, that's not going to last. Back in the day, when we were first getting acupuncture legalized, we liked each other too.

And at the time I was like, wait – what do you mean it's not going to last? (Also – you liked those people?) And I didn't believe him, because let's face it, one thing I've learned by being an acupuncturist for nineteen years is not to readily believe anything anybody tells me about acupuncture or the acupuncture profession. But of course, he was right. The days when everyone involved with this organization was also best friends with each other are definitely over... We're too big to all be best friends anymore, and that's a good thing.

But I do think we must wrap our heads around the idea that having a cooperative together may be less like being in love all the time, and more like tossing each other a mackerel.

(cue mackerel tossing from audience, presenter ducks)

The ultimate goal of POCA is to create a new, sustainable economic foundation for the delivery of acupuncture. Which means, a new acupuncture profession that has many more real benefits to offer both acupuncturists and patients than the current model does. That's a very complex undertaking. It involves lots of people doing things that they wouldn't necessarily do on their own. It involves a lot of us doing things that we don't necessarily feel like doing; it involves all of us learning new, cooperative behaviors. Without some very careful planning, without tremendous intentionality, without patient attention to very incremental changes in our behavior – we wouldn't have a cooperative or a new profession at all. As BF Skinner said: *The original probability of the response in its final form is very low; in some cases, it may even be zero.*

That doesn't mean it's impossible, it just means we have to know what we're doing. We have to know what we're doing with each other.

In this room, many of us are acupuncturists – but I think I can safely say that almost ALL of us are acupuncture patients. Some of us provide acupuncture, and almost all of us receive it. I think I can probably also safely say that all of us are connected to other patients and potential patients – people around the country who need acupuncture; for all of us, there are people we can think of, that it matters to us that they can get acupuncture. In our own lives, and in the lives of people we care about, acupuncture makes a positive difference, sometimes a huge positive difference. So this is what we're trying to do with each other: as acupuncture patients, we're trying to ensure a stable, reliable supply of affordable acupuncture for ourselves and everyone we care about; and for acupuncturists, we're trying to build a collective patient base that is big enough to support all of us to make a living. Obviously, those are not goals that any of us can accomplish alone.

And of course, there are reasons why we don't already have these things: they are, as Dr. Skinner said, "complicated operants which would never appear in (our) repertoire" without conscious intervention. A lot of people are passively waiting for the state of health care to get better, hoping somebody or something is going to save us. POCA's decided not to wait for somebody or something to magically make acupuncture affordable and acupuncturists employed; we are doing it. We're doing it now. And we want to keep doing it at a bigger and bigger scale, and include more and more people, and in order to do that, we have to look at how to shape our behaviors into more and more cooperation. We can do a lot more than we think we can do, and gradually, incrementally, we're proving that to ourselves.

 A lot of acupuncturists get attracted to POCA because acupuncture can be such a miserably lonely profession, and there's so much support and camaraderie here. We're not just here to support each other, though; we're here to train each other. The support and the camaraderie are not our reasons for being – they're the mackerels we're tossing to each other (cue mackerel tossing) on our way to creating the cooperative of our dreams. So this weekend, remember that we might be in love with community acupuncture, but we don't all need to be in love with each other. We came here to make something, something that none of us could make on our own, something big that is ultimately made up of tiny, repeated increments of cooperation. We're here to practice our cooperative behaviors, and we can practice them with people we like, people we don't like, and people we're just getting to know. Because all those people are part of POCA.

So was that a good speech? Somebody throw me a fish. Thank you.

41.

The well is being lined; no blame, says the I Ching. I think this is sometimes an unduly optimistic interpretation. In reality there's often plenty of blame in scaling up, at every level of the fractal. Cooperation's hard. Here's a composite example.

I have a friend, let's call her Gwendolyn, who moved back to where she grew up to open a POCA clinic. She had previously worked for another POCA clinic in a big city, a busy clinic where there was a lot of support and camaraderie. But in the clinic she named Hometown Community Acupuncture, she was by herself and overwhelmed with being a new business owner. She needed help, so she put out a call for volunteers.

Enter Verity (not her real name). Verity's thrilled to volunteer for Gwendolyn because she's fallen in love with the concept of community acupuncture. She's delighted to support a woman-owned business and she has all kinds of useful experience. When can she start, and what can she do?

Gwendolyn puts her to work answering phones on the busiest shift, her most urgent need, but Verity immediately finds other ways to make herself useful during any downtime. Gwendolyn feels embarrassed about marketing her clinic, but Verity's a passionate advocate and she loves promoting Hometown Community Acupuncture. She designs and hangs flyers; she organizes an open house and bakes a cake for fifty people. Gwendolyn feels as if a weight has been lifted from her shoulders now that she doesn't have to think about marketing. Verity's getting a lot of acupuncture, which she needs, and every day she says how much she loves volunteering at such a special place. Mutualism is beautiful and POCA members are a godsend to new clinics. Verity and Gwendolyn are spending so much time together that soon they consider each other friends.

After a month or so of increasing closeness, one day they're sitting in Gwendolyn's living room making to-do lists for the clinic when Verity confides to Gwendolyn that she trained as a feng shui practitioner under a famous master, quite a few years ago. She never did anything with her training, but all the positive energy involved with launching Hometown Community Acupuncture has made Verity reconsider having her own business. Verity's day job is unexciting and she's lacked the courage to make a change, but Gwendolyn has inspired her. Would it be OK, Verity asks shyly, if she practiced her feng shui skills at the clinic?

Of course, Gwendolyn says, wanting to support her friend. What did you have in mind?

Well, Verity says, looking around Gwendolyn's living room with a unfamiliar glint in her eye, would you like a demonstration?

When Gwendolyn's partner comes home, he stops in the doorway and says, Whoa. What did you do in here? I would never have thought of putting the couch over there...but it feels much more spacious. I like it!

A week later, Hometown Community Acupuncture has acquired a few unobtrusive octagonal mirrors and artfully placed new plants, a crystal or two in the windows and a red tassel hanging off the doorknob. Verity is joyful about the experiment and it seems like the schedule is filling up faster; new people are calling to ask about acupuncture and most of them are making appointments. Gwendolyn has a million other things to do, so she notices the feng shui adjustments only in passing, mentioning to Verity that it all looks good and it's nice to see her using her creative talents.

* * *

Two weeks later, Gwendolyn comes into work early and finds Verity already there. (Verity of course has keys to the clinic.) She's showing the space to a potential feng shui client as an example of her work; pieces of conversation Gwendolyn overhears sounds like Verity might be implying that the clinic is hers??? Gwendolyn doesn't say anything until the potential client leaves but then it's awkward. Verity, she says, you know I support your business, God knows you've done so much for the clinic, but...that was a little weird. I need you to ask me first if you're going to use the space to, well, promote yourself.

Gwendolyn chose her words carefully, not wanting to hurt Verity's feelings, but to her surprise Verity isn't hurt, she's offended. Well of course, she says, if that's how you feel. It's just that you're always talking about how this space belongs to the *community*, and I've put so much into it, it never occurred to me you'd have *territorial impulses*.

Just then the phone rings and it's a patient desperate to schedule a labor induction treatment right away, so the conversation ends there. Gwendolyn isn't sure what to do; she's come to depend on Verity and she hopes this weirdness just blows over. Verity makes an extra effort to be pleasant during her shift and it seems like everything is fine...

Until Gwendolyn comes into work one morning and finds the entire clinic re-arranged. Recliners have been taken out of the treatment room and put into storage. Her files have been moved and a red couch has taken their place; her office looks like it's been set up for private consultations. And on the community bulletin board and the front door, there are glossy fliers announcing a series of feng shui classes, eight Wednesday nights in a row right here at the clinic, $300 to $500 sliding scale. Half of the flier is taken up by a headshot of Verity, proud owner of Hometown Community Feng Shui Palace, conveniently located inside Hometown Community Acupuncture.

This time Gwendolyn isn't just taken aback, she's angry, and then it's war.

Verity is shocked and hurt that Gwendolyn is being so unsupportive, so oppressive, so *selfish*. Verity has given so much and she was only trying to help. She has so many innovative ideas to improve the clinic! Ideas that Gwendolyn has never appreciated! It's too bad that Gwendolyn can't see how unwelcoming her space was before Verity fixed it, not to mention there's a crying need for affordable feng shui classes, $300 is just a steal compared to what Verity had to pay her feng shui master for this precious knowledge that she only wants to share with people who need it. What's so special about acupuncture, anyway? The world needs healing in *all* forms, doesn't it? Who does Gwendolyn think she is? And how could Gwendolyn have made Verity work so hard for so long and give nothing in return, it's outrageous!

Verity was in love with community acupuncture, but now she sees it's all a lie. She throws her keys at Gwendolyn and storms out.

Gwendolyn spends the next month trying to clean up the mess, which includes not only Verity's feng shui paraphernalia but:

- A letter that Verity sends to all the other clinic volunteers and some patients describing how badly she's been treated and claiming that though Gwendolyn tries to portray herself as an enlightened healer, she's a fraud and a toxic boss who's taking advantage of all of them;

- Negative Yelp reviews that a friend of Verity's leaves saying there is absolutely no community in Gwendolyn's version of community acupuncture;

- Most surprisingly, a long list of administrative tasks that Verity had promised to do but didn't, which leaves Gwendolyn undecided about whether to feel consoled or indignant that apparently, Verity had been doing only about a quarter of the work she claimed to be doing; and also,

- Handling all the well-meaning people in Hometown who are worried about how Gwendolyn is ever going to get along without Verity's help. Gwendolyn was so good at appreciating Verity in public, so deft at making sure Verity got credit for her contributions, that now the line between Verity's work and Gwendolyn's has gotten blurred. Does Gwendolyn tell them the truth, that Verity's volunteering created so much stress for Gwendolyn that actually, she's relieved? Does she tell them that Verity wasn't doing nearly as much work as everyone (including Gwendolyn) thought she was? There's no polite way to say that.

And sexism being what it is, the most unpleasant part of the cleanup will be dealing with the people in Hometown who think that Gwendolyn's inability to keep Verity happy, to retain such a good volunteer, is proof that there's something wrong with Gwendolyn herself.

Maybe it's because a lot of acupuncturists are women, or maybe it's because the community acupuncture model emerged through a woman's experience; unfortunately, there have been a lot of examples of people projecting what they want to see on to community acupuncture clinics, or on to the movement itself, and then feeling furious and victimized when the clinics and the movement weren't malleable and wouldn't conform to their projections.

Pro tip for budding female-identified social entrepreneurs: if a woman announces in public that she's trying to serve the community, watch out, there may be hell to pay when she needs to put any limits on that service, or when she resists other people's attempts to redefine her work to suit themselves. If you're a woman, be prepared to be told that your boundaries mean you're a fraud. If you're not what people want you to be, you must have deceived them somehow. Be prepared also for dire predictions that whatever you've built is on the brink of collapse, because who's ever going to support you if you dare to have boundaries?

It's sometimes been difficult to explain that making acupuncture affordable for people of ordinary incomes is so demanding in its own right, that efforts to improve (and complicate) what we're doing have the potential to make it outright impossible. Once a clinic is up and running and relatively stable, there isn't much room for innovation, and this will upset or even enrage some people. If you're a woman, brace yourself for people falling in love with you and your work and then falling out of love amid bitter recriminations when you turn out to be exactly what you said you were.

It's inevitable that people will come and go; some of them will go in a huff; some other people will decide that's your fault, and you should worry that everyone is going to leave you.

This cycle has been uniquely odd for me, especially the part where people think I should worry that everyone's leaving. I started out alone with the model and almost all of my work has resulted in somebody, somewhere, getting mad. Being alone and disapproved of isn't my favorite thing, but it's not unfamiliar either, and it's definitely not a deal breaker. I've got my own relationship with the fractal which predates my relationship with everybody else who found community acupuncture. I don't try to control other people's relationships with the fractal, and I don't recommend that you do either. If you're a woman, though, people probably won't understand why you're not trying harder to keep everybody happy.

POCA clinics and the co-op itself have limited resources and not everything is possible. Not all help is actually helpful and we have the right to refuse what isn't. If that makes us unenlightened, unimaginative, unsupportive – and unfeminine – we'll live with it.

42.

A core element of the community acupuncture fractal is acceptance of limitations.

Until the community acupuncture model came along, nobody in the acupuncture profession questioned, at least not in public, the conventional wisdom that all patients could of course afford $50 to $300 for an acupuncture treatment, it's just that some patients didn't want to because (select one or more): they didn't truly value their health/they were ignorant/they had unworthy non-acupuncture priorities. I had plenty of people tell me that there was no point to the model because making acupuncture affordable wouldn't accomplish anything; some of them kept saying that even *after* POCA was providing a million treatments a year and it was quite clear that lowering prices did indeed bring more patients in, not to mention make it possible to get better clinical outcomes.

POCA accepted that our potential patients had genuine limitations in terms of their financial resources. We accommodated them. As a result, we built relationships with all kinds of patients that we would not previously have had access to – and who would not have had access to us – and we found those relationships to be rich and sustaining.

I can trace the appearance of the model back to my realization that I wasn't strong enough to work in public health and I needed to take better care of myself. The model didn't show up until I accepted I had serious limitations (and ignoring them had the potential to be fatal).

However, acceptance of limitations often comes into conflict with ideas about how social entrepreneurship is supposed to work, at all levels of the fractal. Over the years, I've had a range of people ask me why I didn't get more input from patients about how I set up my clinic or even about the model itself. It's impossible to answer that question without having the conversation about limitations, so now that we're having it let me try again, for the record.

First, class cultures come into play. My experience of being working class is that we communicate with actions as much as or more than with words. What people say matters much less than what they do, and follow through is everything. Most of the people who would make up Working Class Acupuncture's patient base didn't show up until it was clear that the clinic was going to stick around. If you have limited resources, you learn not to invest yourself in shiny new possibilities, and if you venture way outside your comfort zone, you've probably done a lot of reconnaissance first. One of WCA's most supportive patients spent about six months watching who came and went through our clinic doors before he made his first appointment. Later on, he would not only refer, but actually pay for first appointments for about fifty of his associates and family members. Working class people invest incrementally when it's clear you're offering something that's worth investing in – but you have to offer something first. Possibilities don't cut it. You have to give people something they can use in real life.

If I had tried to hold a focus group to determine whether or not my neighborhood would support an affordable acupuncture clinic using an as-yet untried model, you know who would have shown up? Not working class people. I probably would have attracted a bunch of well-meaning middle class professionals, and they would have told me to change everything. My focus group, so to speak, was Betty and her family and Chico and Bobette, and they didn't respond to a survey or give me "feedback". The model emerged out of our relationships with each other and our

195

actions in support of those relationships.

Second, and most important, why would I ask anyone for input when I know the odds are that I can't do anything with it? The most difficult balancing act in community acupuncture is charging low enough prices and paying high enough wages, which leaves almost nothing left over. Running the clinic in its most basic form is a low-key kind of miracle. Nobody's underwriting any upgrades, so why would we want to give the impression that we have the resources to do more than we're already doing? The limitations of the model mean that a lot of decisions about how to run the clinic tend to make themselves: things are possible or they aren't, it's as simple as that.

It's the same story at more complex levels of the fractal, which is disappointing to idealists who would like to make improvements.

I've had acupuncturist employees at WCA say (in effect) but it would be so beautiful FOR ME if you could only pay me more/give me a completely flexible schedule/change core elements about how the clinic runs – why can't you be open to these beautiful possibilities? Oh wait, I see...you're a fraud, aren't you? You're pretending to be a humanitarian, but you're just another oppressive boss!

Meanwhile I'm bewildered, because how many times have I said I'm not a humanitarian? And beautiful possibilities just don't compute in my working class brain. I always feel like I'm lucky to have a job at all and I'm surprised when other acupuncturists aren't excited about that too.

POCA is often on the receiving end of its own version of this argument. You're so wonderful, POCA, why can't you be better? If you want us to KEEP thinking that you're

wonderful, you'd better try to improve. You'd better work on
_____.

To which the co-op tends to respond: but we don't care if you think we're wonderful. We've got too much else to do. We're trying to do something tangibly useful with limited resources, and those resources include our members' desire to tackle problems and organize solutions. We don't start things if we don't think we can generate the momentum to complete them, because completing projects is our reward. It's sometimes our only reward. We enjoy getting stuff done. That thing you want us to work on, it might be a worthy project but is it something that somebody in the co-op will enjoy doing – enough to actually get it done? No? Are you yourself willing to join, recruit helpers, and lead the effort? Sorry, then it's not going to happen.

Acceptance of limitations overlaps with the idea of incrementalism (reflected in how acupuncture works clinically and the way most POCA clinics grow) and the Stone Soup strategy, which means creating an experience of the commons by inducing everybody to share a little of what they have. All of these elements intersect with momentum. If you accept limitations, you can work with what you've got. If you can make something useful out of what you've got, people will use it, they'll see that something good is happening and they'll want to join in. You can use what they give you to make more.

It's a recipe. Please note how idealism isn't on the list of ingredients.

43.

The construction phase of POCA made me feel like my head was exploding, mostly in the best possible way. We had to build it based only on educated guesses of how it would work, but the legal and organizational nature of a multi-stakeholder co-op meant that if we got it wrong, we weren't going to be able to go back and change it later. We were lucky or blessed or guided by the fractal or something: when we put all the pieces together, it did what we wanted it to do.

A tricky question was, though, how would we run it day to day? POCA was incorporated in Oregon because that's where WCA was paying the bills for the set up and because Oregon's laws are friendly to co-ops; not all states are. POCA's membership, though, was spread all over North America and beyond. And by then it was clear that POCA reflected another core element of the fractal: it didn't make enough money to pay for management in any traditional form.

We didn't have time to be stumped by this problem, because fate intervened sometime in 2011. One of the other members of the POCA Steering Committee, John (also a longtime WCA acupuncturist) and I had lunch with a couple of consultants who wanted to talk to us about something called sociocracy. I don't remember the details of how that lunch date got set up; I think it was the work of some friends in the UK who heard about the co-op and wanted to help us. John and I were happy to have lunch with anybody who was interested in our problems.

Explaining sociocracy is way beyond the scope of this case study, because it's a complex and technical system in its own right. There's lots on the internet about it if you want to dive down that particular rabbit hole.[37] It's a form of participatory democracy that relies on groups of people reasoning together until they come to decisions that are almost, but not quite, based on consensus. Sociocracy is a structured way of practicing cooperation.

Two points are relevant here.

1) Because sociocracy is complex, we were warned against trying to figure it out on our own or attempting to tinker with it as a system. We were urged to hire consultants to make sure we didn't screw it up. But of course, we couldn't afford consultants. So we figured out how to do sociocracy on our own, we tinkered with it, and our makeshift version has served POCA very well. In our experience, sociocracy's more forgiving than the experts make it sound.

2) Sociocracy uses a system of interlocking circles, which are roughly equivalent to committees. I think of POCA's circles as the flywheels of an engine. POCA as an organization is a lot like a machine, that is if the machine were being operated by a flock of small birds. It hums, but it also warbles and trills; occasionally the gears grind or somebody screeches and you want to cover your ears. But mostly it hums along.

POCA pays a handful of people to do the day to day work of the co-op that's either too demanding or not enough fun to be done by volunteers: IT, bookkeeping, wrangling the details of memberships. All of the management, though, is done by volunteers in circles. Because it's a non-dividend co-op, there's no incentive to volunteer for POCA beyond enjoying the work of building and maintaining infrastructure for community acupuncture.

Being part of a flock of birds that's running a machine is an anticapitalist experience in its own right, and it made my relationship with capitalism more and more tenuous. The appeal of capitalism for me had been that it allowed me to build something I needed – a way to make a living on my own terms. Capitalism didn't give us POCA, though; something else did. Capitalism would in fact have kept us from building POCA if we'd taken its advice. POCA didn't only meet some of my individual needs as a community acupuncturist, it changed my relationship to those needs by locating them within a larger framework. In the long run, individual entrepreneurship didn't do it for me anymore than individual healing did. The flock and the flywheels, though, were a whole different story.

44.

Dear capitalism,

We need to talk.

First, I want to tell you, I've grown a lot by being with you. Relationships change people, and you've changed me. I don't want to minimize what you gave me, just because our relationship has gotten rough.

Owning my own business is one of the best things that's ever happened to me. Anybody's who's known me for a long time can see that. I didn't have a choice about building everything from scratch, but it was a big deal for me to discover I was good at it. I found out I was resourceful and persistent, which is an antidote to the pervasive sexist messages in our culture about women being less capable than men. Double points for what that means for a survivor of sexual violence.

You made me feel like I could *do stuff*.

I like knowing I'm scrappy. I like being an expert at bootstrapping. I like being able to look at men in business suits who work for big corporations – you know, the ones who run the world – and think, Dude, you wouldn't last 10 minutes where I come from; you couldn't hack it. Maybe you can earn a lot of money working in a business, or running a business you *inherited*, but let's see you *make* one. Out of *nothing*. During the 2012 election, when Mitt Romney was talking about being a job creator, I was like, ha ha ha me too! And I bet I started with less than you, Mitt.

You gave me freedom and you gave me confidence, capitalism. I'm never going to try to write you out of my history. But it's complicated now.

* * *

I'm an acupuncturist first. That's what I built my business out of, my skills at relieving people's headaches and regulating their menstrual cycles and releasing their stiff necks (you know how great that is, to put a couple of needles in someone's wrist and all of a sudden, the agonizing crick in their neck lets go and they can turn their head? Best feeling ever!). For better or worse, I look at the world as an acupuncturist; I look at health problems in terms of their root and branch. So you know what our main problem is, capitalism?

You hurt people.

You made my clinic possible but after working in it for a decade, there's just no way around the conclusion that a large proportion of the suffering I see in my patients is coming from you. I started realizing this when I was doing intakes, and I joked with new patients that our name – Working Class Acupuncture – fits because so many people we treat are coming in with work-related problems. So many repetitive stress conditions, so many injuries that turned into chronic pain when people couldn't take time off to heal, so much damage done by grinding minimum wage jobs. People coming to see us because they can't afford to go to the doctor – you know how scary that is, when your patient can't afford their inhalers? People can die of asthma attacks. Or the flip side, people injured by too much medical care that they got thanks to the profit motive in our healthcare system: too many surgeries, too many prescriptions, too many side effects.

Like my colleague Whitsitt said, *The violence of our economic system is written on our patients' bodies and minds.*

* * *

And you know what else is inescapable after a decade of running a community acupuncture clinic: the realization that you're not really on my side as a small business owner, either. You like to pretend you are, but you're not. Everything costs too much because everybody I do business with is trying to pad their bottom line, trying to put a little distance between themselves and the edge of the socioeconomic cliff. Don't try to tell me I'm afraid of hard work – you can't get away with that line with me. I think we've established that I *like* work. I just happen to know the difference between work and running to exhaustion on a treadmill.

It's like so many relationships: in the beginning, I loved your potential. I loved the promise of your possibilities. I loved how you made me feel: like the world revolved around me.

But if I'm honest with myself, a lot of the time you treat me like shit.

Oh, and don't forget my family. You know my father walks with a limp because when he was a kid he got hit by a car and there wasn't any money to take him to a doctor. I don't know how I put that out of my mind when I was so excited about our relationship, capitalism, but I guess I'm good at repressing stuff. For awhile, anyway. But it's too late to pretend that I don't know a lot about violence written on bodies. I know as much about that as I know about running a small business. And I realize now that I didn't have much of a choice about having a relationship with you, since you're the one calling the shots.

Remember what Ursula LeGuin said about you in her acceptance speech for an award from the National Book Foundation? *We live in capitalism. Its power seems inescapable. So did the divine right of kings.*[38]

I'm not going to judge myself, or anybody else, for whatever compromises we need to make with you in order to survive. But from here on out I want to be clear that our relationship is about the power you have over me, that's all there is to it. You don't have my heart or my will or my imagination. I'm not giving you any more creativity or loyalty or hope. You can keep your rewards.

This isn't goodbye because I don't have the ability to leave you, but from here on out I'm putting all my love and belief into the possibilities of what might come after you're gone and what's already happening in spaces you don't completely control – because those do exist, and I even carved out a couple myself without fully understanding what I was doing. I don't mind living in your interstices. I'll be a mouse in your walls. I'll chew through some of your wires if I get the chance.

And I'll wait. Because I believe I deserve something better than you.

Yours truly,

Lisa

45.

POCA's biggest problem was that it had no future.

In the time between when I graduated from acupuncture school in 1994 and when we incorporated POCA in 2011, the cost and length of acupuncture school ballooned. I paid about $21,000 for a three-year Master's degree in acupuncture and Chinese herbology. Today, the same degree costs anywhere from $50,000 to over $100,000. Because of the way my schooling was structured, I was able to work about 30 hours a week and so I only needed to borrow tuition. The increased length of acupuncture programs now means that most students can work less than 20 hours a week at best, and so they end up borrowing to cover their living expenses. Many students graduate with over $100,000 in student loan debt; I've met people who owed over $300,000 in combined loans from their undergraduate and Chinese medicine educations.

There's no way a graduate could pay back those loans by working in a community acupuncture clinic. Which presented us with an ethical problem: how could we encourage POCA's future workforce to go to acupuncture school?

Just as challenging was the problem of retraining graduates to practice using the community acupuncture model after they'd been trained for the conventional model. One recent graduate and new employee at a busy community acupuncture clinic wrote:

The things I learned at acupuncture school are not just irrelevant but in direct opposition to the skills and vision I need to do the work I'm learning to do day in, day out at a community clinic. I had to wear a white coat in student clinic, as an attempt to show that I was as professional as any doctor and to visibly claim a position of power and expertise compared to my patients about their own bodies. Oh yeah, and constant reminders that community acupuncture is a disgrace to the profession. The gulf between with whom and how I wanted to provide acupuncture and the way it was being taught to me was obvious and widening every day during those four years I was in school.[39]

On the other side were frustrated community acupuncture employers struggling to "deprogram" their new employees from a mindset that had prepared them to do very different work with a very different patient population, and which often framed what happened in community clinics as less valuable and less effective than conventional practice.

Back in the 90s, when we were working downtown at Central City Concern, S. coined the term "acupunk". He had taken on some management duties in the acupuncture department and was tired of spelling out "acupuncturist" on memos; in public health work, we had to move fast so who had time for all those syllables? As we developed our own vocabulary for community acupuncture, "acupunk" took on a whole new set of connotations. Eventually it got cut down to one syllable: punk. A punk was an acupuncturist fully acculturated to the community acupuncture model and ready to work. "To punk" was a verb, as in, I'm sorry, I can't make that next POCA Circle meeting, my coworker is on vacation so I have to punk. Speed, efficiency, clinical skill, a strong work ethic and a passionate devotion to patients who needed acupuncture but couldn't afford conventional rates all squeezed themselves into that one syllable – *punk* – and rocked it like a mosh pit.

It was becoming clear to everyone that punks and

conventional acupuncturists were probably different species. Fed up with deprogramming failures, I wrote in 2012:

Genuinely successful community acupuncturists have to refuse to act like acupuncturists, think like acupuncturists – even think of themselves as acupuncturists. The movement has come up with a useful shorthand: we call ourselves acupunks, or often just punks. Upstanding representatives of conventional acupuncture culture in the US are more than happy to agree with us about that: we are the troublemakers of the acupuncture world. An online dictionary (dictionary.com) defines 'punk' variously as:
- any prepared substance that will smolder and can be used to light fireworks, fuses, etc.
- something or someone worthless or unimportant
- a young ruffian; hoodlum
- a style or movement characterized by the adoption of aggressively unconventional and often bizarre or shocking clothing, hairstyles, makeup - and the defiance of social norms of behavior, usually associated with punk rock musicians and fans.

Community acupuncture needs people who are able and willing to smolder, who can light a fuse and stand the heat. Community acupuncture needs people who are untroubled by being unimportant and glad to take care of other people who are unimportant. Community acupuncture needs people who are happy to be seen as ruffians by other acupuncturists, who can defy and shock the social norms of the acupuncture profession. Community acupuncture needs punks.[40]

No existing acupuncture school was willing to train punks for us. This meant that in the long run, all of the POCA clinics with their loyal patients would have no one to operate them. The painstakingly accumulated resources and infrastructure of the cooperative itself would be inherited by nobody. Those of us who were using the model in peak capitalist return mode didn't need to care so much about this; they could treat a lot of patients by themselves until they retired or moved on, and that would be that. But for those of us who felt that community acupuncture clinics meant something in and of themselves to their surrounding communities, it was a painful prospect; we didn't want our clinics to have to fade away when we (inevitably) did. But if we had a punk pipeline, our clinics could outlive us.

I'll spare you all the bargaining I did with God and other educational institutions. By 2012 we'd surrendered to the unavoidable: if we wanted punks, we were going to have to make our own. The DIY aesthetic of the fractal extended farther than we would have liked. We were going to open our own acupuncture school: the POCA Technical Institute.

46.

S. and I had some bitter arguments that sounded basically like this:

S: I've worked in a school and you haven't. This is going to be a lot harder than you think.

Me: We've taught ourselves to do everything else, we'll teach ourselves to do this.

S: Schools can be grim. You don't know.

Me: But we have to, we have no choice.

S: Of course we have a choice, that's ridiculous.

Me: BUT IF WE DON'T MAKE A SCHOOL, POCA HAS NO FUTURE

S: I've worked in a school and you haven't. This is going to be a lot harder than you think.

Rinse, repeat, until one of us stomped away.

I prevailed, but S. was right. Schools can be grim and it was harder than I thought.

Cut to the Chase, Please #7

Oh, come on. Don't be coy. Tell us, what happened?

All kinds of things, but I don't want this book to go on forever. How about I give you one example of how schools can be hard?

All right, but it better be good.

A 2 alarm fire gutted POCA Tech's student clinic about a month after the students of Cohort 1 started their clinical internship. The clinical supervisor called me during a shift and said, I'm sorry, Lisa, but the clinic's on fire.

That good enough for you, capitalists?

Seriously?

Seriously.
Here's a blog post I wrote about it:

Over the last twelve years or so I've gotten to see a lot of community acupuncture clinics in a lot of different phases. I've gotten to see the newly-rented storefronts with nothing in them but potential; the newly-painted rooms with piles of half-assembled IKEA furniture; the carefully arranged recliners all ready for the grand opening; the tiny, warm, super-efficient shared spaces for a slowly-growing clinic – all the way up through the spacious, cozy, well-worn Big Damn Clinics that thousands of people have passed through. I've even seen a clinic in the process of closing, with everything being carefully, regretfully, folded up and packed away.

* * *

But until this morning, I've never seen a community acupuncture clinic destroyed.

It was cold and dark and reeked of smoke. I was standing on a mound of insulation and soaking-wet ceiling tiles that squished when I moved. I looked around the back treatment room at WCA Lents, with blackened wires corkscrewing down from where the dropped ceiling used to be, charred joists above, wind knocking at the boarded up windows where the firefighters had smashed their way through, the walls streaked with smoke and water damage, the IKEA lampshades hanging in shreds, debris in every direction, and all I could think was, "Wow."

The hardest thing to look at was an overturned recliner half-buried under a pile of insulation and what might have been ash. It occurred to me that this was somebody's favorite chair.

You know, it's weird what turns out to be validating.

This was before I saw the torrent of emails that had filled up WCA's inbox, all saying, "I'm so sorry, what can I do to help?"; before the receptor who called all the Lents patients to reschedule them told us that people's responses were so loving that they made her cry; before a dozen people offered to start fundraising for us. I looked at that overturned recliner and I felt it: all these people I won't ever meet have been using this clinic and it means so much to them.

A community acupuncture clinic is basically a nexus where people, ordinary people, come together to take care of themselves. Those of us who work in them are just holding the space, creating the container. There are different aspects to that and the physical room is only one.

* * *

Lisa Rohleder

In a strange way the aftermath of this fire feels like a validation of everything we've said, everything we've done, and everything we want to do but haven't yet been able to. Acupuncture is a tool for communities to take care of themselves. We need physical spaces for that to happen in, but we also need the right kind of education, the right kind of regulation, the right economic and legal structures to serve as a container for that self-care.

Sometimes wreckage makes truth especially visible. When everything's in ruins but the center's somehow intact, you can't fail to notice it.

The whole time I've been involved with the acupuncture profession it seems like it's been obsessed with validation. When will the healthcare system recognize our value? When will insurance companies give us our due? When will we get the respect we deserve – when will the important people acknowledge us, pass laws in our favor, bestow dignity on us?

I looked at that overturned recliner and realized: there's nothing that anybody IMPORTANT could give us that's more important than this. Whether it's a broken, waterlogged, ash-covered recliner upside down in a destroyed community acupuncture clinic or just a regular, shabby, functioning recliner right side up in a regular, shabby, functioning community acupuncture clinic, it's a sign of what we ordinary people give to each other. And there's nothing – nothing! – more valuable.[41]

Cut to the Chase, Please #8

But wait. Hold on just a minute. What do you mean, WCA Lents? Working Class Acupuncture is in the Cully neighborhood.

Yes, it is; but in 2009 we opened WCA Hillsdale, across the river, and in 2012, we opened WCA Lents in outer southeast Portland. They're each about 20 miles away from WCA Cully.

We knew it! You ARE hiding something. There MUST be money to be made with the community acupuncture model, otherwise how did you end up with 3 locations? See, a franchise based on the model COULD be really successful and lucrative!

OK, I guess I'd better tell you that part of the story too. And the truth is, there's a lot about WCA's growth and development that's crucial to understand in terms of the infrastructure that made it possible for us to even consider opening an acupuncture school.

Remember when I said I loved *Banker to the Poor* because it gave me language – the language of social entrepreneurship – for what otherwise just felt like something hammering on the inside of my skull, trying to get out? (Come to think of it, my experience of social entrepreneurship has quite a bit in common with a migraine.)

I've always experienced the community acupuncture model as something large, much larger than me. I remember telling a friend, circa 2003, that I was frustrated because it seemed like a lot of acupuncturists I talked to had a vision of their own practices that reminded me of a model train set: tidy, intricate, extremely contained; absolutely under their personal control; an exquisitely detailed miniature that they could work on perfecting forever. Its function didn't seem to be the point. I listened to people discussing their acupuncture practices and I felt like they were comparing model trains. Meanwhile, what I really wanted was a railroad.

Even after I'd done a reasonably good job of articulating the community acupuncture model, it seemed that the general trend was to try to interpret it at the level of model trains. I was desperate to get people to imagine a railroad.

So when a community acupuncturist I knew had a nasty break up with his business partner, left his clinic, and said he wanted to re-open on the west side of Portland, I said, hey, why don't we just make another WCA location and hire you? By that time, we had a number of patients who were driving 45 minutes or more to get to WCA Cully; one west-side patient told me she crossed the river twice a week to see us even though chronic pain had immobilized her right arm. I pictured her cradling her arm, driving one-handed over the bridge through rush hour traffic. She was getting better with regular acupuncture; I hoped it would be fast enough to prevent her demise in a fiery wreck. The situation was less than ideal.

This is why WCA, unlike a lot of community acupuncture clinics, has debt; we prioritized scaling up, but we didn't have profits or any kind of reserves to pay for it. I kept taking risks in order for us to grow, and I loved trying to create jobs for acupuncturists. WCA Hillsdale would take years to break even, but it had grateful patients from the day that it opened.

And soon as WCA Hillsdale was close to breaking even, I

wanted to open another location. We had acupuncturists who said they wanted to work for WCA; S. and I drove around one day and found yet another storefront that was full of broken furniture, this time in Lents. It had been vacant for 30 years and the windows were pocked with bullet holes. I fell in love. I told one of my regular patients about the fantastic location we'd found and she interrupted me: yes, Lisa, I know exactly where that is; I used to work for the Public Defenders' office.

In order to rehab the space, we got a loan from the Portland Development Commission which S. and I guaranteed with a lien on our house. 3 1/2 years later, WCA Lents was just starting to pay for itself when the fire destroyed it. We had chosen it to host the POCA Tech student clinic because we wanted the students to do their clinical internships in a working community acupuncture clinic in a neighborhood that needed one; the building itself, newly remodeled, was up to code and could meet accreditation standards for school facilities. And besides, it was beautiful. The neighborhood was so happy to have us occupying what had been an example of urban blight that they crowdfunded a gorgeous art mural for the side of the building. (It provided a striking backdrop for the flames shooting up into the night sky.)

Here's the thing, capitalists: the community acupuncture model has fantastic potential for expansion, IF you're a queer white trash girl whose formative adulthood event was a plane crash and you've got a recurrent problem with suicidal ideation. Your own mileage may vary. I'd love to warn you about making assumptions, but if we're talking about a franchise based on the community acupuncture model that you've already invested in, it's probably too late. You saw something that looked like it had capitalist potential and you didn't double check to find out what kind of fuel it was running on.

In part, it's running on nothing. That's the beauty of entrepreneurship, there's always plenty of nothing, right? But it's also running on a combustible mix of pain, rage and passion, and I'm not seeing those in your franchise. Maybe you'll find other kinds of fuel, but I can't help you there, because I've never tried to run it on anything else.

But I digress; what I really want to talk about is building a collective. Remember when I said we figured out there wasn't any money to pay for management at WCA, and we'd have to manage ourselves? Over the course of about 6 years, we slowly converted WCA from a mom-and-pop type business into a version of sociocracy. Here's something I wrote circa 2013, as part of that process:

Stone Soup: The Epilogue

In the process of looking at collectivizing WCA, I find myself thinking about the stone soup story again, and what HAS to happen afterwards. The original story is about something that happens over the course of an afternoon and maybe an evening. Unlike the soldier in the story, those of us who are committed to community acupuncture aren't packing up and leaving town after setting a good example. WCA is almost twelve years old. Now we have POCA, and soon we will open POCA Tech. One good communal meal isn't going to solve our problems. We still need to make a living, and thanks to the acupuncture profession, the famine is still on: acupuncturists don't have enough work, and patients can't get enough acupuncture.

In a sense, you could sum up the whole process of collectivization like this: after a lot of people who would otherwise have gone hungry had eaten some really good food, the soldier stood up from behind his iron pot and announced, "OK, guys – YOUR TURN."

We don't want to re-enact the tragedy of the commons here in the community acupuncture movement. A few people took big risks so that other people didn't have to; a few people did disproportionate amounts of work that everybody – including themselves – benefited from. Now that it's clear that the stone soup trick is good for everyone, it's not fair to require anybody to continue in the role of trickster (or owner/manager of an anti-capitalist business) to keep the soup going. If you ask to keep eating, while at the same time refusing to participate in the core part of preparing the food, you are taking the first step towards re-enacting the tragedy of the commons – you are taking the first step in depleting a shared resource by behaving selfishly. The core part of preparing the food is looking straight at the rock, the empty pot, the skeptical faces, and deciding to do something creative and constructive about it.

One of the reasons that WCA was historically not especially democratic was that we, the owners, thought other people would respond to the famine less creatively and more conservatively than we wanted to. By the time we were able to hire people, we had massed an unfortunate amount of experience with acupuncturists who cared first and foremost about how much money they could make. They wanted nothing to do with risk, especially if the risk was not going to result in potentially more money for them. They particularly did not want to face the truth about the acupuncture profession: that they'd been promised a career that, for their intents and purposes, didn't exist. Even if they could admit that to themselves, they were most likely to get out of the field altogether – not to stay in it and try to change it for the better. They couldn't see the possibilities for something better, and even if they could, they were not about to put themselves on the line to realize those possibilities.

* * *

As a result, we despaired of getting acupuncturists on board with the bigger vision, and WCA for some time looked like a small mom-and-pop business. There were a lot of problems with that, but one of the biggest, in hindsight, was the expectation that in a mom-and-pop business there's a benign owner or owners who protect their employees and treat them well. There's an expectation of a certain kind of paternalism. Which would all be fine and good if we were in a different kind of folktale, but we're not. You'll notice that, in the stone soup story, the hungry soldier doesn't roll into town and find a nice mom-and-pop cafe where he might be able to scrounge a meal. If there were any benign, comfortable, paternalistic entities that employed acupuncturists in large numbers, we would ALL be working for them. There would never have been a WCA, or a POCA. We would not be sitting here with our empty pot, trying to make you understand that capitalism + acupuncture for people of ordinary incomes does not = jobs.

The dream of a mom-and-pop business is a sweet, appealing dream, and both owners and employees are loathe to give it up; we certainly tried to make it work for longer than we should have. Now we see that we have to be ruthless. We can't afford to let people eat our soup who are only worried about themselves, their jobs, their lives. It turns out there is a price tag to this variety of stone soup, and if you are reading this, the check has arrived at your table. If you eat our soup, we are going to require you to worry about other people, other people's jobs, other people's lives; actually, the entire train wreck that is the acupuncture profession.

WCA and POCA are examples of social entrepreneurship. And you know what they say about social entrepreneurship? "Social entrepreneurs are not content just to give a fish or teach how to fish. They will not rest until they have revolutionized the fishing industry."– Bill Drayton

This is the wrong place to work if you just want some fish.

When we were trying to be a mom-and-pop business, a number of our employees were resentful that we put so much energy into the community acupuncture movement as a whole. They correctly surmised that we would all have been making more money if we had ignored the bigger picture and just tried to make WCA more efficient. Their paychecks would have been larger if we had been benign, paternalistic small business owners instead of (harried, frustrated, despairing-but-unwilling-to-quit) social entrepreneurs. POCA and its many benefits didn't exist yet to justify the investment. Now that we are becoming a collective, the collective as a whole runs the risk of hearing this same complaint from new employees. Hence this document.

One of the things that bothers us most about acupuncture in this country is how exclusive it is: it's only consistently available to people who meet a very narrow set of criteria, usually economic, sometimes health-related. We pushed the movement along past WCA because we couldn't stand it that our patients, who could get as much acupuncture as they wanted, had to tell their friends and relatives in other places that they were out of luck. Lots of conventional acupuncturists feel that they are making acupuncture accessible by offering a handful of their patients a discount from their otherwise sky-high fees. It doesn't bother them that this "accessibility" is tiny and narrow. We felt that if all we did with WCA was to make it a successful, comfortable little mom-and-pop business, if we didn't care about anything beyond our own little clinic, we'd be doing the same thing. Without POCA, all of WCA is essentially just another tiny exception for a few lucky people. Because we're committed to inclusiveness in acupuncture, WCA is above all committed to POCA. If you work here, you should ask yourself how committed to inclusiveness you are.

The biggest tangible way that we are about to express our commitment is by becoming the foundation and support for the first campus of POCA Tech. We are working on this document now about our culture, because soon we won't have the energy to do anything like this, thanks to the demands of the school. If you are even slightly dissatisfied now with WCA's failure to take care of you the way a good mom-and-pop business is supposed to, you need to quit before POCA Tech rolls over us all. We really mean this.

Our particular screwed-up fishing industry is never going to get any better until the nature of acupuncture training changes radically. There is no capitalist benefit for us, or anybody else, in changing it. We're going to change it anyway. We have to, because there will never be any fairness in ANY acupuncture business as long as acupuncturists are being lured into the profession under false pretenses. We need an acupuncture school that is radically truthful, and since nobody will give that to us, we have to make it ourselves.

WCA is a stone soup story. Because we were starting from a place where everything was so unfair and so hopeless, the only way to keep moving forward constructively was to focus on behaving as selflessly as possible in reference to the big picture. No other course of action made sense to us, and it still doesn't. If you work here, you have to ask yourself if you are ready to do the same. Do you feel entitled to have a world built for you – and are you disappointed that nobody will do that – or are you stimulated by having to build your own world, with committed comrades to help?

Creating POCA Tech is one of the most important things we

can do to rectify the basic unfairness of the situation that we all, acupuncturists and patients, find ourselves in. However, making a school from scratch is going to demand an enormous amount from WCA. Before we get any further into the process, we need to make sure everybody understands how making POCA Tech is going to change WCA operations.

1) We need everybody who works here to understand and support our culture. We have realized that we can no longer try to just give people jobs. We don't have that luxury. We need people who want to help us build a new world.

2) As part of the process of collectivizing, the work of management has to be shared much more than it has been. A whole bunch of people are going to be learning, through trial and error, how to do necessary administrative work. We expect some bumps, so buckle your seat belts.

3) We need to integrate more POCA volunteers at more levels of WCA's operations. We are building a school for POCA, and we simply can't do it without a lot of help.

4) In a variety of ways, we are going to be making the relationship between WCA and POCA much closer. We need everybody who works here to make an effort to understand POCA, what it does and why it matters. (from the WCA Culture Manual)

By 2014, when POCA Tech opened, a collective was capably running WCA. In 2015, we made WCA a 501c3 nonprofit, mostly because it no longer made any sense for any individual to own it. The most important thing, though, was that we learned the importance of culture. In order to expand, the fractal needed a culture that was characterized by a collective mindset and an acceptance of limited resources.

Lisa Rohleder

47.

But before we get to that, there were three major hurdles to POCA starting an acupuncture school at all.

The first hurdle was money. You can't just bootstrap an acupuncture school the way you do a community acupuncture clinic out of goodwill, cheap rent, and scavenged recliners. Punks need licenses in order to work. In almost all states, to get an acupuncture license, you have to pass the national boards for acupuncturists. In order to be allowed to sit for the boards, you have to graduate from a school approved by the accrediting agency for acupuncturists. The process of getting through accreditation requires that the school construct and maintain its own version of an educational bureaucracy that can meet certain standards, and it also demands fees to the tune of $60,000.

It was highly improbable that POCA would be able to clear this hurdle.

Sometime in 2012, I started doing the math and realized that we probably needed to borrow a couple hundred thousand dollars just to get off the ground. I'd been introduced to a nontraditional lending corporation that made loans to social enterprises, and I went downtown to meet with one of their representatives. As he laid out the loan application process, he was friendly, kind and discouraging. The upshot was, we'd never be able to qualify for a loan of that size.

I left his office and walked around the city for awhile, fighting tears, trying to absorb the disappointment. I leaned against a building, looked down at the sidewalk, and realized three things as clearly as if they'd been written on the pavement:
- This was hopeless.

- Nobody outside of POCA was going to help us.
- I was going to do it anyway.

Lockerbie, 24 years past at that point, was present to me as ever. Of course, making an acupuncture school was hopeless; what wasn't? Given that, why do anything? Or, the interpretation I liked better: fuck it, why not?

So if I was going to do this next hopeless thing, how exactly would I go about it? When I thought about it that way, the steps obligingly laid themselves out. They might all be impossible, but they weren't ambiguous or confusing. As quixotic processes went, it was cut and dried, thanks to the highly-regulated nature of schools. Between what we needed to do for the accreditors, and what we would need to do to get a license in the state of Oregon to operate a private career school, opening an educational institution was a lot like being given a paint-by-numbers kit.

And as for the money, POCA raised $191,462. There were a few unexpected large donations, and thousands of tiny ones.[42]

The second hurdle was what I thought of as the Velveeta problem. As I mentioned earlier, if healing were food, *just putting in needles*, as I'd done with Chico, would be Velveeta. By treating Chico, I'd learned that doing acupuncture the wrong way – the simple, cheap, theoretically unsound way – could get someone kicked out of hospice. Could apparently add five years to someone's life. That's a hard lesson to forget.

But you couldn't base an acupuncture school on Velveeta. For one thing, no punk I knew, including me, was actually *just putting in needles* most of the time. My experience with

Chico hadn't made me throw out everything I'd learned; it had just made me doubt that there was a right way to do acupuncture. On a practical level, in the clinic, I was still doing Jingei treatments on almost all my patients because that was what I knew how to do, and it worked.

To become an accredited school, we'd have to teach an approved curriculum of acupuncture theory; we'd have to teach how to do acupuncture the *right* way according to the establishment. Given that POCA was providing around a million treatments a year by this point, I wasn't the only acupuncturist who'd discovered that acupuncture in the real world, delivered in high volumes to patients of ordinary incomes, was a different animal altogether from the acupuncture I learned in school – in its methods, its results, and its potential.

I wrote in a blog post:
A POCA comrade who now runs a very successful clinic said on the forums that the most essential thing the community acupuncture movement gave him was permission: to do acupuncture the way he always wanted to do it anyway – simply, inexpensively, unpretentiously, efficiently. And a bunch of other punks chimed in and said, yes, that's true for me too, this is exactly what I wanted, but my acupuncture school and/or other acupuncturists had convinced me that I better not, because BAD THINGS WOULD HAPPEN IF I DID. But all that really happened was that a lot of people of ordinary incomes got acupuncture. Most of them felt better; most of them were very grateful, appreciative, and enthusiastic; also, a bunch of punks were able to make a living doing acupuncture (something at least some schools were teaching wasn't possible).[43]

How on earth was POCA's school going to have any integrity? How could we teach acupuncture theory to our students the way that we'd been taught it ourselves, knowing what we knew? That wasn't a rhetorical question or a problem only related to our collective conscience; it was a practical issue. Integrity, along with simplicity, transparency, and solidarity, was part of the fractal itself. The fractal wasn't just the why of POCA, it was the how; it was what allowed us to do what we do. Was having a school going to break the fractal? If so, there wasn't much point to this undertaking.

The third hurdle was the problem of who does acupuncture belong to? This was related to the Velveeta problem, but it had its own political twist.

As I said about my own education: a small group of white students of Chinese acupuncturists had built the acupuncture profession that white upper-middle-class professionals thought the US should have. It's as if there are two different directions in the development of acupuncture in the US, like separate moving walkways in an airport: marginalized communities using acupuncture and Chinese medicine to take care of themselves, and more privileged individuals working to fence it off with a goal of increasing its status.

Acupuncture schools were the fence. And by 2012, the main moving walkway for marginalized people was represented by the National Acupuncture Detoxification Association, which was continuing to train laypeople (many of them people of color) to use the 5 Needle Protocol to treat addiction. In many states, licensed acupuncturists who went to accredited schools were determined to prevent NADA from training acu-detox specialists to provide 5NP in their own communities. They saw NADA as a threat to their professional turf.

A few years prior, I had gone to a NADA conference in

Detroit with my friend Nora of Detroit Community Acupuncture. A presentation that stayed with me was one by a couple of acu-detox specialists who had worked in a refugee camp in a third world country. Given that there were no laws regulating acupuncture there, they had been free to teach the residents of the camp how to provide 5NP for each other. When the political situation surrounding the camp deteriorated, the acu-detox specialists had to leave for some months. When they were able to return, the residents of the camp were eager to tell them how they'd put their training to use. Refugees treating each other reported a range of benefits from 5 needles in the ear: children stopped wetting their beds (a huge quality of life issue in a refugee camp); nightmares went away and sleep improved; people had more patience with each other; but most of all, people reported feeling less overwhelmed by their circumstances of displacement, danger, and deprivation. The refugees said that a significant consequence of the treatment was that they felt they could focus on creating solutions for their problems: they were empowered.

This story reverberated in my ears long afterwards for a couple of reasons. First, the refugees' reports of the global effects of acupuncture echoed my own patients' descriptions. People liked acupuncture because it improved their overall quality of life, and people with chronic illnesses valued it especially because it increased their ability *to cope*. It seemed that whether the acupuncture was 5NP done by refugees or Dr. Tan's Balance Method done by me didn't matter. Second, a major criticism that other acupuncturists leveled at POCA punks was that our work was superficial and not spiritual enough. We were accused of providing the acupuncture equivalent to band-aids, as opposed to helping people transform their perspective and take control of their own lives. We spent so little time instructing our patients in how they should live, how could they possibly make any real progress? But listening to the refugees' report, it seemed that the transformative agents were the needles themselves.

One major purpose of acupuncture schools was to confine the use of acupuncture to people who had acupuncture degrees. POCA needed an acupuncture school mostly because other schools had been so successful in this effort. In the US, acupuncture belonged to acupuncturists. Given where we had come from, though, how could we get behind that? How could we be an acupuncture school and teach our students in good faith? How could we, as a school, answer the question truthfully: who does acupuncture belong to?

48.

Lucky for me, by this time I was a practicing Catholic again.

By 2009 I'd realized that I needed more than my meditation practice; I needed some kind of a spiritual community. But I needed one that would give me what my clinic did: the ability to connect to my own kind. I decided to check out the Catholic parish in Cully, St. Charles Church.

The first time I went I recognized a number of my patients, particularly one Vietnamese lady who had impressed me as almost preternaturally sweet and unflappable in the way she dealt with a frustratingly unresponsive auto-immune condition. So is this where she gets all that patience? I wondered. Sign me up. She came over and hugged me; she was thrilled to see her acupuncturist at Mass.

St. Charles started out as an immigrant parish for Italians and Germans, and 100 years later was a parish for immigrants from everywhere. Over a dozen languages are spoken within the congregation. St. Charles used to be a prosperous lower middle class parish; now it's a hub for organizing in the trailer parks of Cully. When people heard I was no longer an ex-Catholic, they assumed I'd gone back to the church because of charismatic Pope Francis. He didn't have anything to do with it, though. I went back before he was pope, and I stayed because of St. Charles itself. What brought me back to Catholicism wasn't one important person, but a whole community of unimportant people. Which was where I belonged; I was home.

It's hard to explain being Catholic, especially when you're queer. Catholicism as it's practiced on the ground in a poor church is extremely different from Catholicism as held up by the Vatican. I felt accepted and welcome in a way that left out no part of my identity or history. By this time, I'd become a sort of public figure in the acupuncture profession, which took a lot of energy and sometimes made me feel disoriented. I was afraid I was going to forget who I was and why I was doing what I was doing; I craved a regular infusion of working class immigrant spirituality. Every week St. Charles grounded me and made me feel human again.

For the purposes of this narrative, though, what matters most is that I was Catholic again in time for the 25th anniversary of the murders of the Jesuits in El Salvador, which is how I met (posthumously) Ignacio Martín-Baró.

In November 1989, when I was a Jesuit Volunteer, a Salvadoran death squad murdered six Jesuit scholars at the Universidad Centroamericana together with their housekeeper and her 15-year-old daughter. The UCA had become a focal point of opposition to the human rights abuses perpetrated by the US-supported military. My JV community went to services for them and there was a lot of discussion about the state-sanctioned murders: it was martyrdom pretty close to home. But I didn't know much about the martyrs themselves.

Reading about them 25 years later, I discovered that one of the six scholars, Ignacio Martín-Baró, was the founder of Liberation Psychology. He was a social psychologist who directed the University Institute of Public Opinion, which polled poor people about their opinions and revealed the realities of Salvadoran life under a repressive government. I started reading his translated work, *Writings for a Liberation Psychology*.[44] He had found a way, *using the techniques and skills of his profession, and a little imagination... to put psychology in the service of human liberation.*[45] He had a lot to say about how Latin American psychology was failing ordinary people.

* * *

He wrote:

In an effort to gain social status, Latin American psychology has imported all of its theoretical and practical ideas from the US, mimicking models without understanding them. Uncritical acceptance of theories and models is precisely the negation of science's own fundamental principles. And the ahistorical importing of ideas leads to ideological thinking, with mindsets whose meaning and validity, as the sociology of knowledge reminds us, excuse some social circumstances and foreclose inquiry into certain concrete questions.

Status-seeking...ahistorical importing of ideas...uncritical acceptance of theories and models that originated in another culture...concrete questions you're not supposed to ask in public...wow, I thought, this sounds familiar. This reminds me of the acupuncture profession in the US. Tell me more, my brother!

The dominant models in psychology are founded on a series of assumptions that are rarely discussed, and even more rarely are alternatives to them proposed.

For example, the assumption of individualism:

Which proposes the individual as an entity with its own meaning as the final subject of psychology. The problem with individualism is rooted in its insistence on seeing as an individual characteristic that which oftentimes is not found except within the collectivity, or in attributing to individuality the things produced only in the dialectic of interpersonal relations. Through this, individualism ends up reinforcing the existing structures, because it ignores the reality of social structures and reduces all structural

231

problems to personal problems.

You mean like insisting that working class people are unhealthy because of their personal choices, which cause them to spend all their money on beer and cigarettes? You mean like ignoring the documented health effects of economic inequality?

If we want psychology to make a significant contribution...we have to redesign our theoretical and practical tools, but redesign them from the standpoint of our own people...Latin American psychology must stop focusing attention on itself, stop worrying about its scientific and social status, and instead propose an effective service to the needs of the majority of the population.

Just as POCA gave lots of acupuncturists permission to practice acupuncture the way they always wanted to, Ignacio Martín-Baró gave me permission to think radically about acupuncture theory. Not just from a practical and clinical perspective, but from the perspective of how acupuncture theories are constructed as a body of knowledge and situated within a culture. If he could turn this critique on his own discipline, psychology, I could turn it on mine. It wasn't just a matter of saying, acupuncture is a much different thing, in the real world with ordinary people, then it appears to be in the textbooks; I could challenge the textbooks and the academic foundations themselves. I *should* challenge them, because all of Liberation Psychology's basic arguments applied to the state of acupuncture in the US and to my own experience of being a low-class practitioner serving low-class patients. Twenty-five years late, I was calling in my Jesuit affiliation, and unlike Ignacio Martín-Baró, I didn't have to worry about getting shot for being a free thinker.

If we want ~~psychology~~ **acupuncture** to make a significant contribution...we have to redesign our theoretical and practical tools, but redesign them from the standpoint of our own people...~~Latin American psychology~~ **acupuncture in the US** must stop focusing attention on itself, stop worrying about its scientific and social status, and instead propose an effective service to the needs of the majority of the population.

To take on a new perspective (**for acupuncture**) obviously does not mean throwing out all of our knowledge; what it supposes, rather, is that we will relativize that knowledge **(of acupuncture)** and critically revise it from the perspective of the popular majorities. Only then will the theories and models show their validity or deficiency, their utility or lack thereof, their universality or provincialism. Only then will the (**acupuncture**) techniques we have learned display their liberating potential or their seeds of subjugation.

There's your school, POCA, there's your foundation for academic integrity. We'll teach the acupuncture establishment's curriculum, but we'll relativize it and critically revise it. Doesn't that sound like something a school should be doing anyway?

But ~~a psychology~~ an acupuncture of liberation requires a prior liberation of ~~psychology~~ acupuncture, and that liberation can only come from a praxis committed to the sufferings and hopes of the people.

We had a praxis and it was the community acupuncture model, rooted in self-organizing. We couldn't teach acupuncture to our students the way we'd been taught it ourselves, but we could teach an acupuncture of liberation. Or, Liberation Acupuncture. I like to think Father Martín-Baró, the Young Lords and the Black Panthers would have approved.

Lisa Rohleder

49.

What is Liberation Acupuncture?

Liberation Acupuncture is a conceptual framework for acupuncture that affirms that individual health and disease do not exist, and cannot be understood or addressed, apart from social conditions – particularly injustice, inequality, and the pervasive influence of traumatic stress.

Liberation Acupuncture is a praxis that begins with the needs and the perspectives of the oppressed, the exploited, and the excluded. Liberation acupuncture defines what is valuable in acupuncture theory and practice by determining what is useful and valuable to oppressed people.[46]

50.

It wasn't until 2014 – two months after our school had
already started – that I found the Jesuit intellectual
solidarity I needed and Ignacio Martín-Baró gave us the
foundation for our academic work. In 2012, though,
someone else had given us the answer to the question, who
does acupuncture belong to?

Sometime that summer, I went out into the lobby of WCA
Cully to greet a new patient. She was a senior African
American lady who looked a little frail and seemed a little
grouchy; let's call her Elaine. She said she was looking into
acupuncture to help her quit smoking, but that she had a lot
of other health problems she didn't want to go into. Elaine
was accompanied by a younger white woman with wheat-
colored hair and warm brown eyes; let's call her Jenny. I
assumed that Jenny was either a neighbor or a relative of
Elaine's and had driven her to her appointment. We have a
chauffeur policy, I told them. We treat chauffeurs for free.
Jenny, if you want to go back in the treatment room with
Elaine, and you want to try acupuncture too, I can treat you
together. I just need you to fill out a little paperwork first.

Jenny laughed. Okay, she said. Elaine, is that okay with you?

Fine by me, Elaine said shortly. But she seemed a little
happier about the prospect of getting acupuncture if Jenny
got it too.

I don't mind treating grouchy patients; a lot of people in pain
are irritable, and I'd rather treat somebody who's open about
their skepticism. After all, that's how my relationship with
Chico started. I liked Elaine and Jenny right away; they were
just my speed.

* * *

I was surprised and pleased when they came back the next week, and after that when Elaine came for acupuncture alone. She said she was cutting back on cigarettes only a little at a time, but that her sleep had improved quite a bit so she was going to keep getting acupuncture. I was more surprised, though, when Jenny called and asked if she could meet with me outside of my punking hours.

It turned out Jenny wasn't related to Elaine and she wasn't her neighbor; she was her caseworker. Jenny worked for a big insurance company that served low income people, and as part of the health care reform effort, the insurance company had adopted what's known as a hot-spotting program targeting "high utilizers" of the healthcare system. High utilizers ended up getting care in emergency rooms and being hospitalized at rates far beyond the general population, and they were often struggling with poorly managed chronic conditions. Hot-spotting programs originated in New Jersey in 2007, and showed that the people with the highest medical costs were (surprise!) generally the ones getting the worst care.[47]

Let's call Portland's hot-spotting program the Wellbeing Program (WP). Elaine was a WP client. Jenny's job was to advocate with Elaine in the healthcare system to get her what she needed to stay out of the hospital.

Jenny told me that several other WP clients were interested in trying acupuncture. All of them were on a long list of medications, and a non-pharmaceutical approach to managing their health concerns would be welcome. The problem, of course, was funding; her program didn't have any funding for acupuncture. She wanted to know if I had any creative ideas.

Funding for acupuncture's always a problem, I said. You

know, I used to work in public health and this is why I got out. But wait, how many people do you think we're talking about? Total, in a month?

Jenny thought about it. I don't know – 7? Maybe 10 at the most?

At this point, WCA was providing something like 800 treatments a week amongst its 3 clinics. With our volume, I said, we won't even notice 10 more people a month, and anyway, probably quite a few of them will try it and decide acupuncture's not their cup of tea. That's how it works in the general population: a lot of people try it, only some of them become regulars. So let's not worry about the funding, let's just see how it goes. One thing, though – we don't have a lot of resources to explain our systems to people, so if we can make sure the caseworkers bring their clients the first time and walk them through the process, we'll treat the caseworkers for free the first time too. That seemed to work well with you and Elaine.

Really? Jenny said. You're sure? That's a lot of free treatments.

Yeah, I said. Why not? Fuck it. I think we should do this, I don't feel like letting money turn into an obstacle.

I include this exchange not just because it's an important part of the narrative but as further proof that you can't expect me to act like Mother Teresa. I'm pretty sure Mother Teresa never said, fuck it; for me, though, it's basically a guiding principle. And it was the foundation for what turned out to be a match made in heaven: the WP clients and caseworkers with WCA.

The WP clients fit in so well at WCA that we never had any

idea who they were or, unless we looked it up, how many of them we were actually treating. They might be perceived as high maintenance patients in other healthcare settings, but at WCA, they were no trouble at all. In return, they would be the key to identifying two more crucial elements of Liberation Acupuncture: trauma informed care and the preferential option for the poor.

Later, Jenny would write:

People feel welcomed at WCA. This is not always the case in the larger medical system where they may be labeled as problem patients, malingerers, drug seekers, or someone with a personality disorder. At this community acupuncture clinic, there is a predictable structure, minimal talking, and a lot of reliability which allows for relaxed and non-pressured healing relationships.

Unlimited resource sharing is rare for people living in poverty. Having a community acupuncture clinic say that you can come as much as you want is the antithesis of almost all current social resource allocation practices. Everything is limited: money, medical, counseling, food, housing, etc. By having an open door, judgments about self-care do not get in the way of treatment and, in fact, are not a part of the dialogue and culture of this clinic. This cuts down on feelings of guilt which trauma survivors so commonly battle.

This clinic asks little of patients. They don't have to fill out forms or questionnaires every time they visit. They don't have to share an awkward amount of personal information. I think this cuts down on self-care guilt.

For clients with trauma histories, acupuncture provides: relaxation, relaxation while with other people, and access without expectation. It seems to heal the nervous system although I am not sure how. What I see with clients is not that all of their symptoms go away, but they are able to handle things in their lives better. They are able to pause; their viewpoint becomes larger. They are triggered less often and have less anxiety. Being in an environment where you are not alienated or seen as different allows peoples' hyper-vigilance to relax. There is a major component of isolation when it comes to trauma. Community Acupuncture has the potential to heal that part of trauma.

Access to community acupuncture is important from a trauma informed perspective because it offers restoration of dignity. By being welcomed and given unlimited access the message becomes "you know yourself...you know what you need...and the community is here to support you in that effort". This is an important message for someone who is feeling overwhelmed and alienated in society –especially feeling that way when trying to get medical treatment.

People are also getting pain management needs met. For survivors of trauma there is often a long history of being labeled as having psychosomatic symptoms, being hysterical, being drug seeking, or having interpersonal deficits which re-traumatizes people, makes people hopeless, which then increases symptoms of pain. I think of my own situation in which I was told my 3 years of chronic pain was a "stress response" without any direction given, the main message being, "you need to manage your stress better". In general, the message in conventional biomedicine is you are doing something wrong which is causing your poor health/pain and if you would just do "x-y-z" then you would be better/get better/be a better person.

51.

WCA wasn't a perfect fit for every WP client, of course, because people are individuals. In general, though, it was impossible to ignore that the community acupuncture model appeared to have been designed to meet the needs of the most vulnerable users of the healthcare system. We realized that we could explain everything about the community acupuncture model by referencing the WP clients. Why did WCA look more like a living room and less like a hospital? Because that was perfect for partnering with a hot spotting program that was trying to keep people out of hospitals, and for treating WP clients who tended to have difficult experiences with the conventional biomedical system. Why didn't we give lifestyle advice or counsel people on their diets? Because WP clients were usually struggling to meet basic needs already, and they didn't need somebody with a lot more privilege telling them how to eat. Why did we take a nonverbal approach to delivering acupuncture? Because that made it easier for the WP clients to use our services.

In short, we did things the way we did them because that's what worked best for the WP clients. Liberation Psychology had a term for that: *the preferential option for the poor.*

Liberation Psychology, and all other liberation studies, come out of Liberation Theology, which is a universe in its own right and beyond the scope of this book. In Liberation Theology, the preferential option for the poor means that God loves everyone, but God really loves poor and vulnerable people. Just ask Jesus and the prophets. Dr. Paul Farmer, one of the founders of the global health organization Partners in Health, wrote an essay, "How Liberation Theology Can Inform Public Health", about applying the key concepts of Liberation Theology to medicine: *Any serious examination of epidemic disease has always shown that microbes also make a preferential option for the poor.* The people at the bottom of the socioeconomic ladder suffer the most from disease; therefore, why not design the whole system for them?

If our school was a Liberation Acupuncture school (the first of its kind), then we had an unshakable answer to the question, who does acupuncture belong to?

It belongs to the poor and the vulnerable. Laws may have been written to reflect otherwise, but that doesn't change our school's obligation to practice a preferential option for the poor. It might be deeply inconvenient for us, but it's consistent and true.

My personal hexagram 14 finally made perfect sense. The idea that brokenness holds the center and leads was ultimately a reflection of the preferential option for the poor and the role of the WP clients in demonstrating the principles of Liberation Acupuncture. We couldn't have Liberation Acupuncture without the WP clients, because, as Ignacio Martín-Baró wrote:

True practice has primacy over true theory, orthopraxis over orthodoxy. Actions are more important than affirmations in liberation theology, and what one does is more expressive of faith than what one says.

Liberation studies don't work only at the theoretical level; they have to work in real life.

We gave the WP clients a lot of acupuncture treatments, but they gave us something more important: a rock-solid basis of integrity in demonstrating and articulating the preferential option for the poor.

52.

This gets us to one of the acutely messy and unfinished aspects of the community acupuncture movement: its relationship with public health and publicly funded acupuncture treatments. It used to be so nice and neat, back when I was thoroughly done with public health and when I thought bootstrapping was the solution to everything; and damn it, I was so good at that part! The preferential option for the poor is inconvenient for me and my entrepreneurial satisfaction.

That's the thing about hot-spotting programs, though: they'll give you a crash course in the social determinants of health. Recently, the insurance company that manages the Wellbeing Program partnered with other organizations to invest in creating affordable housing. I thought this was a great idea. One of my favorite WP clients got excellent results with acupuncture for pain management, until she was evicted from her apartment. Warm, upbeat and funny, she still managed to come in for treatments while she was staying in a homeless shelter – that is, until she had a heart attack. It's difficult to have an ongoing relationship with someone like that and maintain your enthusiasm for bootstrapping. Some problems require big, structural solutions and bootstraps aren't much good to people who are managing both chronic illness and poverty.

I remembered how I had tried to get some of my working-class patients to come see me downtown at the drug treatment program, and how they wouldn't do it. It turned out that I'd had the arrangement backward: it worked better to create a space for working-class patients and then invite underclass patients in. Other WP caseworkers besides Jenny made a point of telling me how much their clients appreciated being treated with dignity at WCA, how they never felt like they were on the receiving end of charity, how much it meant to them to just be part of a welcoming community. On our side, some WP patients were our most committed regulars; and in a community acupuncture clinic, being a regular implies a contribution to the clinic above and beyond paying a fee for treatment. Regulars help maintain the community itself, by their presence and their commitment to treatment. Regulars are what makes a punk's job possible: if we only treated acupuncture tourists, we'd eventually lose our own faith in acupuncture because we wouldn't get to see clinical results.

In capitalism, working class people and underclass people are pitted against each other (at least in my experience). Working class pride is so much about the ability to work: self-sufficiency, not taking handouts from anybody, not giving in to illness or pain. Working-class people live in fear of becoming underclass people. I was acting out that tension when I initially wanted nothing to do with patients who couldn't afford even modest fees for treatment. WCA's relationship with the WP clients is a way of creating anti-capitalist headspace: a place where that tension between classes can unwind and allow us to be human together.

And also, life's just messy and the line dividing people who can afford $15 for an acupuncture treatment from people who can't is pretty arbitrary. Fifteen years ago, I would have disagreed; I hadn't yet met enough people on both sides of the line. WCA evolved to the point that insisting we couldn't treat patients who couldn't afford the bottom end of the sliding scale would diminish the community that we'd worked so hard to build. Some of these people we could treat for free, but if we wanted to treat a lot of them, we would have to partner with organizations who served people who had no disposable income whatsoever. We'd have to find a way to accept some kind of third party funding without undermining our grassroots, cooperative, self-sustaining model.

Stay tuned for updates. I'll let you know when we figure that one out.

53.

One of the highest priorities for POCA's school was that its graduates not be so burdened with debt from their acupuncture education that they couldn't afford to work in, or start up, a POCA clinic after graduation. We estimated that the entire program shouldn't cost more than $25,000. Then we wrote it into our official goals and objectives.

I wanted something more for the school, though. The big thing about the community acupuncture model, for me, was that it allowed me to treat people like myself; like my family; to organize my work life as if they mattered. I wanted to do the same with the school: to train students from working class and poor communities to go back and serve people like themselves. That felt like the ultimate demonstration that people like us were worth taking care of.

It also addressed a practical problem: a lot of people who had gone to acupuncture schools that promised them they'd be making $100K right after they graduated didn't want to work in POCA clinics. They thought it was beneath them. Twenty years into my career, I continued to feel lucky to be making about $20 an hour and having regular work. It occurred to me that for POCA's survival, we needed to recruit people who would feel the same way, and we'd find them in places where people thought $20 an hour for work that wasn't backbreaking or dangerous was really pretty good.

The good news is: I got what I wanted. Here's an excerpt from a paper written by a POCA Tech student:

Sometimes, the incredible amount of economic inequality that exists fills me with a terrifying amount of rage, but then I have to remind myself to be patient. With patience, I will soon have the means to channel my anger through the most beautiful way I can imagine. And to me, it's a big part of my education. I'm learning how to use this rage constructively but it's taking some time and effort. As I sit across from someone in clinic who is asking for help, I must be as calm and as present as possible in order to be helpful. If I'm agitated, as I learned right-away, my needles will hurt; if I'm calm and present, the treatment benefits. This is how the patient is unknowingly (or knowingly) helping me and this is how, to me, acupuncture can change the world, through a feedback loop of stress-relief and kindness. The community acupuncture treatment/room seems to enforce and reinforce the Golden Rule. To me, the implications of this are profound.

As we are learning, maintaining the framework necessary for this ripple effect of "do unto others" to happen is proving challenging and I admire everyone who helped start it and everyone who has helped keep it going so much. I have to remind myself not to give up. Studying acupuncture through the framework of liberation ideology is helping a lot, but it also helps to recognize my own oppression—not to feel sorry for myself, but to recognize it. I have a lot of privilege, but I'm still part of the greater oppressed class. Because how can I be in solidarity with the oppressed, if I do not recognize that I am also oppressed? I have it better than almost everyone on Earth, but there it is . . . oppression. Getting acupuncture helps immensely with this feeling of helplessness. I get on the bus after a treatment and feel like a different person than the same one who got on the same bus 2 hours ago. I see a frustrated person take their seat and it's hard for me to remember that I resembled that person 2-3 hours ago. Getting over that anger and using it constructively, to me, is the key to fighting oppression. My energy cannot be turned inwards. It must be used constructively. This has quite possibly been the greatest gift that POCA Tech has given me, a vehicle through which to channel both my anger and my good intentions. Anger with nowhere to go is wasted and good intentions are meaningless without action.

For me, attending POCA Tech has been hard, harder than any other school I've attended, not just because it's a new school going through growing pains, but because I have learned a whole new way of looking at the world and have been given the task of applying this knowledge practically in the real world while grappling emotionally and intellectually with identity, politics, economic violence, etc. I'm more stressed than I've ever been, but I am so happy others have made this school possible— through fundraising, filing incredibly boring paperwork, etc. I am eternally grateful for that. I am struggling now; I'm trying to embrace it. I hope to be a great punk someday because of it.

54.

This seems like a good place to take a quick detour from the narrative and talk about punking as a job.

Did I mention that the term itself was controversial? One day in 2013 I logged into my email and found one from an acupuncturist that started, "Hello you Acu-Idiots – I'm reporting you to the boards of CA, FL, NY, NCCAOM etc. for unprofessional conduct."

The email went on to scold POCA for publicly and privately aligning ourselves with the word "acupunk", which in the writer's opinion demonstrated poor judgment in our professional activities as acupuncturists. By calling ourselves punks, he claimed, we promote actions that undermine the value of acupuncture, with potentially damaging consequence in the public's mind; we devalue the meaning and true joy, beauty and light of acupuncture. By destroying acupuncture, we are bringing it down to our own level of marginal skill. We have lost the soul and spirit of acupuncture and are threatening to bring our own darkness to it.

OK then.

Public kerfuffles like that tend to obscure the reality that punking is a complex, subtle, demanding job, and we only realized how demanding when we got the opportunity to train our own punks. As the article about trauma informed care suggests (Appendix E), a punk uses a set of refined, nonverbal communication techniques to reach across barriers that can include language, class, and PTSD in its myriad forms. Those techniques have to merge fairly seamlessly with the punk's clinical strategies; this requires having command of a range of acupuncture treatment approaches so that the punk can choose one that fits the patient sitting in front of them. Maybe you love using acupuncture points on the head, but your patient is wearing a hijab; a good punk can come up with alternatives without missing a beat. A punk is able to think about acupuncture pragmatically: not how they wish acupuncture worked, but how it actually does. One of a punk's most important functions is to act as a guide for patients in how to use a community acupuncture clinic on their own terms, to meet their own needs and goals. This requires good communication, realistic expectations of both the acupuncture and the patient, attentiveness and empathy.

I wouldn't call that constellation of abilities *marginal skill.*

And since any given punking shift is ultimately a series of encounters with pain, punking is also a searingly personal occupation. Unlike some other jobs, you can't hold it at arm's length. It'll hurt. If you do it right, it will also heal you.

Finally, punking requires attracting and maintaining a patient base that's large and consistent enough to provide a living wage. The metaphor I like best is that a punk is the nucleus at the center of a little electron cloud of patients. The punk has to be able to connect with enough people to stay busy, and connection isn't something you can fake; it demands energy, attention, and a steadiness of purpose. The connections have to be genuine, or the bonds dissolve and so does the punk's job.

Recently in a POCA Tech class, I tried to describe how a patient base comes together for a punk who starts a new POCA clinic. Back in 2003, when Dev told me that affordable acupuncture clinics don't grow because there's no market, he wasn't wrong. If you open a clinic and expect to make a patient base just out of people who are looking for affordable acupuncture, you won't be open long.

Those people are out there, and they'll find you early on, but they won't necessarily become your regulars or help your clinic become a local institution. Marketing can bring those people in, but only connection will keep them, and lots of people who already know they want acupuncture aren't going to be open to connection with a punk. They're just passing through your electron cloud on their way somewhere else.

The most important people in building a patient base are the ones like Betty: they don't know they want acupuncture, but they know they're in pain and they need something – and they know *you*. If you happened to be a feng shui practitioner who treated arthritis by painting their kitchen walls blue, they'd probably let you. Since you're an acupuncturist, they'll try acupuncture. Enough of them will get results that they'll begin to tell their friends and relatives, or even bring them in. Their friends and relatives will tell their friends and relatives; eventually somebody will tell their doctor that there's this shabby little clinic down the street that totally cured their intractable headaches, and when the doctor learns your price range, they'll start sending you referrals (but don't expect them to ever call you or want to talk about cases, the way some acupuncture schools tell you they will; they're too busy). If you're lucky, and you will be, somewhere in this crowd of people beginning to gather around you will be one or two people like Donzel: charismatic connectors who will lend you their own social capital out of sheer goodwill.

This process requires a lot of putting yourself out there, a lot of openness and being your authentic self, regardless of people's responses, which will be all over the map. Some people will all but knock you over with their love and gratitude. Some people will grumble about trivial details but become unshakably loyal regulars. Some people will disapprove of you. And a whole lot of people will be indifferent, or think what you're trying to do is silly. One of the hardest parts about being a punk is remaining true to yourself, trusting that if you do, you'll find the people you're supposed to connect with. There's an entire little community of people who need you – yes, you, not anybody else – to give them acupuncture, and if you can keep putting yourself out there, you'll find them.

55.

POCA Tech turned out to be a challenging exercise in cross-class collaboration. Not everybody was working class, just like not everybody who gets treated at a community acupuncture clinic or owns one is working class. Cross-class collaborations are important if you want to build anything that demands more than working-class resources, which both the school and the co-op did. But that also set us up for some culture clashes. Two years into the school, exasperated, I wrote this to the students:

According to classism.org: "Straddler" generally refers to the experience of people who were raised in poverty or working-class backgrounds, but over their lifetimes move into the middle or owning classes. They have the experience of "straddling" two class identities.

I'm a straddler. This means that the organizations I founded, WCA and POCA Tech, are shaped by a complicated class identity.

Here's an example of what straddling is like: I attended a fancy college because I was a smart kid and got scholarships. (I had no idea how hard this experience would be, but that's another story.) Almost all my friends there were in the same boat. During my junior year, while our wealthy peers were doing junior year abroad, some of us scholarship kids decided to create our own version: we'd live off campus. This meant we needed a car.

It wasn't a big deal for me to get a car. There were any number of them, in various states of disrepair, parked on the grass in my family's front yard. These cars circulated in and out of use, based on which one my father could coax into running for awhile (or could persuade one of his friends to try to fix, in exchange for a six pack of beer). I got one of those cars, a hulking, wheezing, decommissioned Checker cab built before I was born, and I drove it to college.

A month or so later, the Checker (of course) broke down. My friend Katie was dating a guy named George who said he knew about cars, who offered to take a look. I warned him that it was probably held together with duct tape, like other things my family owned. I warned him that it had last been worked on by a guy known only as Danny the Thief. George was about six foot seven; it took him a while to maneuver his lanky frame under the Checker. When he finally slid back out, his eyes were bright with wonder. Lisa, he said, this car is held together with–

Duct tape, I said irritably. I know.

Yes! But also – rubber bands. And bubble gum.

I don't remember the details of what George did next, or how the Checker got running again, but somehow it did, and the knowledge of its inner workings didn't deter my friends from getting rides from me.

One of the things about being a straddler that has slowly dawned on me over the years is that there's often a big difference between how people approach new projects based on whether or not they have abundant resources. People who are used to having resources often won't start something new unless they feel they can do it "right". Also, they may conceal their anxiety about doing things right – in the form of judgements about other people and their standards. Whereas people who don't have resources don't have the luxury of doing things "right". If people are used to not having resources, they assume they'll just have to do what they need to do, using whatever they've got, no matter how apparently inadequate; they also experience anxiety, but they have less ability to conceal it, and it generally doesn't come out in the form of judgement about other people. You can see this particular dynamic at play in debates about child rearing, and especially judgements about who "should" have children versus who *does*.

In my professional life, I've often been accused of "lowering the bar" or having no standards. It's taken me awhile to realize that, while it might be good for me to have more positive expectations of the world, I'm never going to be able to reflexively "have standards" in the way that middle-class people do. At a deep level, it's just never going to dawn on me that I shouldn't use rubber bands and bubble gum to hold things together, that I should wait to build something until I have better materials – because I know too well I'll be waiting forever. I come from a long line of scavengers, scroungers, and people who make do.

For perspective, I've been reading Nancy Isenberg's book *White Trash: the 400 Year Untold History of Class in America*. She writes:

First known as "waste people" and later "white trash", marginalized Americans were stigmatized for their inability to be productive... Throughout its history, the United States has always had a class system. After settlement, colonial outposts exploited their unfree laborers (indentured servants, slaves, and children) and saw such expendable classes as human waste. The poor, the waste, did not disappear, and by the early 18th century they were seen as a permanent breed. This way of classifying human failure took hold in the United States. Every era in the continent's vaunted developmental story had its own taxonomy of waste people – unwanted and unsalvageable.[48]

I'm confident that there are two reasons why WCA was the first clinic to try to provide acupuncture to large numbers of people using an economic model based on $15 increments. The first reason is that most people would have calculated – correctly – that $15 increments would not provide the resources to do such a project *right* by good middle-class standards. And the second reason is that the people that WCA most wants to serve are not recognized by society as worth taking care of. Same goes for POCA Tech: no one else has done this because they couldn't *do it right* with the tuition that we charge, and also, no one else really believes our target demographic is worth serving. This may sound harsh to you – but if it isn't true, why are we the first of our kind? So many elements of our model make so much sense, why wouldn't someone else have already done it?

If you get involved with WCA, or with POCA Tech, part of what you need to prepare for is a vicarious, possibly immersive, experience of white trash consciousness. This is one of the main reasons we don't advertise or try to "sell" people on either organization. Some people will find dropping down to our level liberating; others will be profoundly disappointed, even disgusted.

A big problem we have is when people mistake us for idealists or humanitarians. The next step after that misidentification is what I think of is, "You're so good – why can't you be better?" People have demanded, in all seriousness, why I can't be more like Gandhi, or Mother Theresa. The assumption is that I/we should be trying harder to live up to certain standards. This keeps happening and the point that always gets missed is: the basic thing we're trying to do, which is to provide acupuncture to marginalized people on their own terms, in a capitalist society, *is already really hard.*

* * *

It's so hard that nobody else is even trying to do it at this scale.

It would probably be good if more people thought of WCA and POCA Tech not as ends in and of themselves, but as *vehicles*. That's how I think of them. They're not utopian dreams, they're not social justice paradises, they're not going to end up on the list of best places to work because, for one thing, we can't afford to offer health insurance. (Seriously, we can't; the math just doesn't work.) WCA is a vehicle to provide acupuncture to as many people as possible who otherwise couldn't afford it. POCA Tech is a vehicle for getting people who don't have a lot of money to be able to legally practice acupuncture, without burdening them with huge student loan debt. These organizations are all about getting from point A to point B, using the very limited resources that we have.

It would be even better if people thought of WCA and POCA Tech as beat-up cars held together with rubber bands and bubblegum and goodwill, driven on a rough road that is stretching all of those things, all the time. Driven by riffraff who are often tired and cranky. *If you can get a "better" ride, you should.* In fact, please do. We don't want you in these cars if they're too disappointing for you. They're all we've got and believe it or not, we worked really hard on them. We took huge personal risks to get them on the road and we keep taking risks to keep them moving.

The problem of course is that the people with more resources, nice people who drive nice cars, are not offering rides on this particular stretch of road. There is currently no other acupuncture school that offers tuition this low, and no other clinic that is trying to provide jobs for this many acupuncturists. You may feel that if we can't do these things better, we shouldn't be trying to do them at all. That's certainly your prerogative, but if you feel that way, please *get out of our car*. You are, of course, free to wait for somebody more respectable to come along and pick you up.

All of the acupuncturists who work in their various roles at WCA and POCA Tech would make more money if they took the community acupuncture formula (which we made freely available) and set up their own little clinic. The crucial element is to reduce overhead and to make no effort to create jobs or infrastructure for anybody but yourself. All of us are here because we find this work more satisfying; however, we're not saints and negative feedback has the potential to wear us down.

One of our faculty members said recently:
I have never met a student who didn't have some complaints about the school they went to and when I was in school there was lots of stuff that I wished was different and it makes sense. Any type of institution is the way it is and it's impossible to cater to the way each individual would set up the school. So we do our best to make the program work in the best way possible for our vision and mission but unfortunately someone is going to have a problem with one thing that works really well for someone else and so on and so forth. That's just the nature of organization and groups.

I agree with that absolutely and also, I think it's important to remember that being at POCA Tech and/or WCA requires us to focus on the positive to a degree that, to some people, is going to be simply unacceptable. Are we still moving down the road? Are the rubber bands still holding? Well, that's fantastic; good job, everyone.

If you want more from us, you're going to have to step up and help make it happen.

56.

This gets us right back to why I wrote this book: we're trying to train people to use the community acupuncture model, which by definition makes them social entrepreneurs. We've figured out all kinds of strategies for teaching what we call punk skills – good needling technique, empathetic rapport-building practices, everything that goes into providing acupuncture efficiently and in a trauma-informed way – but we're struggling to teach social entrepreneurship.

How do you train people to bring their whole selves into the void?

There's no formula. Working in a community acupuncture clinic will teach you both how much we have in common with each other and how fantastically diverse we are as individuals. Nobody does their healing exactly the same way as anybody else; as a punk, it's endlessly interesting to watch your patients work out their own versions. Similarly, nobody's going to approach the void in exactly the same way as anybody else; how you bring yourself into it will depend in part on the unique shape of yourself. The goal for this book was not to provide a formula, just one example.

That said, you train people to work with the void in part by letting them practice: by letting them – in school – encounter situations where not everything is provided for them, where not everything is spelled out, where they have to manage uncertainty and precarity and make what they need out of nothing. Where they have to self-organize. Fortunately, since our school is held together with rubber bands and bubblegum, there have been plenty of natural opportunities. Unfortunately, some of the students hate that.

I've had several interactions where I wanted to say: you don't understand how close all of community acupuncture is to *nothing at all*. If I had demanded what you're demanding – security and guarantees and affirmation and, basically, not having to risk everything (repeatedly) – we wouldn't be having this conversation because there wouldn't be *anything* here. No model, no co-op, no school. That's concerning, because I'm trying to teach you to do what I do. You won't have to do all of what I did, but the fractal being what it is, you're going to have to do a lot of it. You're going to have to put yourself on the line, in the face of disapproval and dismissal and plain old indifference. Right now you're benefiting from the risks that other people took; don't confuse that with not having to take any risks yourself.

At this point it's clear to me that community acupuncture is about three things: self-organizing in difficult circumstances; solidarity; and suffering. It's about holes. The people who should become community acupuncturists are the ones who need to: either they need to do something useful with their own pain, or they're driven by an empathy so deep it's like pain. It also helps to have had some experience with a brutal capitalist job, either high-paying or low-paying, where you felt like you had to fight to preserve your humanity, so that a modestly-paid punking job, where you can count on feeling better and more human at the end of your shift than you did at the beginning, is something you can appreciate.

And it helps to love prefigurative intervention.

This means recognizing that the world we want to live in is not the one we have. Nobody's just going to give us the one we want, and we don't have the resources to overhaul the whole thing. With effort, though, we can find overlooked spaces, holes in the walls of capitalism – like providing acupuncture to ordinary people at prices they can afford– and by means of cooperation and creativity, we can enact in those spaces the world we want to live in.

That's completely different from looking for a niche to exploit. You don't take anything out of prefigurative interventions; the point is, you get to put yourself in. The point of building infrastructure for community acupuncture – making jobs, making a co-op, making a school – even though capitalism doesn't reward any of that, is that creating infrastructure is a concrete and lasting way of building the world we want to live in. Building infrastructure is a way of saying, ordinary people should be able to get acupuncture on their own terms; not just when an individual acupuncturist decides they want to lower their rates for whatever reason for a few people, but because *acupuncture for ordinary people is part of the world*. It has structures to support it; it won't go away when an individual acupuncturist changes their mind.

Prefigurative intervention, in my experience, is very different from utopian longing. Prefigurative intervention for me isn't about trying to achieve something perfect, it's about building the world I want to live in out of the resources I have – which given who I am, are scraps. It's going to be partial and imperfect; that doesn't stop it from also being a triumph. Partial and imperfect is a long, long way from nothing at all, which is what I had when I started. Infrastructure that demonstrates people like me are worth taking care of is a long, long way from infrastructure that demonstrates that we're not. The latter is all I could see 15 years ago, when I looked around the acupuncture profession. Prefigurative intervention and world-building are active; utopian longing is passive – and under certain circumstances, passive-aggressive.

Like acupuncture points, I think spaces of prefigurative intervention can be containers for an experience of healing.

Not for perfection. The healing that happens in community acupuncture clinics isn't about making people's bodies or minds perfect; it's usually just about incremental relief. And hope. Finding space for hope is worth a lot, to people like me.

Chorus: Epilogue

Well, that was an interesting story but it's a pretty disappointing account of entrepreneurship. A lot of entrepreneurs, especially ones in alternative medicine, recognize that people *create their own reality*. What's the matter with you --why didn't you create a better reality for yourself, where you could make a lot of money?

I'm so glad you brought that up.

From my perspective, this case study *is* about creating reality. For a while, community acupuncture was like my imaginary friend; it was real to me but almost nobody else could see it. One of the main ways my life is different today than it was 15 years ago, is that everybody agrees community acupuncture is real. They might argue about the details, but not about its existence. For example: on May 13, 2015, Self Magazine tweeted to its 477,000 followers: Hold up. Group acupuncture is a THING? with a link to an article about POCA.[49] I was amused; if Self says it's a thing, I guess it's a thing.

But hold on, capitalists, I know what you're thinking: that tweet changed everything, right? That kind of mainstream exposure and validation? No, it totally didn't. An army of spandex-clad women did not swarm POCA clinics, forever altering our demographics and our profitability. Being discovered isn't the same thing as creating reality. Also, being discovered only seems to happen incrementally for POCA anyway.

Eknath Easwaran in his own way was an advocate of creating reality. He recommended that all his students read Somerset

Maugham's novel *The Razor's Edge*, not just because its title
quotes the Katha Upanishad but because its thesis is that
people tend to get what they want. Easwaran believed that
passage meditation could slowly change what people want,
down at the unconscious level; as a result, they could create
lives that reflected the virtues in the passages.

*All that we are is the result of what we have thought: we are
formed and molded by our thoughts. Those whose minds
are shaped by selfless thoughts give joy whenever they
speak or act. Joy follows them like a shadow that never
leaves them.*[50]

So I'm familiar with the concept of creating reality, and I try
to do it consciously. I'd even say I'm a fan: in my experience,
it's been healing, liberating, and most of all, fun.

However, like any big creative project it involved hard work
and hard choices. I've heard a lot of alternative medicine
types talk about creating reality, but I haven't heard anybody
address my experience in that regard. So here goes.

Having a meditation practice helped me enormously with
integrating the parts of my personal history that I'd
repressed. Part of what it did for me was to give me the
capacity to witness the way that child abuse had shaped my
thinking and my life, which in turn allowed me to work on
reshaping them. I haven't heard a lot of acknowledgement
that it takes a tremendous amount of effort to rewire your
brain; not to mention, it's painful. You have to figure out,
and then practice, how to put energy into self-love instead of
self-destruction. And self-destruction is easier, because it not
only feels like what you deserve, it feels true and real and
solid while self-love seems – I hate to say it – kind of iffy.
You have to decide, over and over, not to prove to yourself
that the world sucks by creating circumstances that confirm

it.

I have a lot of relative privilege, and I still have to work at pulling myself out of the groove of self-hatred. I still have to work at wanting good things; unfortunately, things that suck still hold the appeal of familiarity. It's gotten easier, but I don't know that I'll ever be able to take it for granted. I think about the people I met through the WP program, who have to pay attention to a lot of survival-level details, the type you can't ignore when you're living with chronic illness and poverty (not to mention kinds of structural violence I don't have to deal with, like racism and disablism), and I wonder what it would be like to tackle all of that in addition to making the effort to rewire your thinking.

In short, capitalists: *easy for you to say.* Creating your own reality isn't like waving a magic wand; it's incremental and demands resources of time, energy, and support. I like to think that the reality I created not only helps me remember that I deserve good things, it helps people like the WP clients do the same. We all need all the support we can get.

The hard choices were mostly about who I was going to serve with the thing I'd created. I might create my own reality, but it's not like I can create a classless society (if I could, I think I'd also throw in world peace). A core part of making a better reality for myself was being able to have relationships with marginalized people. When it came down to it, those relationships were worth more to me than money.

It would've been much more convenient if my social entrepreneurship had been the variety where I did good and made a profit (reinvested of course) as well as an acceptable upper middle class professional salary. It's inconvenient that I chose to forego the profit and the professional salary in order to treat a lot of people who couldn't afford the low end of the sliding scale; it's inconvenient that I prioritized building infrastructure over things like having health insurance.

I suppose I made a lot of irresponsible white trash choices. As they say, you can take the girl out of South Baltimore, but you can't take South Baltimore out of the girl.

But I confess, not only am I not sorry about that, it was exhilarating to do social entrepreneurship on my own low-class terms. But wow, people get really mad about that. I've been accused of being a victim and a martyr, which is surprising because I think it's clear that as an adult I've done pretty much what I wanted. All this infrastructure that didn't pay me to make it, that included all these low-class people, this *is* what I wanted. I guess that's hard to understand?

I wrote this book not only as a textbook for POCA Tech students, but also as an invitation to anyone who, having read my confession, might want to join me.

Community acupuncture always needs help. The POCA Co-op needs members; POCA Tech needs students who want to serve the co-op as punks. The infrastructure needs resources of time, energy, and support. Maybe you and your talents belong in this particular prefigurative intervention, too.

Alongside the preferential option for the poor, another important concept in liberation studies is accompaniment. In our culture, physical and mental suffering marginalize people; I spent 2 decades as an acupuncturist watching chronic pain push people to the edges of society. I don't think I can overstate how meaningful and powerful it's been for me to reverse that in my own life and work. The point of Liberation Acupuncture is to create community that includes suffering people.

* * *

As it turned out, my entrepreneurship made it possible for me to practice accompaniment. Maybe I could have created a reality in which I made more money, but this reality – where I have the opportunity to accompany and to be accompanied – this is where I want to live.

Acknowledgments

I've been trying to write this book, off and on, for the last 5 years or so. It finally made it into completed and legible form thanks to the assistance of the following people:

Lisa Baird, poet and punk. I'm very grateful to her, not just for editing, but for the encouragement to prioritize writing and take it seriously (which is the only way it gets done, apparently) as well as for ongoing support, cheerleading, and role-modeling.

Other early readers and commenters, including Melissa Tiernan, Cris Monteiro, James Shelton, Kate Kampmann, Sarah Allen, Cera Mae Evans, Cortney Hartman, Amy Vance, Jade Fang, Tatyana Ryevzina, David Lesseps, Ellen Vincent and Josh Whiteley. Thank you, especially to those of you who read it as a serial and encouraged me to keep going.

James Shelton and Kate Kampmann for the beautiful cover art.

Gail Roudebush for patient editing, formatting, and scaling the treacherous heights of eBook publication with me.

Wade Phillips for general IT genius and especially, remembering where the ISBNs were.

Tyler Phan and Andrew Zitcer for amazing conversations.

the students of POCA Tech, for providing motivation (in all sorts of ways).

and S., for pretty much everything.

Appendices

Appendix A

love your microbusiness:

marketing for a community-based acupuncture
practice
the working class acupuncture e-book, 2006
(a little red book in disguise)

contents

love your microbusiness

Most acupuncturists are self-employed, sole
proprietors running a microbusiness. Not a
small business, a microbusiness. Definitions
vary, but usually the legal definition of a
small business is one that has under 100
employees. I've never met an acupuncturist
with 95 employees, have you? A common
definition of a microbusiness is a business
with average annual gross receipts of
$2,500,000 or less over the past three
years. Makes a microbusiness sound pretty
good, doesn't it!
Many acupuncturists are intimidated by the

business end of practice, and indeed by the idea of business itself. Remembering that for most of us, the goal is to create a successful microbusiness can make it less intimidating. For even more perspective and inspiration, it's helpful to read about microbusinesses worldwide. An excellent introduction is the book Banker to the Poor: Micro-lending and the Battle Against World Poverty, by Muhammad Yunus, which describes the birth of the enormously powerful global micro-lending movement. All over Bangladesh and Southeast Asia, people are lifting themselves out of the most grinding deprivation by creating and running microbusinesses. If they can do it there, surely we can do it here.

Being successful in business does not look only like Donald Trump or Martha Stewart on "The Apprentice". Being successful in business also looks like a Third World woman raising goats and selling goats' milk so that her children can afford to go to school. Being a successful acupuncturist doesn't mean you have to dress up in a suit, drive a big car or engage in conspicuous consumption. Part of our culture's problem is that our images of success are so limited and so distorted. The rewards of creating a successful microbusiness are not only financial. Making your living by working for yourself can have a profound impact on your self-esteem. Business success means not only economic self-sufficiency but dignity, empowerment, integrity and creativity.

This e-book consists of marketing

suggestions that have worked for an acupuncturist (me) who consistently sees around 70 patients a week. I consider myself successful, and I haven't sold my soul to do it. You don't have to sell yours either. Creating a successful acupuncture practice has been one of the best things I ever did for myself, and I wish the same success for everyone who reads this book.
Good luck!

know who you are
Be able to answer the following questions:
• What communities do I belong to?
• What communities do I resonate with?
• What kind of people do I like to be around?
• The answers to these questions will describe your
ideal patient base.
For example, if I respond to those questions, here are the answers I get: I'm a white female acupuncturist, age 37, from a working class background, living in a working class neighborhood, a stepmother of three terrific teenagers, a serious meditator, an avid reader, a lousy knitter, a recovering Catholic who thinks a lot about social justice and social entrepreneurship, and backyard chicken-keeper.
Communities I belong to: my neighborhood, working class people, Gen-Xers, parents, meditators, bookworms, knitters, ex-Catholics, activists, social entrepreneurs, self-employed people, acupuncturists, and

urban chicken aficionados.

Communities I resonate with or empathize
with, but don't belong to: single mothers,
caregivers of people with serious illnesses,
artists and bicyclists.

I like being around creative people,
stubborn people, feisty people, people who
persevere through obstacles, people who are
down to earth, people who pray, people who
care a lot about their families, people who
put energy into their communities, people
from ethnic and cultural backgrounds
different from mine, people who are direct
and who say what they think. I don't like to
be around pretentious people, people who
whine, or people who worry a lot about avian
flu.

My patient base, not surprisingly, consists
primarily of working class people as well as
a few college professors, successful
entrepreneurs, and other acupuncturists.
Although Portland is a very white town, my
practice is more ethnically diverse than
many acupuncture practices. I attract a lot
of artists, parents, and activists of all
varieties.

The point is that it's easy to treat who you
are and who you empathize with. The easiest
kind of marketing is to identify target
communities that fit those categories, and
then focus on those communities. You will
know how to communicate to these people; you
will understand their language. Their
communities are places you either already
spend time and know people, or you would
enjoy doing so.

It's much, much harder to market yourself to
people you can't relate to - and harder
still to have a good connection with them as
a practitioner.

know what you like

What kind of acupuncture do you like to do?
Resolve to do that and only that. Having fun
doing acupuncture is not optional or
frivolous, it's absolutely vital.
For instance, I like simplicity. I enjoy
doing a very simple kind of Japanese pulse
diagnosis which results in very simple,
streamlined treatments. If I had to
practice, say, NAET, with all those little
bottles, not only would I do a terrible job
at it but I would also want to shoot myself
in the head. I also don't like billing
insurance - or, God forbid, tailoring my
treatments to what I think insurance will
cover.
Don't ever give up what you like to do
because you think a patient wants something
different. Patients who want something else
can find it somewhere else; there are plenty
of acupuncturists, and plenty of patients,
for everybody. It can be hard to promote
yourself (more on that later); it is
virtually impossible to promote yourself
unless your enthusiasm for what you are
doing is real and contagious.
Nothing is better for your business than you
having fun. I know that a lot of my patients
come to me not only because I can relieve
their pain but because I am always genuinely

happy to see them. This is not something you can fake. It wouldn't happen if I felt obligated to do things for them that weren't interesting to me or that I didn't enjoy. I'm sure that a few of my patients would be thrilled if I suddenly decided that I needed to do half an hour of shiatsu after every treatment. But I wouldn't be thrilled, and after not much time, the spark that currently animates my practice would go out. Over eleven years of being an L.Ac., I've had time to think about what is fun for me and what isn't in terms of treating patients. Several years ago, I decided that if I didn't want to burn out (as I have seen many colleagues do), I would have to dispense with all the parts that weren't fun. It's important to me not to burn out; acupuncture is an art form, developed over many years.

As it turned out, all the parts that weren't fun for me also happened to be unnecessary. I didn't lose any patients over the changes I made. I found LOTS of patients who liked simple treatments (note: many men fall into this category).

Most of my patients don't have insurance that covers acupuncture, and the ones who did, who really wanted to see me, figured out ways to bill it themselves.

take down the barriers
Are there barriers to your ideal patient base actually showing up in your clinic for acupuncture? What are they? Are they

geographical, psychological, cultural, financial? All the marketing efforts in the world will accomplish nothing - except to exhaust you - if you don't identify and take down these barriers. They are walls for you to bang your head against.

But before we talk about specific barriers, there's one point that has to be addressed first. No matter who you listed in your answers to the first three questions about communities, there is one barrier that will be virtually universal to all acupuncturists: *your ideal patients don't know that you're there.*

Lots of acupuncturists are by nature introverts. Nothing comes less naturally to us than standing up and shouting, "Hey! Here I am! Look at ME!!!" Unfortunately, though, this is what it takes to get the people you want to help to realize that you're available. Hanging up your shingle is probably not going to be enough. People are busy, distracted, have learned to tune out a lot just to get through their days. Even after they notice you, they will probably forget about you right away. Yes. Even you. Learn not to take this personally and do everything you can to get over your fear of rejection. Successful marketing entails getting rejected over and over! It's not fun, but it won't kill you.

In my case, if I look at my ideal patient base of working class people (plus the occasional ex-Catholic who knits lumpy little scarves for her pet chickens), I notice several obvious barriers to them coming in to get acupuncture. First, the price of acupuncture versus the amount that they are paid to do what they do for work. The minimum wage in Oregon is $7.50 an hour, and the going rate for acupuncture is $65 per treatment. As barriers go, that's a doozy.

What about insurance? Well, unfortunately, a lot of working class patients don't have any kind of health insurance, let alone the kind that covers acupuncture. Another barrier! And anyway, billing insurance doesn't fall into the category of "things I like".

Many acupuncturists have a "financial hardship" policy; if people say they can't afford it, they'll temporarily reduce their fees or even give some treatments away. What about that as a solution? Actually, if you look closely, that kind of policy is yet another barrier! I know working class people (because I am one) and I know that if I make them feel like a charity case, they will run in the other direction. If they have to ask me about a sliding scale, they won't get treated at all. In fact, a barrier that I have no control over is that many working class patients have done some research, found out what acupuncture costs, and decided that, like health insurance, it's one of the many things they'll have to do without.

While we're examining barriers, let's check out the ones related to "professionalism". In conventional terms, "professionalism" in health care means wearing a white coat, having a spiffy, sterile-looking office, and

a vaguely officious manner. Another thing I
know about working class patients is that
many of them do not have positive
associations with that particular type of
professionalism. They have been put down by
it too often, in too many contexts. A good
way to prevent them from coming to see me
would be to look and act like a conventional
professional. Which, of course, also
wouldn't exactly fit in the "things I like"
box.
Interestingly enough, our state medical
board recently wrote an article on the
characteristics necessary to professionalism
in medicine, and at the very top of their
list was, of all things, altruism. They
defined altruism as the practitioner putting
their patients' needs ahead of the
practitioner's own. So, let's see, I do feel
good about *that* definition of
professionalism, and if I apply it to the
needs of my ideal patient base, it would
actually *require* me to ditch the attitude
and the outfit which function as
psychological and cultural barriers to my
patients' access to care, and to adopt
practices which make them feel comfortable
and welcome.
Just about the only barrier I don't have to
grapple with here is geography; my clinic is
two blocks down the street from my house, in
a working class neighborhood, on two bus
lines and a bike route. Whew.
To make a long story very short, the way to
take down all these barriers - all of them
at once, actually, it was surprisingly

efficient – was to jettison the conventional
business model for acupuncture and to create
a more appropriate one, which suited the
needs of my target patients.
The barriers to your ideal patients showing
up in your office may be different from the
ones I encountered. For everyone, however, I
think it's worth looking how you define
professionalism. If "being professional"
includes even a subtle undertone of "I'm
better than you because I have a degree" you
will be putting up a psychological barrier
to someone. No patient from any community
wants to encounter condescension or coldness
when they are looking for help. Similarly, I
have seen any number of new acupuncturists
acting aloof with their patients or their
potential patients because they thought that
was how to "be professional", and that
patients wanted them to be that way. On the
contrary: patients and potential patients
love it when you are funny, enthusiastic,
and above all, warm; they want to feel that
they can connect with you. Which brings us
back to the beginning: you want to find
patients that you want to connect with.

strive to be useful
Think in terms of service. The idea of
"selling yourself" is not only scary but
vaguely nauseating to many of us, myself
included. And providing health care is not
like selling aluminum siding – or at least,
it shouldn't be! Try thinking about it this
way: there are people out there who need

what you have to offer. Your job is to find them, so that you can make their lives better. Not only is this an uplifting thought, it is absolutely true. No matter who you are, there is somebody out there who needs you, who would really benefit by coming to see you. If your practice makes you feel the opposite way, you are probably targeting the wrong people.

Spend some time consciously putting the issue of money aside (imagine that you're independently wealthy, and doing this just for fun). Concentrate on what a pleasure it is to be useful to someone. Think about how that feels. (If there's no pleasure for you in being useful to someone, you need to get out of health care immediately.) To whom do you want to be useful? How might you do that? Now go find those people. Remember that they don't know to come looking for you.

This point is actually a subset of the first one: know who you are. You belong to certain communities, and you are a resource to those communities. You are the person who can bring Chinese medicine to those people with whom you identify or empathize. They can receive it from you because you understand them. Focus on your function as a useful person, not on your fears about money. In my case, caregivers and single mothers are people I like being useful to, because they are already giving so much to others. Nurturing them feels like bringing some balance back to an imbalanced place. It's satisfying in a way that has nothing to do with getting paid.

enjoy your own marketing

Find ways to get yourself out there that you actually enjoy doing.

A new acupuncturist whom I mentored was a serious skateboarder; in fact, he went to acupuncture school primarily in order to be able to treat his own knees so that he could continue skating. Although he was intimidated by marketing his acupuncture practice, with some encouragement he willingly designed a flier, "Acupuncture for Skateboarders" with a collage of cool images. He enjoyed making the flier; it was creative and it involved paging through lots of skating magazines. Then he took the flier and began hanging around skate parks, looking for people to talk to. It gave him an excuse to skate, a reason to go into skate shops, and an opportunity to have animated conversations with people who shared his passion. Talking about his practice to strangers was still a little scary, but the discomfort of that was offset by the pleasure of being in a community he knew he belonged to. I think of myself as an entrepreneur, and I like going into other self-employed people's businesses and having conversations about what they're doing, how they got started, what obstacles they encountered; it's very interesting to me. I like other entrepreneurs. I like talking to them about business - theirs, mine, anybody's.

Whether or not they ever come and see me for acupuncture, at the end of our conversation, I will have had a good time. I don't think of this as "networking" because that sounds like a chore, and talking to these people is fun. I don't have to force myself to go out and have these conversations, I look forward to it.

If you enjoy your own marketing, other people will too. Just as important, however, is that if you enjoy it you will DO it.

have energy for your practice

You MUST have energy to put into your practice. Where do you get it?

Meditate. Whatever this looks like for you – whether it's a formal practice like Vipassana, prayer, qi gong, or just sitting still. This is very important, because being an acupuncturist entails moving in and out of a lot of different energy fields – some of which are very imbalanced and full of pain. You need a daily practice in which you center and replenish yourself. You will have much more energy to offer to your patients. You will attract more patients because you can handle the increased volume.

Meditation creates more space in your heart for other people. Potential patients feel this and respond to this; I have seen it work for many, many practitioners. Do things that make you feel creative. Good marketing is about creativity. (So is good acupuncture.) Cultivate yours, whether it's painting, cooking, dancing, playing music,

writing, knitting, gardening, or making mud pies with your kids. This kind of play also helps replenish you so that you have something to offer your patients when they come in exhausted and discouraged.
Rest. All acupuncturists who have been in practice for any substantial amount of time know that when they are tired or overwhelmed, their practice will slow way down. It's like magic, but not the kind of magic you want. No energy = no patients.

have patience. then have some more.
Patience, patience, patience. All marketing strategies take
time to work.
Almost five months ago our clinic was on TV. I thought at the time, "Wow, I can see why people want to be on TV; it works faster than everything else" because the phone started to ring before the cameras had left the building, and indeed, we probably got twenty new patients in the next two weeks from that particular exposure. However, five months later, we are still getting calls from people who found out about us from that 3 minutes of airtime. It took them that long to make the phone call! It seems that especially with acupuncture, people tend to think about it for a while before acting. They may be waiting until they are sure that they need you. Don't evaluate the success of any particular marketing effort until at least 6 months after you've completed it. Word of mouth is by far the best

advertising: better than websites, better than being featured in the newspaper, better than going out and giving talks, better than TV, better than any form of advertising known to man. Our clinic has put itself into the spotlight in all kinds of ways (and yes, that was hard for me, because I am an introvert too) but the vast majority of our patients still show up because they know someone who came to see us and told them about us. The thing is, word of mouth takes time.

An exercise that was very useful to me was "the patient genealogy" exercise: drawing a diagram of where all my current patients came from, designed to show how the flow of referrals happened. When I was finished, what I had was not a straight line of one person refers one person who refers one person, and so on, but a repeated pattern of a wheel with a center and spokes coming out of it. Out of a practice of a more than a hundred active patients, I had only seven or eight wheels. Each hub of a wheel represented one patient, and the spokes represented all the patients that person had referred. Some of those spokes in turn became the center of their own wheels. One of the wheels had nineteen spokes: one single patient had referred (not only referred, in his case, but actually paid for) nineteen other people to come to our clinic – most of his large family, many of his friends, a few of his employees. There are certain people in any community who have a lot of influence; you usually can't tell who these people are just by looking. You recognize them by the ripples they cause. This is why the idea of communities is so important.

Communities will do your marketing for you. You just have to keep patiently putting yourself out there – in the right communities – until you encounter enough of these influential patients. And that takes some time, because they are unusual, definitely not in the majority --but that's OK, because you only need a few of them to fill up your practice!

In my experience asking for referrals doesn't work. Not because patients don't want to give them to you, but because most patients don't have the power to make the referral actually happen. A lot of my patients have said wistfully to me, "You know, I've told everyone I know to come and see you. But they just won't." The ones who do have the power to send people to you don't need to be asked. If you are useful to them, they will very naturally and probably without thinking much about it cause their family and friends to show up in your office. It's just a function of who they are.

So have patience. And as they say in the Hitchhiker's Guide to the Galaxy, don't panic. When you feel like panicking, remind yourself to have patience. Then have some more. If you have enough patience, you can't panic; they are mutually exclusive.

* * *

a note on scarcity and competition: they are not
real

But they are nasty persistent illusions, and they can make you miserable. Worse, they can distract you from doing the marketing you need to be doing! Resist them with true stories like this one:

Our clinic, Working Class Acupuncture (which uses a sliding scale for treatment that goes down much farther than people would think possible), takes up a lot of space in a huge old building in Northeast Portland. Part of that space we sublet to two other acupuncturists who have private practices separate from ours. Both of them charge market rates (meaning, two to four times more than we do). Both of them are busy. One is so busy that new patients have to wait a month to see her. (If you want to verify this, we'll give you her number, but don't expect her to call you back right away.) The reason all the acupuncturists in our building are so successful, despite the large and obvious disparity in our prices, is that we all like doing acupuncture and we are all clear on who we really want to work with.

There are plenty of patients for everybody. Scarcity and competition are not real, but diversity is. And diversity is your friend. The patients you are looking for are the ones who will feel just delighted to find you, because you are perfect for them. No one else will be perfect for them, so no one

can take your patients. And you can't take
anyone else's.
Remember also the research that showed that
restaurants that are all lined up in a row
all do better economically than restaurants
that are far away from other restaurants.
People like to have choices. Similar
principles operate with acupuncture
practices. I have four separate patients who
all also periodically see other
acupuncturists who do dramatically different
kinds of work; my patients enjoy the
contrasts. Never waste energy worrying about
competition; it takes away energy you need
in order to treat patients.

www.workingclassacupuncture.org

Appendix B

Keynote to CANference 4/18/2011

One of the things that we at WCA have observed, watching other clinics, is that 100 treatments a week is a kind of ceiling. At first, 100 treatments a week sounds like a LOT of treatments to most acupuncturists, something that it's hard to imagine doing. But almost all clinics need to break through that ceiling to be successful and sustainable. Ideally, each acupuncturist in a clinic can provide 100 treatments a week as a matter of course. I want to frame WHY breaking that ceiling is so important – what it means for individual clinics and what it means for community acupuncture in general.

Right-sizing of businesses

Seth Godin, a famous business and marketing blogger talks about right-sizing. To summarize his post, "An atomic theory of business size":

In chemistry, the periodic table of the elements defines elements by the size of their atoms: a unique number of protons and electrons. An oxygen atom always has 8 protons, and a titanium atom always has 22. That's their atomic number. You can't have an element that is part oxygen and part titanium. The elements are what they are. According to Seth Godin, businesses have an elemental size: a size where they are supposed to be, a size where they really work, where they are stable and successful and sustainable. He says: businesses that exist, exist because the marketplace allows them to function at the right size.

Seth Godin says a mom and pop business is just the right size for mom and for pop. The rent and the overhead are probably relatively low, so it's stable. A mom and pop business doesn't need its own advertising department that costs hundreds of thousands of dollars a year. If you added one of those to a mom and pop, it's out of scale, and the business isn't stable anymore.

He says the next level of business up from mom and pop feels different – different furnishings, different payroll, different everything. It's not an incremental step, it's a quantum leap.

What does all that have to do with us? There are individual implications, and there are professional implications. Let's start with the individual implications.

Finding the right size

One of the big things that keeps community acupuncturists from breaking that 100 treatments per week barrier is a problem with right-sizing. We have an image of an acupuncture practice in our minds, but that image isn't the right size. It's way out of scale. It's like our mental setting for an acupuncture practice is at hydrogen (atomic number of 1), but the elemental size for an acupuncture practice is closer to tungsten (atomic number of 74). It doesn't work at hydrogen; it works at tungsten. But, we keep picturing hydrogen. We've got our attention in the wrong place.

It's almost 9 years to the day that I gave my first "community acupuncture" treatments. 9 years ago, we started the clinic that would end up being Working Class Acupuncture. We got the keys to the space in mid-March of 2002 and started seeing patients in early April. We started using the community acupuncture business model, though of course we weren't calling it that at the time. We didn't have a name for what we were trying to do. We were flailing around, trying to figure out how to make a living doing acupuncture.

In 2002, my mental picture of an acupuncture practice was, like everybody else's that I knew, stuck on hydrogen. Stuck on 1. I didn't know tungsten was an option, because I didn't know it existed, or I didn't know it could exist for me. I'd heard stories of great acupuncturists in Asia seeing a hundred people a day, but nobody I knew did that in America. I knew I needed to see more patients than I was seeing if I wanted to support myself as an acupuncturist, but I didn't really know how many. You all weren't around back then, so we didn't have anyone to talk to about numbers; we didn't have any real support for doing the math. My attention was on doing one treatment at a time, which is where most American acupuncturists' attention is, which is, of course, the wrong place. I thought if I did one treatment at a time, it would eventually add up to enough treatments, but that isn't actually what happened. Adding up one treatment at a time is taking incremental steps. I don't think anybody can get to 100 treatments a week by adding up one treatment at a time. You don't break through the ceiling incrementally, you break through the ceiling with a quantum leap.

Making the Quantum Leap

My patients are the ones who catalyzed my quantum leap. They did it by not cooperating with my idea of one treatment at a time. They didn't show up one at a time. They showed up two or three or four at a time; they showed up late or early; they showed up with friends and family members and coworkers. The space I thought was mine, the acupuncture practice I thought was mine, wasn't really mine. It was theirs. Like most acupuncturists, I thought acupuncture was mine and I was doing a good thing by wanting to share it. Eventually I got it. I learned that acupuncture wasn't mine at all; it wasn't mine to share and it wasn't about me being good. It's about acupuncture being big. Really big. I caught a glimpse of how huge acupuncture really is, and I got that I was supposed to participate in it rather than control it or own it. That was how I discovered tungsten, or my version of it.

When I say that breaking the 100 treatment per week barrier is a quantum leap, I don't mean that it happens all at once, because it doesn't. You're not seeing 30 people one week and then you go through a wormhole and you're seeing 100 the next week. It generally happens over time – more time for some people, less time for others. The important thing to understand is that consistently doing 100 or more treatments a week is qualitatively different – not just quantitatively different – from doing 30 or even 50. There's a threshold that you cross where it's not about providing one treatment after another treatment, it's about taking care of a space where a LOT of people come to use acupuncture in the way they want to use it, which might not be the way you think they should use it. There's a point where the space starts to belong to the patients. That's when your practice is elementally different from a conventional acupuncture practice, when it's stable at a level that conventional acupuncture practices can't possibly be stable. For a lot of acupuncturists getting there is hard because of the way we were trained to think about acupuncture.

In that first week of April 2002, we did about 12 community acupuncture treatments. Now, if you look at the numbers from the 2010 CAN survey, 6783 treatments are happening each week in about a hundred clinics. Not everybody answered the survey, and we know that we don't even know about all of the community clinics, so the actual number of treatments is probably a lot higher. We can say confidently it's not less than 7,000 treatments a week. So from 12 treatments a week to 7,000 treatments a week; that's a 58,000 percent increase. Pretty good for 9 years! I'd call that evidence that the community acupuncture model likes quantum leaps.

We didn't know or guess that a 58,000 percent increase was going to happen. But we did know that the hydrogen scale was wrong, and that we were flailing around, reaching in the dark for what the right scale and size was. We had an inkling that the mindset we inherited in acupuncture school had to be questioned, even had to be discarded.

How does as individual acupuncturist make the quantum leap to 100 treatments a week? It has to start with a feeling that the scale you've got is wrong. I don't mean a feeling of panic as in "OMG I'm not going to make enough money!" Lots of conventional acupuncturists have that feeling too, it doesn't have anything really to do with shifting your scale. The feeling I'm talking about isn't about you, it has nothing to do with your personal success or your failure; it has to do with the nature of acupuncture itself. It's like feeling that maybe the world doesn't work the way you thought it worked, and that acupuncture doesn't work like you were taught to think it worked – it's bigger and stranger and more magical than you expected. It can shift you out of worrying about yourself and your success, because you're no longer just focused on yourself. You're seeing the big picture with you as a part of it, but not at the center anymore. It's not necessarily a comfortable feeling. There is a kind of uneasiness for sure, but there's also a kind of wonder and curiosity. I remember thinking, wow, I guess I was really wrong about everything, and that's probably good.

So first you need to get into a kind of creative discomfort, a kind of suspicion that maybe everything you think you know is wrong, and the truth is actually going to be a relief when you finally find it. The ceiling is, first and foremost, a ceiling in your mind. If you know you're blocked, if you can't break that ceiling, instead of fighting the block, it's generally more productive to be curious about it. You're confused about something and you don't even know what it is that you're confused about, but once you figure it out, you'll be much happier. If you're on the wrong side of that quantum leap, you have to start by just being open to a qualitative solution instead of a quantitative one. A quantum solution instead of an incremental one.

The next step is to really think about how people work, and how acupuncture works, and how they work together in the real world, which is extremely different from how they work in textbooks. In textbooks, if you do the right treatment, the patient gets results; if you're smart enough, you should be able to make a living as an acupuncturist. It's all about your knowledge and your skill. If you start from that premise, you are looking at your practice as a hydrogen atom, atomic number one. It's all about one treatment at a time, because you can only do one treatment at a time, and this is all about you, right? If you just do enough single treatments they should eventually add up to the point where you can pay your bills, and it's OK to have relatively low numbers of patients, as long as you are smart enough to help ALL of them.

The problem with your practice having a low atomic number is that low numbers are not a good fit with how people behave, and your practice is not going to be stable if the numbers are low. Different people can stick with a treatment plan to different degrees; there are a lot of people who, even if you're helping them, are going to stop coming in, because they can't be consistent about anything in their lives, including acupuncture. Other people can be consistent in short bursts, and then they get inconsistent again. People drop in and drop out of getting acupuncture. They get busy;

they get better; they move away; they come back. These are trends that are obvious to anyone who's had a community acupuncture clinic for five years or so – you get to see the way people flow in and out. This means that you have to set your sights on seeing lots and lots and LOTS of people, if your clinic itself is going to be steady. Sometimes I suggest to acupuncturists with new clinics that they should just focus on trying to accumulate a thousand files. Once you accumulate a thousand files, you're in the ballpark for having introduced enough people to acupuncture that some of them are going to be consistent. The most brilliant acupuncture treatment in the world is not going to make an inconsistent person into a consistent person, it can't be done. Part of the quantum leap is understanding that and letting go of all your patients as individuals. You can and should care about them as individuals, of course, but you shouldn't hang on to them as individuals, ever, because you never know what they are going to do.

It's a similar thing for treatments; you have to let go of individual treatments. In the textbooks, individual treatments matter a lot; in real life, not so much. You can't measure the effect of acupuncture in discrete increments; it's more like a big, messy continuum. Acupuncture works unbelievably well for some people and not so well for others. Acupuncture works very slowly over time for chronic conditions and chronic pain; sometimes people can only track the effects by noticing that this month was a lot better than last month. Most of all, acupuncture doesn't work precisely. After 17 years, I'm convinced that acupuncture is not like a laser, it's like a shotgun. You can try to aim it all you want, but its effects still go everywhere. Acupuncture is not really meaningful in small quantities, with small atomic numbers. As an element, it's only stable when the numbers get larger, and then it's a beautiful, amazing thing. You know what tungsten is used for? Making light bulb filaments. It shines.

Atomic Number of the Heart

It doesn't make sense to think about acupuncture in terms of individual patients, or in terms of individual treatments. Once you get that, you need to take a look at all of the ways you put your attention on individuals, and ask yourself if your attention really belongs there. Sometimes it does, and sometimes it doesn't. For example, an acupuncturist who has broken through the 100-treatment ceiling is never scared by a room full of patients; she doesn't get overwhelmed, and she doesn't lose track of people. A full room feels good to her, and it feels good to her patients; everybody is having their own individual experiences, but there's this other thing going on that is much bigger, and she's holding the space for that thing as she's moving from person to person. She's connected to the tungsten element of her practice. But an acupuncturist who hasn't broken through that ceiling has trouble holding that space for tungsten, because she's still trying to hold it for hydrogen – she's still thinking one plus one plus one. She might spend too much time with one patient so that she gets way behind with the next few patients. She might get caught up in what she's doing with a patient and not be able to tune into the room and what the patients are doing with each other (whether they know it or not). She is overwhelmed by a lot of people because she's no longer in total control, and then she can't keep track of everyone. If that's what's going on for her internally, she's not going to be able to attract or retain high numbers of patients. If she's made the shift to a sliding scale, she's dependent on high numbers to make a living, but she hasn't really embraced the limits, and the possibilities, of community acupuncture. She's essentially trying to have her practice be partly one element and partly another, and that's about as unstable as you can get.

* * *

Most of what it takes to break through that 100 treatment a week ceiling is not external – it's internal. It's not about marketing or signage or what conditions you feel confident about treating. It has to do with your ability to be present for people, and how much space you have inside yourself for other people's suffering. You can attract and retain people in direct proportion to how much internal space you have for them. Call it the atomic number of your heart. Of course, it's harder if you're a new parent, or if you're the parent of a child who's having any kind of difficulty; lots of your heart space naturally will be taken up by parenting. Similarly, if you have any kind of troubles or worries you can't put aside, you won't be able to attract or retain people in large numbers. If you have any interests outside of your practice that are seriously competing for your attention, you'll have trouble attracting and retaining patients in large numbers. You have to be fairly single-minded in your focus on making space for people. This is not what they teach in acupuncture school; they don't teach you how to make space for people in your heart, especially lots of people simultaneously. Community acupuncturists all have to learn how to do that for themselves, by trial and error. Lots and lots of error. You can raise the atomic number of your heart; it just requires effort and desire and practice. Maybe desire more than anything. You have to want to help a lot of people.

In the end, it comes down to looking at yourself and your personal relationship to the numbers. Where do you put your attention? What's the atomic number of your practice, really? How much space do you have inside you? What is the atomic number of your heart, honestly? A few months back we held a class for Oregon acupuncturists, and a really interesting combination of people showed up: a lot of very new acupuncturists who weren't doing community acupuncture, and a bunch of hardcore community acupuncture comrades. I remember looking out at everyone and thinking you could tell who's who by their faces. Most of the conventional acupuncturists looked kind of shiny. You could tell that they hadn't seen a lot of people, and that they weren't oriented toward seeing a lot of people. They were oriented towards expressing themselves as acupuncturists, concerned with the individual nature of their practices. The community acupuncturists, on the other hand, looked, well, used. Well-used. You could see that they had been seeing a lot of people, and they were kind of worn around the edges, sand-papered down by other people's pain, but also lit up inside. Tungsten filaments.

Reaching Only One Percent

Let's talk about the profession as a whole. Seth Godin says that right-sizing your business is one of the most important decisions you can make. What if an entire profession hasn't found its elemental number? Businesses that exist, exist because the marketplace allows them to function at the right size. What if each of our businesses is also impacted because the profession that they are a part of is not functioning at the right size? Because the profession never made a decision about right-sizing, never thought about what size it should be because it was too busy putting all its energy into glorifying individuals being individuals? The acupuncture profession is really good at making gurus and specialists and encouraging people to express their uniqueness as a marketing strategy. Does it work?

What does it mean when only a few people are getting acupuncture? 3.1 million in 2007. Most of the profession thought 3.1 million was a great number, even though it's about 1% of the population, which means that 99% of the population in America didn't get acupuncture. That's the size we're at now as a profession. What does it mean for our businesses?

Well, it means that a lot of people may have heard about acupuncture, but the odds are overwhelming that they don't know anybody who's actually using it regularly. That situation seems normal not just to them but to us as a profession. If we think 3.1 million is a great number, aren't we're saying that we're OK with 99% of the population not getting acupuncture? And aren't we saying that we're OK that acupuncture is a secret and reserved for special occasions or special people? How are we supposed to market something that is meant to be a secret? I'm not saying that acupuncturists in general are OK with the fact that the majority of them are unable to make a living. But the discomfort of "OMG I'm not making any money" is not the useful, creative discomfort of feeling that we're at the wrong scale for our businesses. A lot of acupuncturists would be fine with acupuncture remaining secret if they were also able to make a lot of money at the same time, but business doesn't work like that. People can't rave about something they don't know about. If a secret goes viral it's not a secret anymore. I'm afraid a lot of acupuncturists actually got into the profession because few people know about acupuncture. Not in spite of it, because of it. The secrecy and the specialness are part of the romance of being a healer, right? If you've got a lot of ordinary people getting acupuncture, it loses that specialness. And the healers lose their specialness. The whole thing becomes commonplace.

That leaves out, of course, the reality that for each of those ordinary patients getting acupuncture, the experience itself is often magical, amazing, anything but commonplace. Some people say, acupuncture has given me back my life. They say, I had forgotten what it was like to feel good. They say, I feel like myself again. There's the difference between the patients' reality and the acupuncturists'.

Lisa Rohleder

* * *

Patients are quite capable of picking up on the fact that, no matter what the profession is saying, acupuncturists don't really want them to get acupuncture in large numbers. It's clear that, as a profession, we're just not that into them; we're not that interested in them getting their lives back or feeling like themselves again. So they respond in kind. When we have no enthusiasm, they have no enthusiasm. You can't fake enthusiasm. And where there's no enthusiasm, there's no momentum. In theory, there are more than 20,000 licensed acupuncturists in the U.S., and there have been for a while. Yet only 3.1 million people got acupuncture in 2007. If every licensed acupuncturist were treating 1,000 individual patients a year – some of those people consistently, some more of them inconsistently, because that's how people are – there should be more than 20 million individuals getting acupuncture each year. Of course, that's in addition to all of the people who might be getting acupuncture from someone other than a licensed acupuncturist, someone like a medical doctor or a chiropractor or a physical therapist. If you had more than 20 million people getting acupuncture each year, we would start to see some real momentum. The more people get acupuncture, the more people get acupuncture. You can say those words with a few different meanings, and all of them are true. That is what we should be seeing. Instead we're seeing is the opposite – numbers of licensed acupuncturists are stagnating, and in some places, they're actually declining. So the less people get acupuncture, the less people get acupuncture.

Maybe the profession hasn't made the sizing decision consciously, but it's made it nonetheless: we have chosen the atomic size that makes us feel special. It's a very small size indeed. Unfortunately, due to the realities of how acupuncture works, and how human beings work, you don't get to be special as an acupuncturist and also be able to make

300

a living.

Right-sizing the Profession

I'm going to advocate that we revisit that decision about sizing the profession, and this time we do it consciously and rationally. What does it mean if lots and lots and LOTS of people get acupuncture?

If every one of those 20,000 licensed acupuncturists managed to break the 100 treatment per week ceiling – and we give everybody 2 weeks of vacation a year – that would be 100 million treatments a year. It's hard to say how many patients exactly that would be, because some of them would be consistent and some would be inconsistent, but it's probably more than our previous 20 million calculation – because a lot more people would be trying acupuncture for the first time, because they would finally have heard about it from someone they knew. Acupuncture would start to be an ordinary thing for lots of ordinary people. We would start to get the momentum we needed.

Then the marketplace would change. Businesses that exist, exist because the marketplace allows them to function at the right size. Currently we have a lot of acupuncture "businesses" that don't really exist; they don't function as businesses, they function as hobbies. Because they don't have enough patients, there's no incentive for them to keep regular hours. So their patient flow is unstable, and then their hours are unstable, and then their revenues are unstable, which ultimately makes the job itself unstable; and that all culminates in making the patient flow even more unstable. That's the elemental nature of a small acupuncture practice in a wrong-sized profession: unstable. But all that changes if we collectively decide to right-size the profession. We commit to a stable flow of patients at a high volume; we commit to stable hours; we start to reap the benefits of stable revenues and stable jobs, and every year we see the patient flow get more and more stable. That's what we've seen at WCA these last 9 years. If we collectively decide to right-size our own businesses and to right-size the profession as a whole, what the marketplace allows us to do will change.

Sometimes I think that acupuncture in America is trying to right-size itself through us. It's huge, it knows it's huge; it's the acupuncturists who haven't realized that it should be huge. For last 9 years, I've had this feeling that I'm just taking directions from something that knows what it wants – something enormous that already exists somewhere that I can't quite see. I'm trying to run errands for it, get things set up the way it wants them to be set up so that it can do what it already knows how to do...

I want to close with a last quote from Seth Godin's blog post on his atomic theory of business size:

"When in pain, consider your scale. When you're too big or too small for the revenue or the impact you seek, you'll feel it in your bones. Leap."

Just as elements are not constructed, but discovered (tungsten itself was discovered by the brothers Juan José and Fausto Elhuyar in 1783), the community acupuncture model is something we found out about rather than something we made. We are still learning about it. The issue of right-sizing is not limited to how many patients an individual acupuncturist can treat, or how many treatments an individual patient should receive. Acupuncture treatments are not particularly meaningful when considered individually; they don't make sense in small numbers. But when you truly take into account the social business aspect of the community acupuncture model, you have to say the same about acupuncturists themselves: they don't make sense in small numbers either. If the goal is to treat an entire community, then we need to put our attention on acupuncturists not as individuals but as a collective, and on that collective as part of a larger community.

Tungsten is the atomic number of community. And social business requires a quantum leap. What would that look like?

Appendix C

Real Jobs in the Big Damn Clinic

There are a number of possible ways to structure work. Over the last six years of watching a lot of different acupuncturists establish community clinics in lots of different places, we have learned that some structures are more useful than others in achieving ultimate stability and a big damn clinic. Real jobs are an example of the useful structures. People who work in fields that aren't acupuncture are often surprised that we have to spend a lot of time and energy defining what a "real job" is – but we do, because there's an awful lot of misunderstanding about what they are and what they mean. It's especially common for the acupuncture profession to confuse real jobs with "business opportunities" such as renting a room in someone else's clinic, independent contractor positions based on commission, and similar scenarios with no guarantee of an income.

Essentially, when we talk about real jobs in a big damn clinic, we mean that the clinic is big enough and stable enough to employ acupuncturists, preferably full-time, as opposed to the clinic not being big enough or stable enough to do that, which results in acupuncturists having to employ themselves. As I noted earlier, it seems normal to many acupuncturists for acupuncture jobs to be either very part-time or independent-contractor status or both, when they exist at all. Very part-time jobs and independent contractor positions actually contribute to clinics staying small and being unstable; let's look at why.

An independent contractor position is not employment, it's self-employment. The Internal Revenue Service is quite clear on the distinction, and eager to dispense penalties to employers who are mischaracterizing their employees as independent contractors. The crucial distinction for the IRS' point of view is, of course, payroll taxes. From the perspective of the acupuncturists who is self-employed as an independent contractor, however, there are a lot of other important differences between their status and true employment.

This is a quote from the IRS website: http://www.irs.gov/businesses/small/article/0,,id=99921,00.html

It is critical that business owners correctly determine whether the individuals providing services are employees or independent contractors.

Generally, you must withhold income taxes, withhold and pay Social Security and Medicare taxes, and pay unemployment tax on wages paid to an employee. You do not generally have to withhold or pay any taxes on payments to independent contractors.

The general rule is that an individual is an independent contractor if the payer has the right to control or direct only the result of the work and not what will be done and how it will be done. The earnings of a person who is working as an independent contractor are subject to Self-Employment Tax.

If you are an independent contractor, you are self-employed.

You are not an independent contractor if you perform services that can be controlled by an employer (what will be done and how it will be done). This applies even if you are given freedom of action. What matters is that the employer has the legal right to control the details of how the services are performed.

* * *

If an employer-employee relationship exists (regardless of what the relationship is called), you are not an independent contractor and your earnings are generally not subject to Self-Employment Tax. However, your earnings as an employee may be subject to FICA (Social Security tax and Medicare) and income tax withholding.

To make this all a little less dry and abstract, I'll use myself as an example. I am both an employer, because I own the corporation known as Working Class Acupuncture, and an employee, because I have a salaried job with Working Class Acupuncture. Because WCA is a social business, it reinvests any profits it makes as a corporation, so I do not receive any income from being an owner. All my income is through my salary. Let's demonstrate the difference between being an independent contractor and an employee through a dialogue. (I seem to remember that dialogues worked pretty well for Plato when he wanted to make a point.)

Employee Lisa: Hey boss! You know what, I keep hearing from other acupuncturists that you aren't paying me enough. Here I am, an acupuncturist with 18 years' experience, and I only make $35K per year. I want a raise.

Employer Lisa: All right, how about $50K?

Employee Lisa: Wow, that sounds MUCH better! That sounds like a respectable middle class income for an experienced professional! When can you make that happen?

Employer Lisa: Right away. I'll just redefine you as an independent contractor.

Employee Lisa: Really? All this time you could have been paying me $50K instead of $35K? I always suspected that at heart you were a filthy profiteer.

* * *

Employer Lisa: Uh-huh. You know what they say about me, I'm a capitalist in socialist's clothing. Or a socialist in capitalist's clothing, they're not sure. But enough about me, let's talk about your new status. You'll be self-employed, which means technically you won't work for me at all, you'll work for yourself.

Employee Lisa: Good, I don't want to work for you, you remind me of Ayn Rand.

Employer Lisa: So we'll say that you get paid $50K a year for doing basically what you did before – treating 75 people a week or so (80% of your job) and doing your administrative work (20% of your job). But since you're self-employed, you'll have to pay self-employment tax now. This is what the IRS says about that: Self-employed individuals generally must pay self-employment tax (SE tax) as well as income tax. SE tax is a Social Security and Medicare tax primarily for individuals who work for themselves. It is similar to the Social Security and Medicare taxes withheld from the pay of most wage earners. In general, anytime the wording "self-employment tax" is used, it only refers to Social Security and Medicare taxes and not any other tax (like income tax). SE tax is 15% of what you take home. So I won't take taxes out of your paycheck anymore, you'll have to remember to calculate them yourself and pay them quarterly. You should estimate about 30%.

Employee Lisa: 30%?!? But I thought my tax bracket was like 15%. I get a refund when I file my taxes!

Employer Lisa: It was and you did. But that's because, as your employer, I was already paying a portion of your Social Security and Medicare taxes. Now that you are your own employer, you are responsible for paying that. And don't forget, the reason you got a refund when you filed your taxes was because, even apart from what the company was paying for you, the payroll service automatically deducted the taxes you owe from your check. That won't happen anymore. Don't forget to calculate your own taxes and pay them quarterly, or you could owe the IRS in penalties.

Employee Lisa: Don't tell me what to do!

Employer Lisa: Good point. I can't tell you what to do, because you're an independent contractor. But if we want to convince the IRS of that, there are a few other conditions we'll need to meet. For instance, you'll need to buy your own materials from now on.

Employee Lisa: You're going to make me buy my own needles?

Employer Lisa: The IRS is going to make me make you buy your own needles. Also, your own cotton balls, your own insurance, your own Continuing Education, your own licensing fees, your own business cards, let's see, we should keep a list. I mean, I could keep buying those things for you, but if you're really self-employed, you're going to have to pay me back out of that $50K. Because I can only control the results of your work, not how you make it happen. All those details are your responsibility now, not mine.

Employee Lisa: But those details are going to add up! Let's see, I treat 75 people a week and I use maybe 25 needles on each of them. I'll have to buy about 2 boxes of needles a week, 52 weeks a year – hey, what about vacation?

Employer Lisa: Vacation and sick days are a benefit, and independent contractors don't get benefits. If you were to pay for those benefits you currently have – 10 days of vacation and 2 sick days – you would have to pay someone to cover for you, as I currently do. Let's see, an acupuncturist costs around $20 an hour – so your vacation and sick time costs $1536. Subtract that from your $50K and we're at $48,464.

Employee Lisa: So 2 boxes of needles for 50 weeks a year – that's $2000 a year in needles. That leaves me at $46,464. Are you serious?

Employer Lisa: Not nearly as serious as the IRS. Let's move on to insurance and credentialing. Your malpractice insurance costs $672 per year. You'll have to pay that yourself, which gets you to $45,792. As an employee, you're also covered by worker's comp and unemployment insurance, which I pay. As an employee, if your job ends you can claim unemployment benefits. If your job ends as an independent contractor, you're out of luck, unfortunately, you can't even pay to get that benefit back. So then there's your license fee – $300 every 2 years – and 30 CEUs every 2 years too. We pay for all that, or provide the CEUs in house. CEUs cost about $20 an hour. I think that adds up to $300 per year. So your pay is now at $45, 492. Say you'll spend about $200 a year on other supplies like cotton balls and lancets and biohazard disposal containers to make it an $45,300.

Employee Lisa: And I have to pay an extra 15% in taxes on that? 15% of $45,300 is $6,795! That leaves me at $38,505.

Employer Lisa: Yes, but we're not done. If you're really self-employed, you need to chip in for the cost of the receptionists who work on your shifts and for that matter, the cost of the on-line scheduler. Because remember, I can't have any control over how your work is done, only the results – which means I don't want to be responsible for helping you schedule patients. From now on, that's all on you. I think that the receptionist's salary alone for the hours that you work is about $10,000 a year. You should pay at least half that. Let's see...

Employee Lisa: Wait! Stop! I don't want to be an independent contractor at $50K per year, I want to be an employee at $35K per year.

Employer Lisa: Yes, you do.

Employee Lisa: Besides everything else, I hate filling out Schedule C on my taxes. I just want a nice plain W-2.

Employer Lisa: Yes, and you're less likely to be audited that way, too. Amazing how expensive a nice plain W-2 is, isn't it. *thinks about it* Hold on a minute. What's in this arrangement for me? Now that I see how much you cost as an employee, I have to wonder. If I'm really a capitalist in socialist clothing, I should be making money off your labor even when I'm wearing a t-shirt with a red fist on it. But I'm not. In fact, as long as I keep the sliding scale where it is, and you're an employee rather than an independent contractor, I'm never going to make any money off you.

Employee Lisa: No, you're not.

Employer Lisa: So how does my point of view as a business owner make any sense at all?

Employer Lisa: I guess it doesn't. Sorry about that.

Employer Lisa: So I'm not a capitalist in socialist clothes, OR a socialist in capitalist clothes. I'm just an outmoded way of thinking about ownership that doesn't apply to social business! *vanishes in a puff of red smoke*

* * *

Employee Lisa: You've got to be kidding me. Ask for a raise around here and look what happens. Now I'm responsible for everything! Oh my God, I need to get some help.

Appendix D

Presentation to the American Society of Acupuncturists 3/18/17

Thank you for inviting me to present on behalf of POCA.

About POCA Tech

POCA Tech is the POCA Cooperative's acupuncture school. Its mission is to recruit and train students to provide acupuncture to underserved communities through POCA, and to establish an academic foundation for the practice of liberation acupuncture. POCA Tech is a 3-year acupuncture-only program that offers a Master's level certificate in acupuncture. The basic purpose is to provide existing POCA clinics with well-trained workers, as well as to create new POCA clinics in areas that need them.

POCA Tech has Candidacy status with ACAOM.

POCA Tech's first cohort is preparing to graduate this year, and most of them are in the process of applying to sit for the NCCAOM tests (biomedicine, foundations, acupuncture with point location).

I understand there are rumors going around that POCA Tech graduates won't meet ACAOM or NCCAOM standards, and I confess I'm mystified about how to respond to those. First, you can check the ACAOM website for a list of institutions in Candidacy, and we're right there. Second, why would the co-op want graduates that can't get licenses? The whole point is to recruit and train people to work in POCA clinics.

Educational Philosophy

* * *

POCA Tech made a philosophical decision to offer a Master's level certificate rather than a Master's degree. This meant that at the state level, we got a private career school license rather than a degree-granting institution license. State educational licensing varies a lot but in Oregon it's pretty intense. Our state department of education provides a lot of help to people starting career schools, which was great for us in terms of preparing us to apply for Candidacy with ACAOM; a lot of the requirements were very similar.

In Oregon, though, there was an additional requirement for private career schools, which is that our program be consistent with the higher levels of Bloom's Taxonomy. I'm trying not to lapse into educational bureaucratese here, but Bloom's Taxonomy requires some explaining. It's a pedagogical tool in the form of a classification system for the cognitive processes that learners use. See this link for a helpful overview: https://cft.vanderbilt.edu/guides-sub-pages/blooms-taxonomy/

Bloom's Taxonomy creates a hierarchy of educational objectives which is helpful for teachers to understand in structuring their teaching. At the bottom of the hierarchy, there's rote memorization, and at the top, there's creating original work. In between are categories such as understanding, applying, analyzing, and evaluating knowledge. At POCA Tech we're training independent healthcare practitioners, who in addition to practicing on their own as clinicians, may need to be able to create and run their own clinics. Only the higher levels of Bloom's Taxonomy are going to prepare them for those challenges.

It can be helpful to look at Bloom's Taxonomy in the form of verbs.

* * *

Here are some verbs for lower order skills: duplicate, repeat, reproduce; list, exemplify; apply, practice, use.

And here are some for higher order skills: analyze, compare, contrast, criticize; combine, compose, formulate; compare, contrast, justify, select; assemble, construct, devise. And my favorite: *organize*.

So it's important to understand that these are the skills we're working with our students to develop. Equally important is that POCA Tech is a Liberation Acupuncture school.

What's Liberation Acupuncture? Liberation studies, like Liberation Theology and Liberation Psychology, are disciplines applied to the concerns of marginalized communities. Looking back at the history of acupuncture and Chinese medicine in the US, including immigrant practitioners like Doc Hay in Oregon and the survival programs of the Black Panthers and Young Lords in New York, we decided Liberation Acupuncture made a lot of sense.

So... Liberation Acupuncture is a conceptual framework for acupuncture that affirms that individual health and disease do not exist, and cannot be understood or addressed, apart from social conditions – particularly injustice, inequality, and the pervasive influence of traumatic stress. Liberation Acupuncture is a praxis that begins with the needs and the perspectives of the oppressed, the exploited, and the excluded. Liberation acupuncture defines what is valuable in acupuncture theory and practice by determining what is useful and valuable to oppressed people. (from liberationacupuncture.org)

Liberation studies, especially Liberation Psychology, take the perspective that all knowledge has an historical element; you can't take knowledge out of its social and political context and call it objective truth. Consistent with that approach, Liberation Acupuncture teaches that **there is not now, nor has there ever been, one right way to practice acupuncture.** All acupuncture theories exist in a social and historical context and they're all open to critique.

Whose critique? Liberation studies all include the concept of *the preferential option for the poor*. That means we believe that since people at the bottom of the socioeconomic ladder have the worst health outcomes, systems to provide healthcare should be designed from their perspective. So what we want at POCA Tech is for our students to learn a variety of acupuncture treatment approaches, but to be able to critique and evaluate their usefulness in a clinical context for the people at the bottom of the socioeconomic ladder.

The 10 treatment approaches we teach our students to practice in clinic are:
- Auricular treatment
- 8 Extras
- Jingei pulse diagnosis (this is a Japanese interpretation of Chapter 9 of the Ling Shu)
- Korean 4-Point acupuncture
- Master Tung
- Miriam Lee Ten Points
- Richard Tan Balance Method
- Richard Tan 12 magic needles
- Scalp acupuncture
- TCM Zang-Fu

We want our interns to look at the range of possible treatment approaches and *analyze, compare, contrast, criticize; combine, compose, formulate; appraise, justify and select*, in order to discover what kind of acupuncture both fits them as individual clinicians and best serves their patients. This is why one of our main educational evaluations for Year 3 of the program is a completed clinical journal in which students prepare case studies for the 10 treatment approaches that they learned in the classroom and practiced in clinic. This demonstrates their ability to *analyze, compose, appraise and select.*

All liberation studies depend on praxis; they have no meaning if they're only theoretical. The community acupuncture model represents the praxis for Liberation Acupuncture. For POCA Tech as a school, a crucial part of our praxis is an integrative medicine partnership with a hot-spotting program. (For more information about hot-spotting programs, please read: http://www.newyorker.com/magazine/2011/01/24/the-hot-spotters) Clients of this hot-spotting program, who represent the most vulnerable utilizers of the healthcare system, can access unlimited acupuncture treatment through Working Class Acupuncture clinics, which is where POCA Tech students do their internships. Being able to choose from a range of possible acupuncture treatment approaches to meet the needs of the most vulnerable patients is crucial for our interns.

POCA Tech Job Task Analysis

The first question people usually ask about POCA Tech's Job Task Analysis is, why are you doing one when the NCCAOM already does one?

That's easy: from our perspective, the NCCAOM's is predicated on the idea that there is indeed one right way to practice acupuncture, and it's TCM. We're not buying that.

Also, there are a lot of questions we want to ask that the NCCAOM JTA doesn't, particularly related to what kinds of acupuncture people are using in their practices, where they learned it, and how that's working out for them. We want to learn more about how many acupuncturists are doing community acupuncture, whether exclusively or in combination with private room acupuncture. We want to be able to ask questions of people who are no longer practicing. One of the functions of a JTA can be to validate a training curriculum, so we want to find out how people feel about how their acupuncture educations served them.

As some of you know, the accreditation process with ACAOM involves an institutional self-study that ideally includes some research. Given that we're a technical school training people for a very specific job, we think a Job Task Analysis is an appropriate form of research for us. The data will be very useful for POCA Tech in evaluating our own curriculum, but we think it will also be valuable for the rest of the profession.

We encountered a couple of internal glitches in rolling out the JTA, but we're hoping to be in the beta testing phase within 6 weeks or so, and to be launching the survey by early summer. We're grateful for David's help with the survey design, and we're hoping that we'll get a lot of responses from ASA members. Our survey should take about 30 minutes, and we'll be offering incentives, so I'm hoping it's not an onerous request. We're planning to make our data and our analysis public. So thank you in advance!

And thanks for your interest in POCA Tech.

Appendix E

Trauma Informed Care

Trauma Informed Oregon provides the following definitions:

"Trauma is a wound. Typically, trauma refers to either a physical injury, such as a broken bone, or an emotional state of profound and prolonged distress in response to an overwhelmingly terrifying or unstable experience. Some trauma, like wounds, heal relatively quickly, some heal slowly, and many influence life going forward, like scars. Scars and trauma do not result in defects or deficiencies; rather they are markers of life experience one has survived.

Trauma Informed Care (TIC) recognizes that traumatic experiences terrify, overwhelm, and violate the individual. Trauma Informed Care is a commitment not to repeat these experiences and, in whatever way possible, to restore a sense of safety, power, and self-worth."

The federal Substance Abuse and Mental Health Services Administration (SAMHSA) also has developed a Trauma Informed Approach for use in organizations. According to SAMHSA, "A program, organization, or system that is trauma informed:
- Realizes the widespread impact of trauma and understands potential paths for recovery;
- Recognizes the signs and symptoms of trauma in clients, families, staff, and others involved with the system;
- Responds by fully integrating knowledge about trauma into policies, procedures, and practices; and
- Seeks to actively resist re-traumatization.

A trauma-informed approach can be implemented in any

type of service setting or organization and is distinct from trauma-specific interventions or treatments that are designed to address the consequences of trauma and to facilitate healing."

SAMSHA also counts 6 Key Principles of a Trauma Informed Approach:
- Safety – feeling psychologically and physically safe.
- Trustworthiness and Transparency- organizational operations and decisions are conducted with transparency and the goal of building and maintaining trust among staff, clients, and family members of people being served by the organization.
- Peer Support – can take any number of forms.
- Collaboration and mutuality – true partnering and leveling of power differences between staff and patients; recognizing that healing happens in relationships and in the meaningful sharing of power and decision-making.
- Empowerment, voice and choice – recognize that every person's experience is unique and requires an individualized approach.
- Cultural, Historical, and Gender Issues – the organization addresses cultural, historical, and gender issues; the organization actively moves past cultural stereotypes and biases (e.g. based on race, ethnicity, sexual orientation, age, geography, etc.), offers gender responsive services, leverages the healing value of traditional cultural connections, and recognizes and addresses historical trauma.

Similarly, the Trauma Informed Oregon website states: "Agencies demonstrate Trauma Informed Care with policies, procedures and practices that: a) create safe context through physical safety, emotional safety, trustworthiness, clear and consistent boundaries, transparency, and predictability; b) recognize and honor the individual through relationship, respect, compassion, acceptance and non-judgment, mutuality, and collaboration; and c) restore power through choice, empowerment, strengths focus, and skill building."

Trauma Informed Acupuncture

More recently, research has begun to suggest that acupuncture is an effective intervention for post-traumatic stress disorder. One study stated that "acupuncture is a safe, potentially non-stigmatizing treatment that reduces symptoms of anxiety, depression, and chronic pain...." and "acupuncture is a novel and therapeutic option that may help to improve population reach of PTSD treatment."

Per the Adverse Childhood Experiences (ACEs) study, long term traumatic stress in childhood appears to greatly increase the risk in later life not only of mental health problems and substance abuse, but also physical health problems. The study created a scoring system for ACEs to assess long-term risk of chronic disease: a kind of "cholesterol score for childhood toxic stress". ACEs seem to be associated with chronic pain in adulthood due to arthritis, headache or chronic back or neck pain, as well as cardiovascular disease, liver disease, chronic lung disease, and cancer. People often seek acupuncture for the treatment of pain, especially back and neck pain. The ACEs study suggests that trauma is far more widespread in the general population than previously believed. Taking all these factors into account, it is highly likely that many people who are receiving acupuncture treatment have trauma histories, whether or not they identify them to their acupuncturist or even to themselves.

Between the demonstrated effectiveness of acupuncture for the treatment of trauma, and the probability that the population that receives acupuncture includes a high proportion of people with trauma histories, there are compelling reasons to investigate what Trauma Informed Care would look like in the context of acupuncture treatment. How can the delivery model for acupuncture become more Trauma Informed?

The Community Acupuncture Model

There are several possible delivery models for acupuncture. In Asia, it was common practice both historically and in the present day for people to receive acupuncture in a group setting. In the US, auricular acupuncture for substance abuse treatment is typically delivered in a group setting. Over the past forty years, as many non-Asian practitioners have entered the profession, the conventional setting became similar to the setting for massage or a physical exam: one patient in a cubicle on a table, often delivered by a practitioner wearing a white coat.

The model that is known as "community acupuncture" dates to the 1970s, when the Young Lords and the Black Panthers pioneered the use of auricular acupuncture in a group setting for community-based detoxification in New York. The Black Panthers went on to establish the Black Acupuncture Advisory Association of North America and the Harlem Institute of Acupuncture. The National Acupuncture Detoxification Association (NADA), founded in 1985, promoted the use of auricular acupuncture and established many public health programs. One challenge that all community-based or public health acupuncture programs face is funding: because acupuncture is considered an alternative modality, it is often difficult to support with federal or state funding.

The community acupuncture model began to develop in a different direction in 2002 in Portland, Oregon, when two public health acupuncturists lost their jobs due to budget cuts and set out to replace them. They founded Working Class Acupuncture, which currently includes 3 clinics and provides over 50,000 treatments per year. One of the founders came from a working class/working poor family, and also happened to have a high ACE score. As a result, the community acupuncture model took shape with an emphasis on sustainable self-funding, accessibility to working class people, and – fortuitously – trauma.

The People's Organization of Community Acupuncture (POCA) is currently one of the largest and fastest-growing acupuncture organizations in North America. It is a multi-stakeholder cooperative with about 200 clinics that provide over 1,000,000 treatments per year. As POCA's website explains:

Community Acupuncture offers acupuncture:
[?]   in a setting where multiple patients receive treatments at the same time;
[?]   by financially sustainable and accountable means; and
[?]   within a context of accessibility created by consistent hours, frequent treatments, affordable services, and lowering all the barriers to treatment that we possibly can, for as many people as possible, while continuing to be financially self-sustaining.

Community Acupuncture is not just a description of acupuncture in a group setting, but also describes who is served by acupuncture: our communities. Community Acupuncture is not a one-way relationship of acupuncturists to their communities but the relationship of communities to acupuncture, the clinic, practitioners, and other staff. Community Acupuncture represents the connection and the contract between Acupuncture and Communities."

* * *

The first clinic of the POCA Cooperative, Working Class Acupuncture, uses recliners in a living-room type arrangement. Patients make individual appointments, but receive treatment in the same communal space. The clinic is self-funded with fees on a sliding scale of $15 -$35, with patients choosing what to pay based only on what they feel comfortable with. Patients rest with their needles in for as long as they want, so what you see when you enter the clinic space is a softly-lit room full of peacefully dozing people.

Because acupuncture as a modality is at least 2,000 years old, and because it has been practiced in different cultures all over the world, there are many different ways of doing it. The World Health Organization formally recognizes 361 "classical" acupuncture points and 48 "extra" points. In addition to these, there are a number of "microsystems" or acupuncture points located on only one part of the body which are used to mirror and treat the whole: the ear, the hand, the scalp, the wrists and ankles, the face, and even the nose. Furthermore, there are many separate "lineage" systems, using points that were carefully protected family secrets and never included on the classical lists. While there is an emerging body of research on the efficacy of acupuncture in general, there is no research or data that compares the efficacy of different styles or systems of acupuncture. Anecdotal reports suggest that all systems and styles seem to work equally well.

The community acupuncture model did not invent any clinical strategies for acupuncture. Community acupuncture clinics, however, have opted to use styles of acupuncture that emphasize so-called "distal points" as opposed to "local points". For example, there are a number of popular distal point strategies for the treatment of back pain which focus on acupuncture points on the hands, feet, and head rather than on the back itself. Distal points and microsystems lend themselves easily to a setting in which patients are being treated in recliners and are not removing their clothes.

Community Acupuncture as Trauma-Informed Acupuncture

Because of the history of community acupuncture, core elements of the model align themselves neatly with core elements of Trauma Informed Care. In economic terms, community acupuncture is all about low cost and high volume, and it would not have been as successful as it has if many people were not willing to try it. The low cost is certainly a major factor in attracting hundreds of thousands of patients to POCA clinics, but it seems likely that another reason is that the model works for people with trauma histories. This means:

1) Safety: physical and emotional

Acupuncture is an extremely safe modality compared to other forms of medical care. Serious adverse events are rare. The acupuncture profession in the US has almost universally adopted single-use disposable needles, which further decreases the risk of infection and bloodborne pathogen transmission. And community acupuncture is even safer.

The most serious adverse events in acupuncture involve organ puncture, most often of the lungs due to needling too deeply on the upper back and trapezius areas. In community acupuncture clinics, the points that are most often chosen are located below the elbows, below the knees, and on the head. Points on the neck, upper chest, and on the abdomen, may be added as a supplement but are not usually essential to treatment.

Another characteristic of community acupuncture is that a key clinical strategy is "needle retention": allowing the patients to rest with the needles, often for as long as they want. This contrasts with clinical strategies that rely on the practitioner stimulating the needles by twisting, thrusting, and/or twirling them. Strong and deep needle stimulation over organs is more likely to lead to organ puncture. Needle retention, by contrast, often involves shallow insertion: the practitioner simply inserts and positions the needle just deeply enough so that it will stay in place and the patient can relax.

Emotional safety can be more difficult to achieve in the delivery of acupuncture, especially if the patient is alone with the practitioner and partially clothed and lying on a table while the practitioner is standing up, wearing a white coat, administering an unfamiliar, potentially painful modality. This scenario is potentially overwhelmingly vulnerable, even re-traumatizing, for a person with a trauma history whether that history is conscious or not. Community acupuncture intentionally circumvents it.

One of the beauties of the diversity of acupuncture clinical strategies is that treatment can be adjusted for a patient's comfort level. In community acupuncture clinics, it is typically suggested to patients that they take off their shoes and socks, roll up their pant legs above the knee and their sleeves above the elbow. If a patient who has heard this suggestion sits down in a recliner without doing any of those things, the community acupuncturist can assume that the person is uncomfortable with having their feet, legs, or arms needled. The next step would be for the practitioner to ask, "Is it OK if I try a point in your hand?" Or ear, or head, or any other easily reachable microsystem – until the patient gives their consent. There is no need to push the patient to expose any part of their body. There are enough options that most people will be able to be needled in a way that makes them comfortable.

Similarly, in a community acupuncture setting, it is rare that a patient will be alone with a practitioner. There are always other people present and close by, even if they are asleep. Certainly, the group setting is not going to work for every person with a trauma history, since every person is unique. However, the prevalence of sexual abuse in particular makes it worth taking into account that the experience of being alone and unclothed in a room with someone who has more power is likely to be problematic for a significant percentage of the population.

Community acupuncturists have discovered that a happy consequence of the group setting is that new patients very often come for treatment with a friend or relative who has already tried acupuncture and liked it. If new patients are nervous, they can watch their friend or relative be treated first, and then they can relax with their needles side by side. This kind of social support creates emotional safety.

Another important element of emotional safety has to do with disclosing information. One of the other beauties of the diversity of acupuncture clinical strategies is that many methods of diagnosis do not involve the patient having to verbally tell the acupuncturist much in order for the acupuncturist to successfully choose useful points. In certain kinds of acupuncture, great emphasis is placed on intakes that are similar in detail to a physical exam or to psychotherapy. However, there is no evidence that this kind of extensive questioning produces better clinical outcomes than strategies that are mostly non-verbal. Community acupuncture intakes rely on a relatively brief health history plus a short conversation with the patient about their goals. The assumption is that trust will grow in the process of treatment and patients may feel more comfortable disclosing more information over time, if needed. However, it would be a mistake to assume that level of trust at the beginning of the relationship. The reality of how acupuncture seems to work, though, is that there is rarely any need for the acupuncturist to ask invasive questions, and patients never need to disclose anything that would make them uncomfortable.

"Working in a Trauma Informed way does not require disclosure of trauma; rather there is a recognition of the need for: physical and emotional safety; choice and control in decisions affecting treatment; and practices that avoid confrontational approaches." Cheryl S. Sharp, MSW, "Becoming Trauma-Informed"

2) Trustworthiness, transparency and predictability

The practices that keep a community acupuncture clinic's costs low enough to offer treatments at an affordable rate also enforce a certain kind of transparency. The communal treatment room itself as well as whatever marketing the clinic does are examples of areas where simplicity, straightforwardness, consistency and trustworthiness are required if the clinic is going to function at all, let alone be financially self-sustaining. These qualities are not a question of virtue but of survival.

Everything that happens clinically in a community acupuncture clinic happens in the open. Patients can see their practitioner talking (briefly) with and treating other patients in the community room. This requires the acupuncturist to have integrity in their interactions; if they don't, everyone will notice. Similarly, patients can know what to expect by observing what is happening. If a community acupuncture clinic is functioning smoothly, there are rarely any surprises.

* * *

The purpose of a first visit and intake in a community acupuncture clinic is to orient the patient to the clinic and to give them enough information to decide if acupuncture is something they want to use. The message to the patient is, "Let's see if you like this." The acupuncturist's role is to facilitate, and to let patients draw their own conclusions about acupuncture. Clinic processes have to be transparent and comprehensible.

The low cost of individual treatments has several consequences: one is that a lot of patients have to try, and like, acupuncture for the clinic to survive; another is that there is little or no budget for marketing. Community acupuncture clinics must rely on word of mouth to bring in new patients. Because acupuncture is unfamiliar to many people, if a community clinic is to attract enough patients to be financially self-sustaining, consistency is of paramount importance. People need to be able to explain to their friends and family what will happen if they get acupuncture, and what they said will happen had better be what happens when their friends and family show up at the clinic. Otherwise word of mouth marketing doesn't work and the clinic will fail.

Finally, treatments in a community acupuncture clinic are simple. The process is almost always the same: the patient arrives, checks in, settles into a recliner, the acupuncturist finds them and asks, "what can I do for you today?", there is a conversation that lasts less than five minutes, the acupuncturist puts in the needles, the patient relaxes for anywhere from 15 minutes to several hours, the acupuncturist takes the needles out, the patient leaves. Acupuncture in a community clinic is not like massage, or therapy, or a doctor's appointment. It's just acupuncture, and generally very predictable. For many patients, a weekly treatment is a kind of ritual of self-care, a comforting habit. The transparency and predictability give everyone, but especially people with trauma histories, a sense that they are in control of their treatment.

3) Peer support

Many community acupuncture patients have volunteered that being in the presence of other people receiving acupuncture feels supportive and encouraging. "All these other people, just trying to take care of themselves" was how one person put it. The shared intention to heal is something people can lean on without ever having to talk about it.

For people with trauma histories, being able to relax is never a given. Sitting quietly in a room with other people who already are relaxed can be a step in the right direction. It's a good thing to try, and virtually no interaction is required. A patient can answer the acupuncturist's question, "What can I do for you today?" with just one word, "Stress" – and that can be the extent of it. The treatment allows people to turn inward and pay attention to themselves, while being surrounded by half a dozen other people doing the same thing.

4) Respect, compassion, acceptance and non-judgment

Because there is a long tradition of food therapy and lifestyle practices associated with Chinese medicine, some kinds of acupuncture treatment can cross the line into life coaching or health coaching. While many patients find such conversations valuable, many others do not. An unfortunate consequence of the combination of lifestyle advice with acupuncture in a one-on-one treatment setting is that acupuncturists can feel such pressure to deliver results that they begin to push their patients hard to make changes, even "firing" them from acupuncture if they refuse to change their diets, take up exercise or learn to meditate. "I just can't help you if you don't help yourself," is a common refrain.

What community acupuncturists have found is that acupuncture itself often can help, whether or not patients change anything else. Acupuncture reduces inflammation, promotes better sleep, eases pain, reduces stress, and gives people more energy. Getting regular acupuncture can also lead to other lifestyle changes without the acupuncturist saying a word about it, as a result of patients sitting quietly with themselves and becoming more aware of their own bodies and minds. As a result, the community acupuncture model explicitly discourages giving lifestyle advice.

One of the primary goals of community acupuncture is to be inclusive. Many clinics have succeeded to the point that their patient populations include a striking array of cultures, languages, and lifestyles. It is dangerous to dispense advice about how to live when you have no knowledge of how that advice might be received in light of a patient's religious practices, cultural norms, or personal circumstances. Community acupuncturists avoid the topics of weight loss and smoking cessation: if patients bring them up as goals, community acupuncturists may respond supportively and choose points appropriately, but they should never initiate such a discussion.

Community acupuncture can be uniquely helpful for people with trauma histories, because the model is designed to avoid interpersonal pressure of any kind. Community acupuncture recognizes that patients are taking a personal risk by trying something unfamiliar. Everyone who shows up in the clinic deserves respect, compassion, acceptance and non-judgment, particularly since they are already extending themselves. The goal is simply to welcome them and to encourage them to use the clinic to take care of themselves.

5) Collaboration and mutuality

The one-on-one acupuncture setting can unfortunately emphasize the power differential between practitioner and patient. This differential can feel highly charged to people with trauma histories. Lying down on a table is a physical demonstration of passivity and vulnerability. A practitioner wearing a white coat is a demonstration of social power and authority. The cubicle space is dominated by the practitioner's presence. This setting can highlight the premise that the practitioner has potent, secret knowledge about how the patient's body works, and so the practitioner's instructions have to be obeyed. Giving lifestyle advice can seem like the practitioner is trying to take control over how the patient eats, exercises, and even practices spirituality. The indicators of a medical environment themselves can communicate to a patient with a trauma history that they are "broken" while the practitioner who is supposed to "fix" them is presumably whole.

Community acupuncture seeks to construct a different narrative. A large, open room with more patients than practitioners communicates that the space belongs to the patients, and the practitioner(s) are moving around in it to serve patients. When a patient enters the room, they choose their own recliner and make themselves comfortable as they would as if they were at home. Sitting in a chair – even one that reclines – is a significantly more active position than lying flat on a table. Most community acupuncturists do not wear white coats, so in a clinical setting there may not be immediate visual cues about who is a practitioner and who is a patient, other than that the practitioners are working and the patients are relaxing. Community acupuncture clinics are intended to convey a soothing ambience rather than a biomedical one.

Since the clinical interaction is brief and focused on the patient's goals – "what can I do for you today?" – there is less room for the feeling that the practitioner has potent, secret knowledge as well as social power over the patient. The setting emphasizes that what matters is for the patient to be able to connect with themselves through the experience of acupuncture. Refraining from giving lifestyle advice allows space for the patient to listen to their own experience and draw their own conclusions. The role of the practitioner is to partner with and facilitate for the patient, rather than exercise authority over them.

All these efforts to defuse the power differential between the patient and the practitioner, as well as the presence of other relaxing people who are setting the tone for the space are typically reassuring to people with trauma histories. Furthermore, efforts to level relationships are not confined to the treatment space: they extend throughout the structure of the clinic to include financial relationships.

In our society, money and power are inextricable and the healthcare setting is no exception. For people of limited means, seeking care can be a humiliating experience. One-on-one acupuncture is too expensive for most people to pay for out of pocket, but insurance that covers it is also usually too expensive for the average person to afford. If people are fortunate enough to have that kind of insurance, they still have to deal with elaborate gate-keeping procedures to access acupuncture, and the odds are high that their coverage will be limited – possibly too limited to ensure any clinical results.

In community acupuncture clinics, all patients either pay a

low flat rate or they choose what to pay on a sliding scale. Many POCA clinics explain up front to patients that there are no third-party payers involved and the clinic itself runs on a shoestring. The only way the clinic can function financially is if a lot of people are getting acupuncture, they genuinely feel good about what they are paying, and they spread the word. POCA clinics depend on their patients for financial survival; nobody else is underwriting them.

The POCA Cooperative itself as an overarching structure is an expression of the mutualism of the community acupuncture model. Patients can become members of the cooperative, serve on the Board of Directors, and vote in elections. Many patients opt to join the Cooperative in order to volunteer for jobs like writing the monthly newsletter, participating in membership drives, or helping with conferences. Many POCA clinics also allow POCA patient members to volunteer directly in clinics by working at the front desk, putting up flyers, or helping with laundry. This gives patients a direct sense of ownership in the cooperative and creates another opportunity to build relationships where healing can happen.

6) Empowerment and Choice

Just as collaboration and mutuality are built into the systems of a community acupuncture clinic, so are empowerment and choice. For example, as part of the process of receiving treatment patients choose how much they want to pay, where they want to sit, and how long they want to retain their needles. Where the needles are placed may be a topic of discussion between the acupuncturist and the patient, but the patient always has the final say.

Beyond the process of an individual treatment, though, the overarching question for any patient of a community acupuncture clinics is: how do you want to use acupuncture to give yourself a better quality of life? This question comes from a very practical perspective: for acupuncture to be effective, people have to show up and get it. For many chronic conditions, they have to show up regularly for months or years and get a lot of it. The part of the treatment where the patient shows up and sits down in the recliner is equally as important as the part of the treatment where the acupuncturist inserts the needles. It's vital for everybody involved to be clear about this.

Community acupuncturists always suggest a treatment plan. The frequency of treatment is based on the intensity of the problem: for example, if a patient reports 8/10 pain on a scale of 1-10, the acupuncturists will recommend treatments at least 3 times a week. However, the treatment plan is a recommendation; the patient is the authority. People can only answer the question, "How do you want to use acupuncture?" by finding out how acupuncture feels in their own bodies and how it impacts their particular issues. There are any number of parameters at work, and most of them are only going to be sorted out by the patients themselves.

Particularly in the case of chronic illness and/or chronic pain, successful management usually requires a highly-individualized approach. Most patients need to tackle their problem as if it were a unique jigsaw puzzle of interventions and personal practices. For any given patient with a chronic illness and/or chronic pain, acupuncture may be a piece of the puzzle or it may not. The only way to find out is to try and see if it fits. It may be a larger or a smaller piece, a frequently occurring or an occasional piece. Trial and error is almost always involved.

Patients may choose to use acupuncture for prevention, for maintenance, for acute problems, or only in dire situations when nothing else has worked. They may choose acupuncture to manage stress or to treat the side effects of chemotherapy. From the perspective of a community acupuncture clinic, all of these choices are equally valid.

The financial structure of a community acupuncture clinic also supports this kind of empowerment and choice. Patients may adjust what they pay on the sliding scale if they feel they need to come in more frequently for a given issue, and community acupuncturists encourage this. At Working Class Acupuncture, it is common practice to suggest that patients pay less than the low end of the sliding scale if necessary. The high volume of the clinic means that it's possible to make individual adjustments to make sure people can get as much acupuncture as they need or want, while still keeping the lights on.

Many one-on-one acupuncture practices focus on insurance billing in order to be financially viable. It is difficult or impossible for a clinic with a sliding scale to bill insurance, since insurance companies are not receptive to the idea of different patients paying different amounts for the same service and may even consider it fraud. In any case, the infrastructure required to bill insurance would require a community acupuncture clinic to raise its fees, which would defeat the purpose. Moreover, it is arguable that freedom from third-party payers makes the community acupuncture more Trauma-Informed with regard to empowerment and choice.

Among the numerous downsides of insurance are the need for the patient to have a "billable diagnosis" initially, and for the acupuncturist to prove the "medical necessity" of treatment in order to continue it. From a patient perspective, this means that someone in authority gets to judge whether your distress is valid and deserving of treatment. Dealing with gatekeepers can be demoralizing for anyone, but particularly for people with trauma histories. Being able to decide how much acupuncture you think you need, for whatever problem you define, without consulting anyone but yourself, is potentially healing in its own right.

7) Strengths Focus and Skill Building

Relaxation is a skill. Accessing support is a skill. Using a community acupuncture clinic to manage acute and chronic physical, mental and emotional issues is also a skill. Because the setting of a community acupuncture clinic emphasizes that patients are active participants rather than passive recipients, many people develop a sense of competence around getting acupuncture without even needing to talk about it. All community acupuncture clinics depend on a core group of "regulars" that grows over the years, and all of those regulars, one way or another, approach the clinic as a tool that they use to manage their particular circumstances.

8) Cultural, historical, and gender issues; recognizes historical trauma

Community acupuncture only exists as a model because the Young Lords and the Black Panthers organized to address the needs of their communities and chose acupuncture as one way to meet those needs. The goal of the model is to treat all patients as humans deserving of dignity and care. The model's functions include mixing people from different cultures and socioeconomic backgrounds in the same space and also breaking down the isolation that people with chronic illnesses and chronic pain often suffer. Making community acupuncture clinics more welcoming and inclusive to everyone is a never-ending effort, but it is an effort that the model itself is designed to make.

* * *

One aspect of historical trauma that many communities have in common is the experience of being cut off from access to resources. The structure and processes of community acupuncture clinics are meant to communicate that you can have as much acupuncture as you want; the supply is unlimited.

The POCA Cooperative recognizes that addressing cultural issues and historical trauma will require having more acupuncturists who represent underserved communities, particularly acupuncturists of color. Training these representatives is a long term of goal of POCA's new acupuncture school, the POCA Technical Institute.

The People's Organization of Acupuncture and Trauma-Informed Care

"(Social safety): The sense of feeling safe with other people... There are so many traumatized people that there will never be enough individual therapists to treat them. We must begin to create naturally occurring, healing environments that provide some of the corrective experiences that are vital for recovery."[51]

Community acupuncture will not necessarily be useful to every person with a trauma history, since everyone is unique and has different needs. However, the model is designed to offer a sense of social safety to large numbers of people. The POCA Cooperative is in the process of learning more about Trauma-Informed practices and is exploring their implications at different levels.

In 2014, several acupuncturists who identify as trauma survivors began a public conversation about working with trauma in POCA clinics through presentations at POCA's biannual conference (POCAfest) and on the POCA Forums.

Beginning in late 2012, Working Class Acupuncture began a collaboration with a Trauma-Informed program that provides better care to "high utilizers" of health care services, especially emergency rooms. Clients of the program are likely to have multiple chronic illnesses and to face intersecting oppressions (racism, classism, disablism, etc.). Many also have trauma histories. The premise of the collaboration was that any program client who wanted could receive unlimited acupuncture. (Initially WCA donated the treatments.) It became clear that: the community acupuncture model was a good fit for the clients who chose to use it; the partnership was easy and productive; "high utilizers" of health care with complex, chronic problems are not at all difficult or burdensome for the clinic; and what works best for clients with trauma histories is also what works best for the general clinic population.

In 2014, POCA opened its own acupuncture school, the POCA Technical Institute. Its Director, one of the aforementioned acupuncturists with trauma histories, had had a difficult time with her own acupuncture education due to some of the potentially re-traumatizing aspects of the one-on-one delivery model and how that delivery model is taught in acupuncture schools. It is clear that people with trauma histories potentially make very good acupuncturists, but not all of them can make it through acupuncture school. POCA Tech began incorporating discussions of trauma into the curriculum and began exploring how to modify teaching policies and procedures to better accommodate students with trauma histories. POCA Tech is exploring what it would mean to become the first Trauma-Informed acupuncture school.

Appendix F

WCA New Hire Manual 2017
by Cera Mae Evans L.Ac.

Welcome to WCA! We are excited to have you as part of our team.

Working Class Acupuncture has two simple goals: we want to provide acupuncturists with jobs, and we want to make acupuncture accessible to people with ordinary means. Doing both of these things and being successful at it means that we have limitations. Mainly, we cannot be everything to everyone. This is not the dream job for some people, nor is it the perfect clinic for some patients. That is OK. This document is intended to help you to understand how our business works because it is different from a lot of other jobs you may have had. Also, treating people in this setting is likely different from any clinical experience you have ever had.

If you have ever been employed anywhere before, it is most likely that you worked for a large company with a lot of resources. We are not Starbucks or Whole Foods. We do not have multi-million dollar budgets and our goal is not to increase profits for our shareholders. WCA is a social business and reinvests any profits back into the community. Usually this means incremental raises for punks and opening more clinics.

We are not just a regular Community Acupuncture clinic. We are the *original* Community Acupuncture clinic and therefore an example to the entire country. Our example helps hundreds of other acupuncturists run successful clinics and we take that responsibility very seriously. The systems that we have in place are the result of 12+ years of trial and error - both ours and theirs. We are hesitant to change a lot of our core functions because they work. The following is a list of our limitations and we ask that you are honest with yourself about your own limitations as well.

First of all, there are a lot of things that WCA <u>can</u> offer:
1.   A predictable livable wage in the field that you trained for, plus the opportunity to be a part of health care reform.
2.   An existing infrastructure that is built on the sacrifices and efforts of many people, so that you can show up to work and have a huge patient base to treat.
3.   The privilege of treating a **ton** of people. You my realistically treat more people in one shift than your colleagues do in an entire week or month.
4.   A free POCA membership, which includes a support network of hundreds of punks who are happy to share all of their "secrets" and help you succeed.
5.   Coworkers who are happy to share their successful distal treatment strategies and help you succeed. Plus, the chance to interact with colleagues and not feel isolated.
6.   We pay your malpractice insurance, Oregon license renewals, and some, if not all, of the CEU's required for Oregon license renewal.
7.   If you become full-time (salaried or not) you may qualify for Public Service Loan Forgiveness with your student loans.
8.   Resources to learn about Liberation Acupuncture & practice Trauma Informed Care.

Secondly, here are some things that WCA cannot offer:
1.   We are unable to offer Health Insurance or a 401K.
2.   We do not offer holiday pay. We do not guarantee weekends or holidays off, nor can we guarantee that you can take long, extravagant or frequent vacations.

3. We cannot offer massage tables, moxa, e-stim, cupping, or an extensive herbal pharmacy. This will never change.
4. We cannot change who we are to make you feel more comfortable.

We create jobs but our priority is not that they be perfect. Benefits do not fall from the sky and it takes a lot of work to create and offer them. Do you feel strongly that we should be offering health insurance or a 401K? Great! Work your way up through the ranks, become part of our collective management, and help us figure out how to accomplish this task. Until then, please do not gripe about our limitations. If our limitations are deal breakers for you, please do yourself a favor and seek work elsewhere.

Some people find their dream job here at WCA. These are the folks you will meet who are salaried, have a module, and are running the machine. Some think that this will be a good job for them and only end up working here for a few months or a couple of years. That is fine, too! Part of providing acupuncture to people in need is hiring people for a limited time so that we can feel each other out. Sometimes you don't know if a workplace culture is a good fit until you have tried it.

We have a tiered hiring system based on whether we are a good fit for each other, and reflects your commitment to us. We do not expect to be a perfect fit for each other right away, so we like to give people plenty of time to develop. You will notice that no one is around to micromanage how you do things. We are all too busy keeping the machine running! If you feel lost or confused please ask for a check in with a senior punk. We are happy to help! Otherwise, we will assume that you are doing OK. This goes both ways: no news is good news. If you don't hear anything from us it is because we all think that you are doing fine. We tend to cringe at the idea of "employee evaluations" and instead rely on check-ins. If we get feedback from patients or coworkers that you need improvement with something we will check in and give you a chance to work on it.

Here is a look at the different employment tiers:
1.   Substitute (Irregular hours @ $18/hr):
      a.   New hires at WCA usually start out as a sub. You fill in for shifts when our regular employees need days off. This is a good way to see if CA is a good fit for you.
      b.   Commitment level: Casually Dating
2.   Part time hourly (<20 clinic-schedule hours/week @ 18/hr):
      a.   If things seem to be going well we will probably offer you one or two regular shifts. This gives you a chance to build up your punking skills and get further exposure to our organization culture. It also gives you a chance to build up a patient base and sink your roots into a clinic.
      b.   Commitment level: Still dating, but a little more exclusive
3.   Full time hourly (20 hours/week @ 18/hr):
      a.   If your punk skills are developing well, and you are keeping up with busy shifts, we might offer you a full-time position. This is a point where we feel like you are a good fit and want to give you a shot at a career at WCA. You will be given the opportunity to build up your patient numbers and really become a solid member of our co-op. You will work 5 consecutive 4-hour shifts, including one weekend day.
      b.   Commitment level: Things are getting serious and we moved in together.
4.   Full time salaried (20 clinic-schedule hours/

week @ 29K):

      a.   Once you are solid in your punking and seeing 90 patients/week on a consistent basis, you are given a chance to advance to a salaried position with WCA. We expect you not to have another job at this time and to be fully committed to WCA. You now have access to, 2 weeks paid vacation, and our phone plan.

      b.   Commitment level: We are engaged and plan to be married.

5.   Full time salaried + module (roughly 32 hours/ week @ 36.5K)

      a.   Yay! You are a superpunk! You love your job and are great at it! Patients are filling your schedule and you are routinely seeing 100 patients every week. We could use a hand with all of the administrative stuff that goes on behind the scenes, so here is your chance to be a part of our Management Collective by taking on a module. Modules are primarily "telecommuting" and your hours will vary. You will self-manage your workload, but we expect your time commitment to be roughly 7 additional hours per week. Sometimes it is less, and sometimes it is more, but it should all even out.

      b.   Commitment level: We're hitched.

It is important to know that if you are not completely invested in WCA, we will not be completely invested in you. It's nothing personal. There are plenty of wonderful acupuncturists who are not a perfect fit for WCA. If you love community acupuncture but don't' love WCA, please feel free to work for a different clinic or start your own! Nothing would make us happier. We are of the strong opinion that there is plenty of room for more CA clinics out there and that each POCA clinic should have its own personality. Check out the POCA forums for more info on how to do this.

You will hear a lot of talk about "deprogramming" at WCA. One huge part of the learning curve of becoming a Super Punk (aka high-volume community acupuncturist) is letting go of a lot of the stuff you learned in school (if you didn't attend POCA Tech) and/or may have served you in private practice. You do not have to take elaborate patient histories, give elaborate interviews, palpate, talk a lot, or give lifestyle and dietary advice in order to give effective treatments. Keeping things simple is EFFECTIVE. Please trust us on this point. If you try to do all of these unnecessary things with patients you will become exhausted, burned out, and you will confuse our patients.

We give you a lot of trust and independence because we really want you to be here. Please remember that you are an employee, not an independent contractor or owner. As an employee of WCA there are certain things that we require of you. Do you truly believe that you can help people with needles? Are you willing to do so without the help of herbs or lifestyle advice? Are you willing to try new things? Are you teachable? Just like you applied yourself to your training in acupuncture school, we ask that you apply yourself to being a helpful and useful part of our team. Senior punks are always willing to help you or point you in the right direction if there is something that you struggle with.

Remember that the sacrifices of many people over many years created the infrastructure that you are now enjoying. It is exhilarating to treat this many people, but they didn't find that recliner by sheer magic. Please do not expect us to change our policies or how we run our company unless you show us that you are committed to sticking around and help with the workload. Any changes that we make take a lot of work and are decided collectively. The way that things currently operate is a deliberate result of over a decade of trial and error. Consistency in our systems allows our clinic to be one of the most successful acupuncture clinics in the country. Last year WCA provided acupuncture for 50,000 people and that number continues to grow.

As we mentioned before, our prime directive is to (1) create jobs for acupuncturists and (2) offer acupuncture to as many people as possible. Here are some common questions we get from new employees. If you have any other questions after this please just ask.

Frequently Asked Questions

Q: Can't you pay more? Those salaries sure look pretty low.
A: It is true that starting out part time at $18/hour is not a lot of money. As it was explained before, we are still feeling each other out and neither of us has a lot of skin in the game. If you stick around and become salaried, you will be earning a wage that is consistent with, if not better than your colleagues, and will only be working about 25 hours/week max.
(https://www.pocacoop.com/prick-prod-provoke/post/what-acupuncturists-earn)
If you also take into account the value of not paying self-employment taxes, insurance, licensing fees, and the possible forgiven student loan debt... you could very well have between 12-25K in benefits. This means that you would literally need to earn an *additional* 12-25K in private practice annually to have the same quality of life and pay for those things yourself.

Q: Why don't you offer Health insurance?
A: We can't afford it. Every single year our personnel circle and our Accountant discuss the topic, and every year the answer is the same: we cannot afford to offer it at this time,

and even if we did the coverage would be so expensive that most people couldn't afford it. We hope that changes, but it hasn't yet.

Q: Can't we put up a few tables around here? It would be nice to give a back treatment sometimes
A: No. WCA used to have tables and they became a problem because they interfered with our ability to give consistent care. The constant problems were not worth it and we removed the last table in 2015.

Q: I really love herbs and wish that we had more of them for people.
A: Some of us love herbs, too, but our clinic is not set up to give comprehensive exams and dispense TCM herbs. This is one of our limitations but honestly we find that people benefit so much from regular treatments that we oftentimes don't need to prescribe them. We carry a few ITM patents which we use sparingly. If your patient is interested in more herbs, please refer them elsewhere. If you strongly wish to be working more with herbs, please find a clinic where that is appropriate. We know of a few and can help you locate them and see if they are hiring.

Q: Why don't we do moxa, cupping, estim, and other modalities. They are so helpful!
A: That's true, those things can be really helpful. However, we (and many other clinics) have never been able to successfully incorporate those types of modalities into our clinic without compromising our values of accessibility and consistency. If you are unsure how to turn a breech, induce labor, or treat pain without these modalities please ask a senior punk. We are happy to help.

Q: I learned a lot about diet and lifestyle in school. I can help so many more people if gave them advice!

A: I know it seems that way, and it is tempting to share your beliefs as an effort to be helpful. However, we have patient-centered care. That means that our prime directive is to meet people where they are at and not to make assumptions about how they need to change. We don't know their situations or the implications of our advice. We are willing to hire you whether you smoke, drink, or eat fast food. Please do our patients the common courtesy of extending the same respect. It is never your place to give lifestyle advice at WCA and that is not a policy we are willing to budge on.

Q: I apprenticed with a master, have a martial arts background, and/or studied some esoteric system that is really important to me. Can't I just talk about/do a little extra with my patients because that is the type of practitioner I am?
A: Excellent, don't use it here. Again, we keep our systems consistent so that our patients know what to expect. While we want you to show up and be yourself, we still need for you to adapt as part of the team and hold yourself to the same standards of treatment that we do. Excessive pulse taking, talking about qi cultivation, and other subtle systems can give the impression that we are psychically "seeing things" or makes our medicine look exotic. This causes patients to develop "guru mentality" toward some punks and distrust others. This is not trauma-informed care. Just like you wouldn't show up at a fertility or orthopedic sports medicine clinic planning to only use 5 element treatments, do not show up at WCA planning to treat patients differently than the rest of us. If you are unsure how to incorporate your unique style into this setting please just ask! We are more than happy to help you and show you how to be successful within the limits of what we offer.

Q: I read your culture manual and it sounds really political and/or angry. Can't we all just focus on the good and manifest positive energy?

A: We do not require our employees to feel passionate about the exact same things that we do, but we do expect to be accepted for who we are. Many of the folks who are part of our collective management feel passionately about social justice. That passion and anger paved the way for millions of people to get acupuncture every year, and opened an affordable acupuncture school. It is the reason that we are even able to offer you a job in the first place.

Q: Who can I turn to when I have questions? It is hard to tell sometimes.

A: WCA is governed by a sociocratic structure, meaning that we have several overlapping circles and it can all get very confusing at times. We meet every week to discuss operational aspects of WCA. Usually, your best bet is to ask your Clinic Manager if you have general concerns or problems. If your clinic manager cannot help you they will point you in the right direction.

---

[1] Yunus, Muhammad. Jolis, Alan. *Banker to The Poor: Micro-Lending and the Battle Against World Poverty.* United States: Public Affairs, 1999. Paperback.

[2] Bornstein, David. How to Change the World: Social Entrepreneurs and the Power of New Ideas. Oxford University Press, 2007.

[3] Solnit, Rebecca. *Hope in the Dark: Untold Stories and Wild Possibilities.*

[4] http://www.yesmagazine.org/issues/love-and-the-apocalypse/don-t-wait-for-the-revolution-live-it-andrew-boyd

[5] Rohleder, Lisa. *Fractal: About Community Acupuncture.* POCA, 2013. https://www.amazon.com/Fractal-Acupuncture-Lisa-Rohleder-L-Ac-ebook/dp/B00CPTJDFM/ref=sr_1_1?s=books&ie=UTF8&qid=1486424373&sr=1-1&keywords=lisa+rohleder

[6] Rilke, Rainer Maria. *Letters to a Young Poet.* W.W.Norton & Co., 1934, 1962, 2004

[7] **Twin Verses,** *The Dhammapada.* https://www.bmcm.org/inspiration/

passages/twin-verses/

[8] Lee, Miriam. *Insights of a Senior Acupuncturist*. Blue Poppy Enterprises, Inc., 1992

[9] Tyler Phan, *Smashing Chinoiserie Vases*, POCAfest lecture 9/27/2015

[10] Le Guin, Ursula. *The Wave in the Mind. Talks and Essays on the Writer, the Reader, and the Imagination*. Shambhala, 2004.

[11] Balkin, Jack. *The Laws of Change: I Ching and the Philosophy of Life*. Schocken Books 2002. Hexagram 48 is pages 475- 481, Hexagram 14 is pages 216-221

[12] https://www.pocacoop.com/prick-prod-provoke/post/the-practice-of-cooperation-presentation-by-dr.-andrew-zitcer

[13] Beckett, Samuel. "Waiting for Godot".

[14] Hawken, Paul. *Growing a Business*. Simon & Schuster, 1987.

[15] http://www.medicalnewstoday.com/articles/150999.php

[16] http://www.newyorker.com/magazine/2017/01/23/the-heroism-of-incremental-care?mbid=nl_170117_Daily&CNDID=19980709&spMailingID=10245691&spUserID=MTMzMTc5NzIxNzg3So&spJobID=1081397176&spReportId=MTA4MTM5NzE3NgS2)

[17] http://www.telegraph.co.uk/news/health/news/9757450/Benefits-of-sleeping-pills-come-from-placebo-effect.html, https://blogs.scientificamerican.com/cross-check/are-antidepressants-just-placebos-with-side-effects/

[18] More about him also in a few chapters. He's prominent in a film that my friend Brian Lindstrom made, "Finding Normal" and you can watch him. The last 48 seconds of the trailer, there's the lightning: https://www.youtube.com/watch?v=1WnoyorpbXM. The entire movie has recently been released by Dark Hollow Films.

[19] Yunus, Muhammad. Jolis, Alan. *Banker to The Poor: Micro-Lending and the Battle Against World Poverty*. United States: Public Affairs, 1999. Paperback.

[20] https://www.pocacoop.com/prick-prod-provoke/post/best-practice-for-who

[21] https://revsponderings.wordpress.com/2013/10/16/thomas-merton-a-letter-to-a-young-activist/

[22] Solnit, Rebecca. *Hope in the Dark: Untold Histories, Wild Possibilities*. Page 81

[23] Hawken, Paul. *Growing a Business*. Simon & Schuster, 1987. pg 79

[24] which is where you can find the details if you want them: https://www.pocacoop.com/

[25] Sarah Lefkowich (founder West Philly Community Acupuncture), POCA forums

[26] Solnit, Rebecca. *Hope in the Dark: Untold Stories and Wild Possibilities*.

[27] https://www.pocacoop.com/prick-prod-provoke/post/stone-soup-and-social-business-a-confession

[28] Lund, Margaret. Solidarity as a Business Model. Cooperative Development Center at Kent State University, 2011.

[29] De Lisovoy, Noah. Means, Alexander J. Saltman, Kenneth J. *Toward a New Common School Movement*. Paradigm Publishers, 2013

[30] http://www.truth-out.org/opinion/item/22113-creating-a-pedagogy-in-common-excerpt-from#14872925887461&action=collapse_widget&id=0&data=

[31] Lorde, Audre. *A Burst of Light: Essays*. Firebrand Books, 1988

[32] https://www.pocacoop.com/prick-prod-provoke/post/the-untapped-potentials-in-community-acupuncture-response-to-lonny-jarrett

[33] https://www.pocacoop.com/prick-prod-provoke/post/the-untapped-potentials-in-community-acupuncture-response-to-lonny-jarrett

[34] https://www.pocacoop.com/join-page

[35] BF Skinner https://blogs.scientificamerican.com/thoughtful-animal/what-is-operant-conditioning-and-how-does-it-explain-driving-dogs/

[36] http://www.aragues.com/nyt_training_husband.html Sutherland, Amy. *What Shamu Taught Me About Life, Love and a Happy Marriage*. Random House, 2008.

[37] http://www.sociocracy.info/

[38] http://www.yesmagazine.org/happiness/ursula-k-le-guin-calls-on-sci-fi-and-fantasy-writers-to-envision-alternatives-to-capitalism

[39] https://www.pocacoop.com/prick-prod-provoke/post/dear-prospective-punk-from-a-recent-grad-and-new-punk-or-why-we-need-poca-t

[40] https://www.pocacoop.com/file_attachments/JCM98_FINAL_22-25_Community%20Acupuncture.pdf

[41] https://www.pocacoop.com/prick-prod-provoke/post/nothing-like-a-2-alarm-fire-to-give-you-some-perspective

[42] https://www.pocacoop.com/prick-prod-provoke/post/what-would-poca-tech-do-without-poca-no-seriously

[43] https://www.pocacoop.com/prick-prod-provoke/post/all-the-things-that-didnt-happen-and-some-of-the-things-that-did

[44] Martín-Baró, Ignacio. *Writings for a Liberation Psychology*. Harvard, 1996.

[45] https://liberationacupuncture.org/node/65

[46] https://liberationacupuncture.org/

[47] http://www.newyorker.com/magazine/2011/01/24/the-hot-spotters

[48] Isenburg, Nancy. *White Trash: The 400-Year Untold History of Class in America*. Viking, 2016

[49] http://www.self.com/story/should-you-try-group-acupuncture

[50] https://www.bmcm.org/inspiration/passages/twin-verses/

[51] Bloom, Sandra L. *Creating Sanctuary: Toward the Evolution of Sane Societies*. Routledge, 2013

Made in the USA
Middletown, DE
25 August 2017